Suddenly there were hundreds of planes filling the sky. The fleet shifted into antiaircraft formation. Speeding at 27 knots, the ships opened fire against their aerial foes.

Yamato's 150 antiaircraft and machine guns raised a curtain of shellfire into the sky. Planes were shot down, but new attack waves came on incessantly. It was simply a question of how long *Yamato* could endure their onslaught . . .

"A must for anybody writing about the Japanese Navy for a century to come."

—ARMY-NAVY-AIR FORCE JOURNAL & REGISTER

THE END OF THE
IMPERIAL JAPANESE NAVY

MASANORI ITO
WITH ROGER PINEAU

TRANSLATED BY ANDREW Y. KURODA
AND ROGER PINEAU

A JOVE BOOK

THE END OF THE IMPERIAL JAPANESE NAVY

A Jove Book / published by arrangement with
W. W. Norton & Company

PRINTING HISTORY
W. W. Norton edition published 1962
Jove edition / December 1984

ISBN: 0-515-08176-0

Jove books are published by The Berkley Publishing Group,
200 Madison Avenue, New York, N.Y. 10016.
The words "A JOVE BOOK" and the "J" with sunburst
are trademarks belonging to Jove Publications, Inc.

PRINTED IN THE UNITED STATES OF AMERICA

CONTENTS

ILLUSTRATIONS

Photographs between pages 126 and 127

Maps and Charts

viii

THE END OF THE
IMPERIAL JAPANESE NAVY

1
FORMATION OF THE FLEET

聯合艦隊

1. Foreword

TO THE JAPANESE PEOPLE "Rengo Kantai" is a familiar and honored term meaning "Combined Fleet." When World War II began, the Japanese Navy—the third most powerful in the world—included some of the mightiest ships in naval history and was a force worthy of the pride and trust of the Japanese people. Then, in less than four years, this great war machine fell from glory to oblivion. Of ten battleships riding in Hiroshima Bay in December, 1941, nine were sunk. The lone survivor, *Nagato*, died at Bikini Island as a target in an atomic bomb test

As early as the spring of 1946, *Bungei Shunju* magazine urged me to write of the last days of the Combined Fleet. I refused because I did not wish to disturb the dead bodies of my friends. Even if I had forced myself to write, I would not then have been able to assemble all the material now available to me. In the years since Japan's defeat, the war-troubled mind of the people has been calmed, but I find that there is still nostalgia for the Combined Fleet in many hearts. It was at the request of Japanese readers that my newspaper articles were assembled into this book.

Movements to romanize our language may some day succeed, but the ideographs for *Rengo Kantai* will always stir Japanese hearts, just as do some of Admiral Heihachiro Togo's famous words. His dispatch as battle was about to be joined at Tsushima Strait: "The enemy has been sighted; the Combined Fleet is moving to annihilate him. The waves are high but the day is clear." And his famous Z-signal: "The rise or fall of the nation is at stake in this battle; all hands are exhorted to do their utmost," are quotes known to everyone.

We like to recall stories of bravery such as this incident in the battle of the Yellow Sea during the Sino-Japanese War. The enemy flagship *Ting-yuan*, almost twice the size of any Japanese ship present, had scored a direct hit on flagship *Matsushima*. A fatally injured sailor named Torajiro Miura asked a passing officer, "Sir, is *Ting-yuan* not yet sunk?"

Deeply moved, the officer replied, "Rest easily. *Ting-yuan* has been knocked out of action."

With a smile of satisfaction Miura said, "We are avenged," and he died. This story is told in a martial song which closes:

> "Is *Ting-yuan* not yet sunk?"
> The brief remark is forever engraved
> In the heart of the people,
> The bulwark of the nation.

2. The "Unsinkable" Warships

One of the most ambitious naval projects ever undertaken was the construction of Japan's three superbattleships of World War II. Each displaced 72,000 tons, as against the British standard of around 35,000 tons. To attempt such construction was audacious, to achieve it was amazing, and to maintain secrecy of the construction fantastic.

The Japanese public, who knew little of these three ships, wrote many letter when my articles appeared after the war. These letters reflected a deep affection for an interest in the Navy. In substance they said:

Reactions to the war must not be limited to lamentations over our defeat. We have a right to be proud of our ability to build the world's largest warships. That we could do this should serve as an inspiration in the reconstruction of the nation.

Aside from this, however, we are interested in knowing why these ships were built. Why did these unsinkable ships sink? Did these giants have inherent defects, even as a great *sumo* wrestler may have some physical shortcoming which proves his downfall? Or were they lost through operational errors? We would like to know the truth.

These are good and reasonable questions, whose answers tell the whole story of these great ships. The stories of *Yamato, Musashi*, and *Shinano* describe the alpha and omega of the Japanese Navy in World War II.

In a sense, these mighty warships were doomed even before their keels were laid. The result of Japan's determination to scrap the disarmament treaty of 1922, they played a part in the new arms race before their first rivet was driven. *Yamato*'s keel was laid at Kure in 1936. *Musashi* and *Shinano* were building soon thereafter at Nagasaki and Yokusuka. Fences of unprecedented size were set up to shield the construction areas, and strict security measures were taken to keep secret what went on inside.

While Japan observed the letter of the disarmament treaty before 1936, its spirit was violated in the very planning for the superbattleships. Japan's intention to vitiate the treaty was apparent.

Just as the warship-building race between Great Britain and Germany had been a factor leading into the First World War, there was always the chance that naval rivalry between Japan and the United States, with British involvement, might touch off another war. Therefore, Japan, Great Britain, and the United States concluded a naval disarmament treaty at Washington in 1922. By this treaty they agreed, among other things, to build no new battleships. The treaty was hailed as a great success, earning high praise for the Japanese participant, Fleet Admiral Tomosaburo Kato, and adding to the prestige of the Japanese Navy. This Washington Treaty was still in force when peril of war gripped the world early in 1936.

Japan's remarkable achievement in becoming one of the three leading powers in the 1920s was mainly the result of her great national growth and increased naval strength, but much credit for her rise in international prestige must go to Admiral Kato. As a correspondent in Washington at the time, I had opportunity to observe him in action. He often took the initiative in breaking conference deadlocks, and soon proved his stature as equal to that of such statesmen as Arthur James Balfour of England, and Charles Evans Hughes of the United States.

After the Washington Conference Kato returned to Japan as Prime Minister. In this role he laid down and faithfully followed a policy of abiding by the Treaty. Content with Japan as the third-ranking power of the world, he regarded the Imperial Navy as a deterrent force and reduced it in size by one half. He sought to guide the nation toward enhancement of its world position through peaceful means. His leadership was so firm that no one in either the Army or Navy dared to oppose him.

Kato met an untimely death in 1923, before he could eliminate the influence of the factions vehemently opposed to the 5-5-3 ratio established under the Washington Treaty. Upon his death these small groups of men became vocal. They demanded either a more favorable ratio or renunciation of the treaty. Kato's influence, however, survived his death long enough to dominate the Japanese delegation at the London Disarmament Conference of 1930. Strategic posts in the Navy were still held by his followers. Such men as Admirals Keisuke Okada (later Prime Minister), Takeshi Takarabe, Kichisaburo Nomura, Katsunoshin Yamanashi, and Teikichi Hori kept the Navy in line with the government in accepting the agreement at London. Admirals Mitsumasa Yonai (later Prime Minister) and Isoroku Yamamoto were also followers of Kato's policies.

The "tough policy" faction of the Navy, however, took advantage of the political atmosphere created by the abortive coups of 15 May 1932[1] and 26 February 1936,[2] and started to gain control of the Navy at the policy-making level. It appeared early that the disarmament agreement would be at stake in 1935 at the Second London Conference. The outlook was so grave that a preliminary conference was held in London in 1934. Isoroku Yamamoto, still only a rear admiral, was a delegate. He had the confidence of both factions of the Navy, and a promising future.

Upon his return from the 1934 meeting in London, Yamamoto talked with me at length about his experiences and observations. He had spoken privately with Prime Minister MacDonald and thought him "a truly great statesman." But Yamamoto confided to me, "The outlook for next year is almost hopeless. We will have to think in terms of second-best measures."

Yamamoto was a firm believer of Kato's ideas, but he was only a very junior flag officer. It was unlikely that he could make his influence felt against the tough-policy group.

As predicted, the conference of 1935 failed. The Japanese delegation seemed determined not to reach any agreement. The only real hope was that battleship construction might be suspended for another five years, while some compromise was achieved. It was on this thin strand that Great Britain and the United States depended in their efforts to preserve peace, feeling that a naval race could be prevented only if the construction of battleships was not resumed.

That autumn Japan declared that any extension of the Washington Treaty would be useless, and gave notice that she was withdrawing from its accords. The decision was reached

---

[1] Known in Japan as the "May 15 Incident." Premier Tsuyoshi Inukai was a victim.

[2] Known as the "February 26 Incident." An attempt was made on the life of Premier Keisuke Okada. His residence was attacked, but a brother-in-law saved Okada from the assassins at the sacrifice of his own life.

only after prolonged consideration, with full knowledge of its grave consequences. Japan's elder statesmen were deeply apprehensive about the danger of war and, within the Navy, moderates tried their utmost to restrain the tough-policy group. No one, however, could now stop the onrushing waves.

3. Building Warships, but not for War

As notice of Japan's withdrawal reached Washington, the keel of battleship *Yamato* was being laid in Kure Naval Yard. It was, of course, impossible to start building such a giant battleship without long and careful preparation. The decision to build these ships had been made two years earlier. Blueprints were complete, a construction slip in the Navy Yard had been ready for almost a year, and building materials had been stockpiled.

Japan, like Great Britain and the United States, had not built battleships for fifteen years, and had never built a warship in excess of 35,000 tons. H.M.S. *Hood* was 42,000 tons, but she had been built in 1920 and was already in commission when the disarmament treaty was signed.

It is astonishing that Japan should have even tried to build a 70,000-ton warship. The audacious plan was aimed at giving Japan a sudden and decisive superiority in warship quality. She realized that once a building race was underway she could not match the other leaders in quantity. She also figured that the United States would build no ships too large to pass through the Panama Canal.

Thus the plans for *Yamato*'s construction were completed while the treaty was still in effect. The giants of Japan's Navy were good ships but they were built in bad conscience, and all three were lost. It must be made clear, however, that although the planning for these ships violated the spirit of the treaty, they were not built as a step toward war. Japan's aim was to enhance her international standing by becoming a great peacetime naval power. Admiral Kato's strategy still controlled the

Navy. The 70,000-ton battleships would provide great bargaining power in negotiations with Great Britain and the United States, and would also serve as "iron security" to command the respect of all nations.

It was in affirmation of this position that Navy Minister Mitsumasa Yonai announced unequivocally on the Diet floor in the winter of 1937: "The Imperial Navy has no force to match the combined strength of Great Britain and the United States. It has no intention of building its strength to such a level." This statement is significant when one recalls that *Yamato* was on the ways, and *Musashi* and *Shinano* were already scheduled.

It should also be remembered that Yonai and his Vice Minister, Isoroku Yamamoto, were vigorously opposed to strengthening Japan's ties with Germany and Italy. Yamamoto, especially, never yielded on this point, despite tremendous pressure from the Army. He killed a compromise plan the Army tried to push through, and he persisted in his stand even though it placed him in danger of assassination. It was Yamamoto's firm opinion that "Japan should never be so foolish as to make enemies of Great Britain and the United States." Battleship *Yamato* did not change this conviction.

Japan's new program of naval construction was gloomy news to the rest of the world. I observed this during a six-month tour, starting in the fall of 1937, which took me to Europe and the United States. People everywhere asked about or commented on Japan's construction of big warships. The great English journalist and good friend of Japan, Mr. G. Wynn of the *Morning Post*, spoke frankly with me and said, "The building of battleships may be a plus for Japan's naval strength, but I am afraid it will end up as a minus for her in international relations."

I spoke with equal frankness, saying that Japan would probably have been content with a ratio of 10-10-7, instead of the 5-5-3 of the treaty. If Great Britain and the United States had yielded an additional ten percent the problem would have been solved. Mr. Wynn agreed and expressed regret that the necessary insight had been lacking.

I talked with naval editor Hanson Baldwin of the *New York Times* and was surprised at his vast fund of information. He said, for example, "I have heard that Japan is building a battleship which will have two dozen 5.5-inch antiaircraft guns." (That was the actual number of such guns installed in *Yamato*.) As I took leave of Mr. Baldwin in early 1938 he said, "For the time being we cannot talk of arms reductions. We may have to have another war before there can be a real disarmament conference."

4. Confident Army, Skeptical Navy

Even with the building of *Yamato* and *Musashi* war could have been avoided if the Navy had pursued an unswerving policy of peace at any cost. The Council of Senior Statesmen recommended Admiral Yonai to the Emperor as their choice for the next Prime Minister. This was a good choice but the Army, dissatisfied, stalled in selecting a Minister of War. After urging by the Emperor, the Army agreed to accept General Shunroku Hata as Minister of War, and the Yonai Cabinet was formed on 16 January 1940. When Hata resigned shortly thereafter because of ill health the Army refused to name a successor and the cabinet fell within six months of the time it was organized. The Army thus had its revenge for the Navy's rejection of a strong Japan-Germany alliance, and also clearly demonstrated that it would block any cabinet which did not comply with its wishes.

With the fall of the Yonai Cabinet the stage was set for the appearance of General Hideki Tojo as Minister of War in the Konoye Cabinet, which was formed in late July. Thereupon the reckless young Army officers spoke more brazenly of "war against Great Britain and the United States," and began to interfere openly in political affairs. A small group of field-grade officers soon took over complete control of the Army. These men, with their narrow outlook on world affairs, were violently pro-German and anti-American. Lieutenant General

Kanji Ishihara's urgings to concentrate on the development of Manchuria were ignored. Talk of war emanated from the General Staff Headquarters at Miyakezaka and spread to the four corners of the country. The few informed Army officers with foreign experience and knowledge, men like Colonel Hideo Iwakuro who had served in Washington and London, were quickly sent to posts far from Tokyo.

Admiral Isoroku Yamamoto was named Commander in Chief Combined Fleet, and at the time of his appointment was at sea in his flagship. A member of the Supreme War Council told me, "We sent him to sea purposefully because he would have been assassinated if he had stayed in Tokyo, and that would have been a great loss to our country." The rank of Commander in Chief, Combined Fleet, was the Navy's highest honor and even Yamamoto could not decline it. He was thus transferred from the nerve-wracking political position of Navy Vice Minister to duty at sea, where there was strict adherence to the Imperial Rescript, "Men of the services should not participate in politics."

Had Yamamoto remained in Tokyo he would gladly have risked his life in opposing the German alliance and war against Great Britain and the United States. It was unfortunate for Japan and the world that he was on board his flagship. Without the Navy the Army could not have started the war no matter how loudly the sabres rattled.

In our last talk before his going to sea, Yamamoto told me, "Zengo Yoshida is a good Navy Minister and he will be able to take care of the Department without me. He is every bit as stubborn as I am. We can rest assured as long as he is in charge."

Unfortunately, the overburdened Yoshida became ill and was forced to resign. Those who followed him had wisdom but lacked courage, and the Navy was soon dragged along to the point of no return.

Koshiro Oikawa took Yoshida's place in September 1940. Prime Minister Fumimaro Konoye was concerned about his new Navy Minister, who showed himself to be, unlike Yonai and Yamamoto, quite accommodating to the Army and its point of view. When Yamamoto returned to Tokyo a year later he was invited to "Tekigaiso," the Prime Minister's residence. Konoye wanted to know if there was a chance of victory for Japan in a war with Great Britain and the United States. Yamamoto replied prophetically, "I can raise havoc with them for one year, but after that I can give no guarantee."

Both men knew the British and Americans well enough to realize that, in spite of the much-vaunted "*Yamato* spirit," neither people was inferior to the Japanese. It is clear from Yamamoto's words that he saw defeat for Japan in a prolonged war.

This advice must have assured Konoye that his policy of avoiding war at any cost was correct, and he concentrated on creating a better understanding with the United States. This policy angered the Army, however, and Tojo soon began to take more direct control of state affairs.

It may be unfair to say that the nation was imperiled upon Tojo's coming to power. No matter who had headed the Cabinet at this time, he could not have resisted the pressure of the Army. Army leaders, and even some leading civilians, were for war and promotion of the Greater East Asia Co-prosperity Sphere. Many who today speak and write unabashedly about peace and neutrality were then eager to curry the favor of the Army, and they branded negotiations with the United States as "soft diplomacy." In order to win valuable time for war preparations, Kichisaburo Nomura and Saburo Kurusu were duped into carrying on diplomatic conversations at Washington. They were still negotiating when "the holy war" began with a surprise attack.

Since both Great Britain and the United States had strong navies, Japan could not invade their homelands. The question, therefore, was whether the islands of Japan could be protected from attack, and the answer could come only from the Imperial Navy. The decision for war or peace had to be left to the judgment of the Navy.

Unfortunately, the naval high command did not advise Tojo in the clear and direct way that Yamamoto had advised

Konoye. The Navy not only failed to object to war, it failed also to point out that defeat for Japan would be inevitable in a long-drawn-out conflict. Instead of standing its ground, the Navy yielded and went along with Tojo. Was this inevitable? One critic has said, "Primary responsibility for Japan's going to war rests on the Navy. We cannot really blame the ignorant and reckless Army. Neither public opinion nor even the Emperor could have halted the plunge toward war, but the Navy could have. The Navy alone was in position to stand firm against Tojo and, had it done so, Japan could not have gone to war. The Navy, with its broad outlook on the world, yielded to the narrow-minded Army. The Navy is to blame." I am in general agreement with this opinion, but wonder if it does not overestimate the Navy.

Yamamoto felt that Japan had no chance of victory in a war lasting more than one year. It is regrettable that other Navy leaders lacked his courage and conviction. As Vice Admiral Tomiji Koyanagi has written, "Reluctantly we (the Navy) were gradually dragged to war. We are still sorry about the vacillating and capitulating that went on in the Navy's high command."[3]

5. *Japan Builds Warships*

At today's unit cost of two million yen per ton, it would take 150 billion yen to build battleship *Yamato*. Since this amount is the entire annual budget for Japan's national defense, it is obvious that she will not be building such a ship. Great technological skill was needed to build ships big enough to mount nine 18.1-inch guns. It was an unprecedented undertaking.

Japan was a relative newcomer to the field of warship construction. At the time of the battle of the Japan Sea, in 1905, every ship of the Japanese Navy had been foreign built. Once

[3] Tomiji Koyanagi *Reite Oki Kaisen* [*Battle off Leyte*], Tokyo Kobundo, 1950, p. 58.

she began building warships, however, Japan's construction and design achievements were second to none. Her capabilities were first recognized abroad when she abandoned traditional battleship bows. Until then battleships had been built with bows protruding far forward below the waterline, for ramming purposes. Japan realized that this protuberance was no longer practical and was, in fact, detrimental to high-speed maneuvering. Accordingly, in 1907, Japan began building warships with a receding bow line which eliminated the bulky protrusion and increased ship maneuverability. Japanese warship development continued to make great strides thereafter. It would be wrong to ignore or depreciate Japan's attainments simply because the nation was defeated in World War II.

At the Washington Disarmament Conference in November 1921, Japan's new battleship *Mutsu* was the subject of lively debate. At the outset U.S. delegate Hughes had proposed the scrapping of certain old capital ships as well as all then under construction, including *Mutsu*. Delegate Kato objected strongly since *Mutsu* had just completed her maiden voyage the previous month. The ensuing debate lasted for three weeks. Japan's unyielding attitude was erroneously ascribed by some foreign newsmen to the fact that this ship had been named after Mutsuhito, the personal name of Emperor Meiji.[4] Actually, like all Japanese battleships, this one was named after an ancient province of the homeland.

Great Britain and the United States would have found it advantageous if *Mutsu* had been scrapped along with U.S.S. *Colorado* and H.M.S. *King George V*. Although the three ships were of similar size, *Mutsu* far exceeded the others in fighting power. Kato's statesmanship was proven when he was able to save *Mutsu* on terms agreeable to the other conferees.

Japan's shipbuilding technology continued to advance during the 1920s. Warship *Yubari* was revealed to the world as a 3,000-ton light cruiser possessed of armament such as appeared only in ships double her size in the British and U.S. navies. Parallel superiority was achieved by Japan in other

[4] Born 1852; reigned 1867–1912.

classes of warships as well, as can be seen by comparing her 10,000-ton *Nachi*-class cruisers with similar British and American ships:

	NACHI[5] (JAPAN)	KENT (U.K.)	PENSACOLA (U.S.)
Guns	10 8-inch	8 8-inch	9 8-inch
	6 4.7 inch	4 4-inch	5 5-inch
Torpedoes	12 24-inch	8 21-inch	6 21-inch
Speed	34.5 knots	31.5 knots	32.5 knots
Armor	side 4-inch	magazine 4-inch	side 2-inch
	turrets 3-inch	other 1-inch	turrets 2-inch

In 1929 flagship *Kent* of Britain's Far Eastern Fleet put in at Yokohama where her officers were invited to visit on board *Nachi*'s new sistership *Myoko*. One of the visitors exclaimed, "Now *this* is a real warship. *Kent* is a luxury liner by comparison!" Even allowing for the courteous language of diplomacy, the comment must be recognized as the sincere appraisal of a professional.

A similar reaction came from a London *Times* reporter who inspected heavy cruiser *Ashigara* when she was in England for the coronation of George VI in 1937. The newspaper account of his visit to the Japanese warship was entitled, "Greetings to a Wolf of the Sea."

Japanese warships differed from those of other nations in that they were designed exclusively for fighting. This singleness of purpose reflected the spirit of the entire Imperial Navy. *Yamato*, a product of this spirit, embodies all the experience and technology that could be incorporated into a fighting ship. Her building was no chance thing, and no outside help was required to produce her. She and her two sister ships were designed and built entirely by Japan. And all three were destroyed within a period of six months, victim to Japan's "decisive battle" complex.

---

[5] The others of this class were *Myoko, Ashigara,* and *Haguro.*

6. "Invincible Armadas"

Like an unsinkable battleship, an invincible armada is a mere figure of speech. If the Spanish Fleet of 1588 was the first Invincible Armada to be vanquished, the last was probably the Japanese Fleet at Leyte Gulf in 1944. Not until this miserable defeat did Japan realize how empty had been her pride in an unbeatable Combined Fleet.

Japan's ten prewar battleships—*Mutsu, Nagato, Fuso, Yamashiro, Ise, Hyuga, Kongo, Hiei, Haruna, Kirishima*—placed her on a 3-to-5 firepower ratio in capital ships with the United States. With the addition of giants *Yamato* and *Musashi* this ratio rose to about 4 to 5, and Japan thereupon became a formidable naval power against which not even Great Britain and the United States would have declared unprovoked war. Wisely used, or even unused, Japan's Navy could have remained an invincible defensive armada.

Like the Imperial Fleet, the United States Navy held the traditional concept of crossing the ocean to duel with capital ships. Gradually, however, it came to realize that the required westward extension of supply lines across the Pacific Ocean would lead to an attrition war—difficult to win, but easy to lose. This realization resulted in a relaxation of strategic thinking which enabled the U.S. Navy to adapt itself quickly and successfully to the idea of a mobile task force. Aircraft carriers were the heart of the force, closely surrounded and protected by battleships, cruisers, and destroyers. A watchful vanguard of aggressive submarines would reduce the surface strength of the enemy by attrition, and the following surface units could then engage to advantage.

Foreseeing these tactics, Japan's basic strategy lay in letting the opponent come to her. However powerful an approaching enemy might be, Japan's far-ranging submarines would whittle down that power far at sea by repeated torpedo attacks so that a surface encounter in homeland waters would find the remaining forces on equal terms. Japan's fleet could then move into decisive battle with a fair assurance of victory. In this vanguard role submarines were to play a vital part; so their strength, capabilities, and training were of great importance. This explains Japan's tenacious struggle for 78,000 tons of submarines at the London Conference in 1930. Perhaps because Great Britain and the United States were aware of this strategy, they had since 1922 been advocating the abolition of submarines as inhuman weapons. In any case, after a long and heated debate at the London Conference it was agreed that each of the three powers have 52,700 tons of submarines.

The Naval General Staff in Tokyo was enraged at this. Equality of submarine tonnage was totally unsatisfactory. Japan's war games had shown that she needed an absolute minimum of 78,000 tons. A strength of 52,700 tons would leave her short by two squadrons—16 boats—of what her planners considered necessary to a strategy of attrition. The results of the London Conference were thus looked upon as having placed Japan's national defense in jeopardy.

This provoked an unfortunate and serious conflict between the Navy Ministry and the Naval General Staff. Its ramifications were many and widespread, among them, on 14 November 1930, the attack on Prime Minister Osachi Hamaguchi in a Tokyo railway station. The submarine problem also led to a conflict between civil and military authorities over the prerogatives of the supreme command, and this dispute came to cripple Japan's whole parliamentary system.

7. Submarines Which Don't Return

Japan's submarines played a key part in her "Invincible Armada," and their design was quite properly a matter of great pride. The I-class fleet submarine was capable of cruising to California and back without refueling, an achievement in its time parallel to the modern accomplishments of the atomic-powered U.S. submarine *Nautilus*. Even the smaller *RO*-class boats (500–1,000 tons) could cruise to the Hawaiian Islands and return on a single fueling.

Submarine *I-401* was specifically planned for the purpose of destroying the Panama Canal, but that mission was never attempted. The boat's design displacement of 4,000 tons was increased during construction to more than 5,000, and the deck hangar space for two seaplanes was enlarged to hold three seaplane bombers.

Prior to World War II, Japan's submarines seem to have been the single weapon most feared by the United States and Great Britain. In December 1941 the Imperial Navy had 64 submarines ready for action, and 126 new boats were built during the war. In spite of its size, spirit, and reputation, this redoubtable force proved to be an almost total failure. At war's end not more than 50 Japanese submarines were still in existence, and most of them were inoperable because of damage or lack of maintenance. The rest had vanished, achieving little more than a remarkable score for the enemy.

One of the main causes for this submarine failure was lack of habitability in the boats. Too much emphasis was placed on making a war machine, and not enough on living conditions for the crew who had a minimum of space and creature comfort. The confined quarters might have been adequate if there had been enough men to rotate the crews for proper rest and rehabilitation after each mission. But there never were enough trained men. As time passed, the efficiency of submarines deteriorated even faster than their numbers decreased. Training in homeland waters had not prepared them for arctic and tropic extremes, where man and machine betrays unexpected weaknesses. The results were disastrous.

Japan's submarine force started the war with seeming advantages and the appearance of tremendous strength. United States submarines began at great disadvantage. Having no Far Eastern bases near Japan, they had to operate from Hawaii and Australia. Their unreliable torpedoes were sadly outperformed and outranged by the remarkable torpedoes of Japan's arsenal. While Japan's submarine weaknesses increased, those of the United States were compensated for and corrected until the once-great threat of Japan was reduced to impotence. U.S. submarines, on the other hand, proved to be the single most potent weapon against the Imperial Navy in the Pacific War.

The greatest cause for the failure of Japanese submarines was their unfortunate diversion from offensive to defensive assignments. Designed as weapons of attrition, they came to be used, instead, as mere supply ships for bypassed garrisons. At the same time, U.S. submarines became increasingly aggressive and destructive. Thus Japan's hopes for her submarine force were doomed, while the validity for her original plans was proved by the enemy's successes.

The enormity of Japan's failure is dramatically pointed up by a few simple statistics:

JAPANESE OCEAN-GOING VESSELS

December 1941	5,900,000 tons
Built during war	4,100,000
Total	10,000,000
Sunk during war	8,617,000
Heavily damaged	937,000
Total loss	9,554,000
Cause of loss	
Submarines	54.7% (63% of the sinkings)
Air attack	30.9%
Mines and other	14.4%

Japan's skill in night actions, in which the Navy had such great pride and confidence, proved to be equally fruitless in the long run. This skill paid off at Savo Island and other early battles in the Solomons. At the time it was said that Americans built things well with their modern methods, but that their blue eyes were no match for our dark eyes in night surface actions. This saying was soon rendered meaningless by the genius of American technology. Effective search radar proved superior to any human eyes, and when the marvel of radar was applied to gunfire control the brilliance of our training for night battle, like the difference in eye coloring, was immaterial. Radar enabled the enemy to fire accurately on Japanese ships while still beyond visual range.

Japan developed radar during the Pacific War. But, as with most of our wartime efforts, it was too little too late, and neither the equipment nor its technicians ever equalled those of the enemy.

8. *The* Shinano *Tragedy*

The keel for a third ship of the *Yamato* class was laid in May 1940 at Yokosuka. During the construction of this battleship, however, it was decided to convert her into an aircraft carrier. The decision for this change was made in June 1942 as a result of the Pearl Harbor and Midway lesson that carriers, not battleships, would be the most important warships of World War II. This lesson reinforced the memory of the May 1941 sinking of Germany's battleship *Bismarck* by British ships in the North Atlantic, and the sinking of Britain's "unsinkable" *Prince of Wales* by Japanese planes off Malaya on 10 December 1941.

The U.S. Navy knew that battleships—even monsters such as *Yamato*—could be sunk by air attack, but battleships with 18.1-inch guns would have a tremendous advantage over smaller-gunned ships in a purely surface action. Not until October of 1944 did the giants of Japan's Navy come to grips with enemy surface forces. *Musashi* was sunk at this time, *Yamato* succumbed six months later; both were victims of aerial attack.

Carrier *Shinano* was completed in November 1944. As a result of the change in plans during her construction, she was three years longer in building than her battleship "sisters." This 71,000-ton hybrid was a carrier-of-battleship-born, but she must be distinguished from hermaphrodites *Ise* and *Hyuga*, whose two main after turrets were merely replaced by small platform decks. *Shinano*, with her 70-plane capacity, was a wonder of the naval world. Her flight deck, made of special steel, 30 centimeters thick, over a layer of concrete, was built to withstand any aerial bombing attack. All her equipment was of the latest design. Her very existence was a serious threat to the enemy.

U.S. Navy Secretary James Forrestal made a postwar plea for the building of a giant aircraft carrier. Its design was completed, but budgetary demands met with such strong opposition in Congress that the idea was dropped. Shortly thereafter Mr. Forrestal became ill and met an untimely death. Within three years of his death, however, his dream was realized and a 59,000-ton carrier bore his name. This monument to a great man may also serve as a reminder that the Japanese Navy's 71,000-ton *Shinano* had been completed a decade earlier. It, too, was a monument; a monument which, despite its tragic fate, is deserving of recognition as a milestone.

Long years of effort reached a point of fruition on 11 November 1944, when the waters of Tokyo Bay first floated the leviathan *Shinano*. It was the anniversary of the armistice of World War I—a day far removed from one war, but in the midst of another which was becoming increasingly unfavorable for Japan. The Imperial Navy had lost most of its carriers in the Marianas and Leyte battles, and it now awaited *Shinano* as a parched earth waits for rain. Because of the pressing war situation, *Shinano* was commissioned before final testing, before her crew had been trained, indeed, before all her equipment had been installed; and she was underway for Matsuyama, the Combined Fleet training area in Shikoku.

At 1800 hours on 28 November she sailed from Yokosuka toward Osaka Bay on the first leg of her maiden voyage. Her escorts were battle-tested destroyers, *Hamakaze*, *Isokaze*, and *Yukikaze*. The wind was from the north at six meters (per second); the moon shone cold in the wintry sky.

The next day was but half an hour old when *Shinano* lookouts reported a dark object on the horizon. Escorts were alerted and all ships started to steer a zigzag course. Peering through binoculars, the Officer of the Day and the Executive

Officer concluded that the dark object was merely a low-hanging cloud. The alert was cancelled and all ships resumed a straight southward course.

At 0312 horrified lookouts spotted the first of four torpedo wakes only 100 meters away from *Shinano's* port side. There was no time to dodge. The first hit came just beneath the waterline. Three more hits followed almost instantaneously, tearing a gaping hole in the ship's center, causing an influx of water that no pumping system could possibly counteract.

Captain Toshio Abe, full of pride in his new ship, steamed on at 20 knots. He feared no serious danger to his mighty, new, "unsinkable" command; hence he gave no thought to grounding her, or even to considering the nearest port of safety. Gradually, then suddenly, *Shinano* listed until a foot-hold was impossible. Kumano Sea water poured into the hull and, finally, 100 miles south of Shio-no-misaki, the order was passed to abandon ship.

Captain Abe remained on the bridge to the last, assuming full responsibility for the fate of his ship. Nearby stood a young officer with *Shinano's* flag draped over his shoulders. Ensign Tadashi Yasuda, top man of the Academy class of 1943, calmly had kept a detailed log from the moment of the first hit. His sense of duty was in the highest and best tradition of the Navy, and it won the admiration of all his colleagues. Captain Abe and Ensign Yasuda were last seen on the bridge as *Shinano* disappeared beneath the waves. They were not among the 900 who survived the tragic sinking.

Another hero was Lieutenant (jg) Sawamoto, who gave his life to save the Emperor's portrait. When Abandon Ship was ordered, he got the picture from the captain's reception room and brought it topside wrapped carefully in canvas. Before going down with *Shinano* this loyal officer handed his precious package to a sailor who floated with it until rescued by destroyer *Hamakaze*.

Five hundred men perished with her when *Shinano* sank at 1055 on 29 November 1944.[6] The eight hours which followed

---

[6] The position was lat. 32°00′ N, long. 137°00′ E. *Shinano* was a victim of submarine *Archerfish* (Cdr. J. F. Enright).

her first torpedo hit would have been ample time to make port in Ise Bay, but she was maintained on course and speed because of Captain Abe's mistaken reliance on her unsinkability.

Basic responsibility for *Shinano*'s loss lies with the high command for having resorted to a nighttime transit of waters in which enemy submarines were known to be operating. It would have been far safer to navigate these waters by day, when land-based planes could have flown in escort. It is not known who decreed the night passage, but this was another of the many unfortunate decisions made by Navy leaders in the closing months of 1944.

Events of the previous month should have discouraged the moving of *Shinano* at night. On 22 October, Admiral Kurita's task force had sortied from Brunei anchorage to attack American ships supporting the invasion of Leyte in the Philippines. Moving northward that evening Kurita's ships were sighted by two American submarines. They pursued the force and attacked just before dawn, sinking two heavy cruisers.[7] Yet five weeks later, invaluable *Shinano* put to sea at night without special precaution.

A board of inquiry into *Shinano*'s loss was convened in December 1944, but its findings were never released, and all records of the board were destroyed at the end of the war. One of the board members has informed me that her loss was laid to the commanding officer's overconfidence in the ship's seaworthiness, which caused him to maintain a speed of 20 knots after serious damage; and to poor damage control by the untrained crew, because proper counterflooding could have corrected her list and saved the ship.

This brings to mind the sinking of battleship *Musashi* in the Sibuyan Sea a month earlier. On 24 October she was hit by at least ten torpedoes from American planes, but so perfect were the damage control efforts of her skilled crew that the fatally damaged ship was maintained on an even keel until the sea

---

[7] These were *Maya*, sunk by submarine *Dace* (Cdr. B. D. Claggett) in lat. 09°22′ N, long. 117°07′ E; and *Atago* by submarine *Darter* (Cdr. D. H. McClintock) in lat. 09°28′ N, long. 117°17′ E.

closed over her decks. In the hands of such a skilled crew *Shinano* could have been saved.

Of 1,400 men on board *Shinano*, 850 had never sailed in a warship before. *Shinano* never fired a shell, and never launched a plane. Her most notable deed was in going to the bottom of the sea within seventeen hours of the first time she left port. *Shinano* was probably the shortest-lived capital ship in history.

The fruit of years of planning and labor thus disappeared in a single day. This was more than accident. It was a tragedy and a terrible loss to Japan. May not this, like Japan's many great losses of World War II, be laid to the wrath of a vengeful god?

2
PEARL HARBOR

聯合艦隊

1. Surprise Attack

THE PACIFIC WAR BEGAN on 7 December 1941 with a Japanese surprise attack on Pearl Harbor which all but destroyed the United States Pacific Fleet. Plans for this attack were known to only a few high-ranking officers at Imperial General Headquarters. The assault by carrier-borne planes—the most powerful weapons of the day—began thirty-five minutes before official notice of the severance of diplomatic relations was delivered to the United States Government. Today a similar attack delivered simultaneously against the major cities of an enemy, without warning and employing modern nuclear weapons, could determine the outcome of a war at its outset. Accordingly, the United States is not likely to slacken her present vigilance and preparedness against a surprise attack by the Soviet Union. At least in part, her concern for preparedness is rooted in the memory of her unpreparedness on that 7 December.

These repercussions, like the general facts about the Pearl Harbor attack, are common knowledge. I will, therefore, mention here only those aspects of the attack which are not so well known or understood. It was not really a battle, because the United States had no opportunity to respond in force, and so it cannot be assessed on the basis of ordinary tactics. In its consequences, however, it was an event without precedent.

The success of Japan's effort depended on the following factors:

1. Development of plans to achieve the tactical and strategic objectives.
2. The ability of a naval task force to traverse thousands of miles of the Pacific Ocean and approach the target undetected.
3. Precise skill in aerial bombing and torpedoing.
4. Divine assistance.

This last point is a universal yet imponderable factor which can never be measured. A study of the first three, however, indicates the effort put forth by the Japanese Navy in those closing days of 1941.

The operation was feasible only if surprise could be achieved by the attacking force. It was essential that the aircraft carriers move unnoticed to the launching point, 200 miles north of Oahu. If the striking force had been detected early, and itself had been taken by surprise, as happened six months later at Midway, the Japanese fleet and all its plans for conquest in the Pacific might have been destroyed at the very outset. The Pacific War initiated by Japan could have been decided against her on the opening day. It was a gamble of great magnitude.

The Japanese Navy's Pearl Harbor Attack Force was assembled at Tankan Bay (Hitokappu Wan), a remote anchorage in the Kurile Island of Etorofu. Participating ships had arrived there singly or in pairs from all parts of the Empire, taking varied and different routes to avoid attention. Until the time of sortie the mission of the force was unknown even to ship captains. It was almost beyond imagination that distant Hawaii could be the target.

The last ships arrived on 22 November 1941, crowding the usually desolate bay. The organization of the force was as follows:

Pearl Harbor Striking Force

Attack Force, Vice Admiral Chuichi Nagumo
  Carriers *Akagi, Kaga, Soryu, Hiryu, Zuikaku, Shokaku*

Support Force, Vice Admiral Gunichi Mikawa
  Battleships *Hiei, Kirishima*
  Heavy Cruisers *Tone, Chikuma*

Scouting Force, Rear Admiral Sentaro Omori
  Light cruiser *Abukuma*
  Destroyers *Tanikaze, Hamakaze, Urakaze, Asakaze, Kasumi, Arare, Kagero, Shiranuhi, Akigumo*

Supply Force, Captain of *Kyokuto Maru*
  Tankers *Kyokuto Maru, Kyokuyo Maru, Kenyo Maru, Kokuyo Maru, Shinkoku Maru, Toho Maru, Toei Maru, Nippon Maru*

Three submarines, commanded by Captain Hidemitsu Imaizumi, were to reconnoiter along the route in advance of Nagumo's task force. Destroyers *Akebono* and *Ushio*, under command of Captain Kaname Konishi, were assigned to destroy the enemy air base at Midway Island.

The target and plan of attack were first disclosed to the officers and men of the fleet on 23 November. Young aviators shouted with joy at the news, thrilled at the chance to bomb and sink American warships. The elation of commanding officers and their staffs was more subdued. They knew that the success of the operation depended upon their ability to cross

3,000 miles of Pacific Ocean in complete secrecy. The warships would have to fuel at sea and sail undetected deep into an area patrolled by the United States.

In the months of November and December the North Pacific is usually calm about one day out of four. The striking force was favored, nevertheless, by perfect air and sea conditions on its outward passage. Also favorable, not a single foreign ship was encountered, and the carriers arrived at their launching point precisely on schedule.

The Navy General Staff had at first been opposed to the Pearl Harbor operation because of the great risks involved. The original strategic concept for the war had been to concentrate on operations in the southern regions. After quick subjugation and consolidation of the desired areas to the south, it was planned that the United States Fleet could next be successfully engaged in a decisive battle in the western Pacific. This had been a traditional naval plan since 1909, when the "National Defense Policy" was first formulated. This policy regarded the United States as Japan's hypothetical Enemy No. 1, and its fundamental strategy held that the Japanese Navy would wage decisive battle on an Inner South Seas line along the island groups of the Marianas and the Marshalls. For thirty years Combined Fleet's planning and training had been conducted upon this premise.

It was Admiral Isoroku Yamamoto who, as Commander in Chief Combined Fleet, changed all this when he promulgated the idea of attacking the United States Fleet in the Hawaiian Islands. After long debate his proposal was finally accepted on 3 November 1941 by Admiral Osami Nagano, Chief of the Naval General Staff. It was then determined that the attack on Pearl Harbor should be carried out in early December.

In discussing the various requirements for the success of his plan, Admiral Yamamoto declared, "Divine assistance must be with us if this operation is to succeed. If the plan miscarries it will be a sign that divine guidance is lacking and we should abandon the whole strategy."

By "the whole strategy" he may have meant simply the attack against the United States Fleet at Pearl Harbor, or he may have been speaking of the whole concept of war. In either case, his words show that he recognized the very considerable risk involved.

2. Concept and Training

The strategic plans for the Pearl Harbor assault were not seriously considered by the high command until May of 1941. The traditional battle area had been bounded on the east by the line of the Bonins and the Marianas, but in 1939, when Yamamoto became Commander in Chief Combined Fleet, the line was extended to include the Marshall Islands. By July 1940 he had stretched this line eastward to include the Hawaiian Islands. This final extension of the potential battle arena came about as the result of the spring fleet maneuvers of 1940.

It was during these maneuvers that Admiral Yamamoto, after witnessing demonstrations by carrier-based planes, first conceived the idea of a surprise air attack on Hawaii. This was contrary to the traditional defensive strategy of the Japanese Navy, but Yamamoto realized that there was great advantage to be gained by heavy assault on an enemy strongpoint at the outset of hostilities. The air training program would have to be adapted to meet the special requirements of such an attack. Thus the air arm of the Navy was recognized and established as a factor of primary importance. Most important, however, was the extension of Japan's defense line to include Hawaiian waters so that the attack could be justified.

In January 1941 Admiral Yamamoto summoned the Eleventh Air Fleet Chief of Staff, Rear Admiral Takijiro Ohnishi, and instructed him to study the feasibility of an aerial attack on the island of Oahu. Ohnishi's report, which was completed in three months, convinced Yamamoto that it was possible to make a successful attack on the great fleet base at Pearl Harbor. Yamamoto presented the idea to his staff in May as a subject for further study. They voiced much skepticism, and Ohnishi himself cautioned that there was only a fifty-fifty chance for success. Yamamoto had become obdurate, however, and in July he ordered special training procedures for all the air fleets of his command. Combined Fleet training and employment were responsibilities of its commander in chief, who had to insure that all strength was used for maximum benefit. Pilots of these air fleets had gained experience, skill, and confidence in oversea air attacks as early as 1937 in raids on Nanking.

It was customary for the Naval General Staff to set up a war game objective each year and for the Combined Fleet to develop plans to achieve that objective. For more than twenty years the objective had been "the annihilation of the United States Fleet." The only difference in the summer of 1941 was that the means and area for achieving this goal had been changed from surface battle in the Marshalls to air attack on Hawaii.

The principal training ground for this venture was at Kagoshima Bay in southern Kyushu, where residents referred to the rigorous daily exercises as the Navy's aerial circus. Planes roared in low over Shiro Mountain, dove precipitously into Iwasaki Valley and followed its winding bed to the shore, where they would skim over the waters of the bay and release torpedoes. The pilots themselves did not know that this perilous practice simulated conditions in the narrow confines of Pearl Harbor, but they drilled faithfully and well. With the thousands of flights involved in this training "circus," there was not a single accident or casualty.

In late October a huge crate was delivered on board carrier *Akagi*, flagship of the First Air Fleet. It contained a mock-up of Pearl Harbor, showing all possible details of the harbor and its surrounding terrain. Day after day Commander Minoru Genda,[1] staff officer in charge, studied the model, as did Commander Mitsuo Fuchida, the attack leader. They became familiar with every feature of this miniature and the area it

---

[1] General Minoru Genda is Chief of Japan's Air Self-Defense Force today.

represented. At the same time, participating pilots continued to train and practice at Kagoshima, Izumi, Kanoya, Saeki, and five other locations on Kyushu.

Training and practice were not the only problems in preparing for this operation. It was also necessary to develop and perfect the required weapons. Special armor-piercing bombs had to be built and tested to find their most effective drop altitude. The greatest weapons problem lay in obtaining new torpedoes suitable to the shallow waters of the target area. Conventional torpedoes were useless for launching in shallow water where the run was as short as it would have to be at Pearl Harbor. After seemingly endless experimentation it was found that 80-per-cent accuracy and effectiveness could be expected under the following conditions:

LAUNCHING ALTITUDE	LAUNCHING SPEED	LEAD ANGLE
(A) 10–20 meters	160 knots	0° (level)
(B) 7 meters	100 knots	4.5°

Design of the special torpedoes was completed and they were put into production in mid-September. They were not all finished, however, by the time the first fleet units left the homeland for the Kurile rendezvous. Accordingly, carrier *Kaga* was detained until 18 November to receive the last of the torpedoes from the factories. These were distributed to the other carriers when *Kaga* arrived at Tankan Bay.

It is important to understand that Admiral Yamamoto's basic plan for an attack on Hawaii was not conceived with the idea of precipitating a war with the United States. He was, on the contrary, consistently and vigorously opposed to such a war. In our long and close personal acquaintance he often expressed the view that a war with the United States would end disastrously for Japan. His words on the subject to Prince Konoye, the Prime Minister, have been quoted frequently: "In the event of such a war, the Navy could give the enemy great trouble for six months or a year. After that I do not know." These are not words of aggression to inspire war.

Yamamoto also said, in a letter to a friend: "If we should go to war against the United States we must recognize the fact that the armistice will have to be dictated from the White House." These words, meant to convey the impossibility of victory for Japan, were misquoted and misinterpreted in World War II propaganda.

When Yamamoto saw Admiral Nagano in Tokyo in early November, they drank toasts to the negotiations being conducted in Washington. They hoped that these negotiations would avoid the need for war.

3. *Timing and Accuracy—Excellent*

The Pearl Harbor Attack Force sortied from Tankan Bay in the morning of 26 November. On 2 December His Imperial Majesty's Cabinet made the final decision in favor of war with the United States and this was communicated to the task force next day by means of a coded message, "Climb Mount Niitaka!" Thereupon, barring circumstances which in the opinion of the force commander might require a change in plans, the die was cast. Seas, weather, and fortune all favored the attack force in its approach to the scheduled launching point, some 230 miles due north of Pearl Harbor.

The local time was 0600 hours on 7 December (1330 of 8 December in Tokyo) when the first wave of attack planes was launched. The seas had built up in early morning so that the carriers pitched as much as fifteen degrees, but all planes—51 bombers, 89 torpedo planes, and 43 fighters—were launched without incident. One hour later the second wave, consisting of 78 bombers, 54 torpedo planes, and 35 fighters, was launched, also without mishap. The estimated flying time to Pearl Harbor was one hour and fifty minutes.

American radar installations at Oahu were capable of detecting the approach of planes at a range of fifty miles, and a set located at Opana did, in fact, pick up the first attack wave at 0730. But the young officer in charge of that station, thinking these planes to be an expected flight of friendly aircraft, took no action.

Mention is made of this "chance" to detect and be aware of the approaching attack force because it could have made a difference in the tactics employed by the attacking planes. The Japanese plan embraced two possibilities. If the element of surprise could be maintained, the attack was to be opened by torpedo planes, followed closely by level bombers, and lastly by dive bombers, which could best make their way through the smoke from the earlier attacks to find suitable targets. If surprise was lost there would be a "storming assault," wherein the fighter planes would have to gain control of the air over the targets, before the bombers and torpedo planes came in to do their work.

Each method required different approaches and movements. The decision as to which type of attack should be used was difficult because the choice had to be made while the planes were still at an altitude of 10,000 feet.

When Commander Fuchida arrived over the target that Sunday morning the sky was clear, the harbor calm. He decided that surprise had been achieved, and ordered the entire force to attack accordingly, leading off with torpedo planes which began launching their missiles at 0755.

By the time the second attack group reached Pearl Harbor an hour later, the sky was so filled with smoke that the new arrivals had to sweep low to catch sight of the targets. Some planes came in so low that they returned to their carriers with electric lines dangling from their tail wheels.

It was astonishing and beyond all expectation that of the 350 planes engaged in attacking Pearl Harbor all but 29 returned safely to the carriers. Simple statistics indicate the value of a surprise attack and the virtue of rigorous training and preparations, but the basic wisdom of the Pearl Harbor strike must be considered from the standpoint of over-all strategy in the Pacific War.

Results of the attack as acknowledged by the United States were as follows:

Sunk
> Battleships *Arizona, California, Oklahoma, West Virginia*
> Minelayer *Oglala*
> Target ship *Utah*

Damaged
> Battleships *Maryland, Nevada, Pennsylvania, Tennessee*
> Light cruisers *Raleigh, Honolulu, Helena*
> Destroyers *Cassin, Shaw, Downes*
> Seaplane tender *Curtiss*
> Repair ship *Vestal*

Thus it appeared that a critically large portion of the Pacific Fleet had been disabled. It was fortunate for the United States Navy, however, that none of its aircraft carriers were in Pearl Harbor that eventful day. Prime targets for attack, they would almost certainly have been sunk. That they were absent, and thus spared, was to be of great significance in months to come.

The official Japanese report of the attack did not differ greatly from the damage acknowledged by the United States. The accuracy of the claims made by the Japanese pilots was remarkable, and indicative of their skill and training. Hits were achieved with 55 per cent of the torpedoes launched; in bombing, the successes were 25 per cent for high-level releases and almost 50 per cent for dive bombing. These scores were as good as any achieved in practice.

In addition to the damage inflicted on warships at Pearl Harbor, there were 219 enemy planes destroyed on the ground and in the air. Included in this number were many B-17s which had begun arriving at Oahu at 0800, just as the Japanese attack was getting underway.

4. Special Attack Submarines

The brilliant success of the Japanese air strike at Pearl Harbor obscured the comparatively unsuccessful effort made by Japan's midget submarines. They derived from the "human torpedoes" idea of the Russo-Japanese War. Their construction program was started in 1939 and the first ones were commissioned the following year. Some twenty of these curious little craft had been built by 1941. They were designed to be launched during the confusion of a great surface battle, where they could slip close to the enemy and raise havoc with his capital ships. The midgets displaced 46 tons, were 24 meters long and not quite two meters in diameter, and were powered by electric batteries capable of propelling them submerged for five hours.

In the summer of 1941 Lieutenants (jg) Naoji Iwasa and Keiu Matsuo produced a plan for using these small submarines at the very outset of a war. Admiral Yamamoto rejected the scheme on the ground that the crews could not be rescued after launching their two torpedoes. The two young officers worked out a method of recovering the little submarines, and petitioned for the Admiral's reconsideration. This time Yamamoto was persuaded that their proposal had merit. He ordered a full-scale study of the small boats with special attention toward increasing their range and perfecting methods of recovery. By early November the cruising range had been increased to sixteen hours and plans had been worked out which gave the midgets a fair chance of being recovered by large submarines. It was thereupon decided to make them a part of the Pearl Harbor attack.

Operation of these little submarines was difficult and risky but there were many volunteers for this duty. The ten men honored by being chosen for the Pearl Harbor attack were Lieutenant Iwasa, Lieutenants (jg) Furuno and Yokoyama, Ensigns Hiro and Sakamaki, and Petty Officers Sasaki, Yokoyama, Ueda, Katayama, and Inagaki. After intensive training they were assigned in pairs to the five craft allocated for this operation.

Each of the small boats was transported to the vicinity of Pearl Harbor by a fleet submarine whose afterdeck was fitted with clamps for carrying the infant. The "mother" submarines left from Kure on 18 November and arrived in the delivery area before dawn of 7 December. Four released their charges within minutes after 0300, but the fifth was two hours late in loosing the midget.

The crews had been ordered to enter Pearl Harbor, fire on targets of opportunity, and rejoin the parent submarines at a rendezvous seven miles west of Lanai Island. The only entrance to the harbor was a shallow and very narrow channel protected by antisubmarine nets, which were opened only to permit the passage of friendly warships. Thus the tiny subs, to accomplish their mission, had to pass through the nets in the shadow of an American ship.

The midgets first attracted American attention at 0342 when minesweeper *Condor*, patrolling outside the harbor, sighted one. Two managed to get through the entrance channel and were sunk, as were the other two outside the harbor. The late-starting midget experienced various mechanical troubles, drifted around to the eastern end of Oahu, and ran on a reef the next morning. Her commanding officer, Ensign Kazuo Sakamaki, managed to straggle ashore, where he was taken prisoner, the only survivor from the midget submarines.

Even though the aerial attack at Pearl Harbor greatly overshadowed the midget submarine activity, the nine young men who gave their lives were lauded in Japan as outstanding heroes of the Pacific War. Lieutenant Matsuo, who had helped in the planning for the midgets, was bitterly disappointed that he had not been selected to take part in this initial operation. His disappointment was overcome when he was permitted to volunteer for a midget submarine operation into Sydney, Australia, in May 1942, from which he never returned.

5. Strategic Defeat for Japan

From the standpoint of tactics, the Pearl Harbor operation was one of the most successful surprise attacks in history.
Admiral Yamamoto, though not an aviator himself, had enjoyed several tours of duty involving naval aviation, and the
Combined Fleet maneuvers in 1940 had firmly convinced him
of the importance of naval air power. This conviction was
strengthened the following November when twenty-one carrier
planes of the British Mediterranean Fleet struck Italian warships anchored at Taranto in a night attack, and sank three
battleships with a loss of only two British planes.

It is interesting to note that the United States Navy drew the
same lesson from the British attack at Taranto. Navy Secretary Frank Knox sent to Army Secretary Henry L. Stimson the
following memorandum: "The success of the British aerial
torpedo attack against ships at anchor suggests that precau-
tionary measures be taken immediately to protect Pearl Harbor against surprise attack in the event that war should break
out between the United States and Japan. The greatest danger
will come from aerial torpedoing. Highest priority must be
given to getting more interceptor planes and antiaircraft guns,
and to the installation of additonal antiaircraft radar equipment."

Secretary Stimson agreed and instructed the Hawaiian
Defense Command to strengthen its facilities against a possible surprise air attack. When, in spite of this warning, the
Hawaiian Command was caught off guard, a sudden sense of
outrage galvanized the American people into action as nothing
else could have. President Roosevelt's promise that Americans
would never be sent to fight overseas was instantly nullified,
and America went to war to the cry of "Remember Pearl Harbor!" It is significant that the attack on Pearl Harbor, despite
its immediate success as a tactical operation, is characterized
by American historians as a strategic defeat for Japan.

Admiral Yamamoto had planned that the attack on Pearl
Harbor should commence one hour *after* Ambassador Kichisaburo Nomura had notified Secretary of State Cordell Hull

of the severance of diplomatic relations between their two countries. Ambassador Nomura had been instructed to deliver the note to the United States Government at 1300 hours on 7 December, Washington time. But the note was 5,000 words in length and the deciphering of its fourteen parts took more time than had been anticipated. When the Japanese Ambassador finally rushed to the Department of State with his note the time was 1420. Secretary Hull was already apprised of the attack, which had started 35 minutes earlier. Thus did Japan enter into a state of war without formal declaration.

This same coded message, announcing the severance of relations, had also been deciphered in Washington by the United States Navy at 0800—a little less than five hours before the attack—and was delivered to official Washington within two hours. Though this was not strictly a proclamation of war, the local authorities in Hawaii and the Philippines were later of the opinion that if its contents had been forwarded to them promptly they could have avoided being taken completely by surprise. As a matter of fact, the Army Chief of Staff, General Marshall, did dispatch the essence of the note to overseas commands, but it was not delivered in Hawaii until after the attack had started.

The American failure to act or react in time, and the personal responsibilities for that failure, are problems for the United States to ponder. As for Japan, she can never eradicate or alter the fact that she started the war with a surprise attack.

Regardless of diplomatic problems and later strategic results, the attack on Pearl Harbor was an operational masterpiece. Tremendous damage was inflicted on the target, with miniscule losses to the attacking force. As a result, Japan was able to complete her southern conquests even sooner than she had expected.

There was, however, an ironic and disastrous element in the victory. The United States Navy was operating under a war plan called "Rainbow 1," which had been drawn up in contemplation of possible conflict with Japan. This plan called for the abandonment of the Philippines and other American outposts in the Western Pacific at the beginning of hostilities, but it also called for a decisive battle with the Japanese Fleet within six to nine months in the vicinity of the Marshalls or Western Carolines.

Had Admiral Yamamoto been aware of this plan he would have realized that the attack on Pearl Harbor was not necessary. The battle area envisaged in Rainbow 1 fitted exactly with the traditional strategy for which Combined Fleet had been planning and training over a period of thirty years. When Japan's decision was made for war, however, it was the consensus of her high command that the United States Fleet would move immediately to the Western Pacific and there threaten Japan's southern operations. The attack on Pearl Harbor was executed to prevent this threat at the outset of hostilities. In short, the entire Pearl Operation was the result of a strategy based on an erroneous hypothesis.

Much criticism has been directed at Admiral Nagumo for withdrawing his force after making the single, two-wave attack. Defenders of his decision point out that the prompt withdrawal was entirely orthodox, since he had inflicted a decisively heavy blow while suffering only minute loss. They argue that to have remained in the vicinity of the Hawaiian Islands to deliver another attack would have exposed his force to losses out of proportion to the amount of additional damage that might have been inflicted. Nagumo decided against the second attack despite the urgent pleadings of Rear Admiral Tamon Yamaguchi, the commander of Second Air Fleet.

There have been many critics of Japan's failure to make another attack. Their judgment springs primarily, of course, from the benefit of hindsight—an advantage not available at the time and place of action. But it is now clear that if the fuel tanks and naval repair facilities at Pearl Harbor had been destroyed—and one more attack could easily have accomplished that—the United States Navy would have been delayed much longer from taking offensive action, and Japan's early success would have been the greater for it.

聯
合
艦
隊

3

EARLY VICTORIES CONTINUE

1. Battle off Malaya

A GREAT CHANGE in the character of naval warfare occurred on 10 December 1941 with the battle which took place off Kuantan, Malaya. Up to that time naval experts had debated vigorously and long the question of who would win a contest between planes and capital ships. Taranto and Pearl Harbor had not provided the answer because in both cases the ships were "sitting ducks." But off Malaya, for the first time in history, battle was waged between planes and capital ships underway.

British battleship *Prince of Wales* and battle cruiser *Repulse*, with escorting destroyers, were attacked by 95 land-based planes of the Japanese Naval Air Force. A fierce battle, which lasted only an hour and a half, resulted in the sinking of these two powerful and modern warships.

Great Britain, the United States, and even Japan were stunned by this astounding aerial success. The step-by-step developments of this battle, which led to new concepts of naval warfare, can now be told.

Japan's final decision for war was made on 2 December 1941, and the Malayan Expeditionary Force was that day mustered in full strength. It sailed from Hainan Island on the 4th to make surprise landings in Malaya on the 8th. Naval support for the convoy and landing operations was provided by Vice Admiral Nobutake Kondo's Second Fleet and Vice Admiral Jisaburo Ozawa's Third Fleet.

The Pearl Harbor Striking Force had been able to choose a fairly isolated course toward its target in the Hawaiian Islands, but the way for the Malayan Expeditionary Force lay through the narrow South China Sea and athwart the busy sea lane between Singapore and Hong Kong. It was thus exposed to the observation of numerous merchant ships and, in addition, there was the ever-present possibility of its being sighted by land-based scout planes of the Royal Air Force. As might have been expected, the Japanese force was sighted off Pointe de Damau, at the southern tip of French Indochina, by an R.A.F. patrol plane on 6 December. Admiral Ozawa promptly ordered that any plane should be destroyed on sight, and one was shot down that very afternoon.

The Japanese ships proceeded on their scheduled course and, starting at midnight, 8 December, landed troops at Singora and other points along the eastern coast of the Malay peninsula. Japanese landing operations went smoothly everywhere in Malaya except at Kota Baru, where enemy air raids provided some slight interference. The really formidable opposition in this area was yet to come.

On 2 December Great Britain had announced the formation of her new Far Eastern Fleet. This fleet traditionally consisted of a cruiser squadron whose flagship was the 10,000-ton *Kent*. It came as a shock to the Japanese Navy, therefore, to learn that the new battleship *Prince of Wales* and battle cruiser *Repulse* had been added to the British Far Eastern Fleet. The presence in the Far East of *Prince of Wales*, which, along with *King George V*, was considered the strongest ship in the Royal Navy, indicated Great Britain's determination to maintain her position of strength and deter Japan's southward expansion.

Japan's old battleships *Nagato* and *Mutsu* were no match for Britain's *Prince of Wales*, and superbattleship *Yamato* was not yet commissioned. Second Fleet Battleships *Kongo* and *Haruna* were in the area, but their 14-inch guns did not compare with the new 15-inch weapons of *Prince of Wales*. Admiral Ozawa's carriers had been detached for the Pearl Harbor operation, so he had only five cruisers (*Chokai, Kumano, Suzuya, Mikuma, Mogami*). The two modern British warships easily outclassed any surface force Japan could muster in the vicinity.

The British ships were first sighted south of Poulo Condore Island off French Indochina by Japanese submarine *I-6*, at 1410 hours on 9 December, and were reported promptly. Japanese transport vessels engaged in landing operations immediately fled to Thailand Bay. As soon as the transports were headed for safety, Admiral Kondo ordered land-based planes to shadow the British warships while he led his own surface forces to engage them. He planned to have Cruiser Division 7 (four heavy cruisers and three destroyers) and Destroyer Squadron 3 (ten ships) attack the enemy during the night. The Second Fleet, with its two battleships and two heavy cruisers, was to arrive at dawn on the 10th, when all ships would join in a daylight attack.

At this early point in the war the aggressive spirit of Japanese Navy men was not dampened by the fact that their ships' guns were shorter ranged than those of the enemy. The contest would be resolved by a long-distance duel between the two big ships on each side. Although the British would have a 60 per cent advantage in gun range, the Japanese counted on superior skill in gunnery and tactics, on spiritual power, and superior numbers to gain them a victory.

The gods smiled frequently on Japan's Navy during the early part of the Pacific War. On this occasion they smiled fondly on Kondo's warships, which never met the southward-speeding enemy. The British ships were sighted by a scout plane from heavy cruiser *Kumano*, and also by submarine *I-59*, but both contacts were quickly lost in tropical squalls. It was fortunate for Kondo that he did not have to engage this powerful enemy force.

2. *Planes Sink Battleships*

In early November the Japanese Navy had stationed the First Air Group, consisting of 6 reconnaissance planes, 39 fighters, and 99 bomber and torpedo planes from Genzan, Mihoro, and Kanoya in the homeland, at three fields in French Indochina. These 144 planes scored the brilliant victory over British surface forces off Malaya on 10 December.

The First Air Group received word of the movement of enemy ships in the vicinity of Malaya at 1710 on 9 December. It was too late in the day to launch an aerial attack, but at 1800 a token group of four reconnaissance planes was sent out, followed within an hour by eighteen bombers and fifteen torpedo planes. They searched throughout the night for the British ships while the other planes were being prepared for dawn takeoff.

Two nine-plane formations were sent off at 0625 on 10 December to search arcs of 250 and 600 miles from their bases. The First Air Group launched 34 bombers at 0750, and 50 torpedo planes at 0930.

The general direction of all planes was toward Singapore. No enemy planes were sighted on the outward flights and, reluctantly, the Japanese pilots started back to base. Then, by extraordinary luck, one plane sighted *Prince of Wales* and three escorts cruising to the south, 50 miles off Kuantan.

At news of this sighting the entire group headed full speed for the indicated area. They came within sight of the British ships at 1156, five and a half hours after take-off. These Usui Unit planes of the Minoro Air Group, though very low on fuel, made their first bombing run at 1214. It was close to 1300 when the next three units, torpedo planes from the Kanoya Air Group, joined the battle. Time was running out for the attacking planes.

The aerial attack on Pearl Harbor was much more widely publicized, but it was in no way superior to the performance of the Japanese planes which struck the British naval force off Malaya. Here the targets were powerful modern battleships, under way and in fighting trim, fully prepared with the latest in antiaircraft guns and equipment.

Prince of Wales was slow in avoiding torpedo attacks, but her antiaircraft fire was heavy and far surpassed any that might have been produced by a Japanese battleship at the time. Eight planes of the first attack group were hit at an altitude of 3,000 meters. Enemy fire was so rapid and heavy and the bomb explosions so fierce that torpedo planes of the Ishihara Group, in the second attack wave, lost sight of their companions attacking from the opposite side of the targets. The antiaircraft fire from *Prince of Wales* was relentless to the last, and damaged five of the eight Takeda Group bombers which delivered the *coup de grâce* to the valiant warship.

Battle results showed that of 84 planes used in the attack, three were shot down, one crash-landed with heavy damage, two were heavily damaged but landed safely, and twenty-five were slightly damaged. The guns on *Prince of Wales* were used well, but British fire was less effective against torpedo planes than against bombers. This may be explained by the fact that British torpedo planes of that time launched their weapons at speeds no greater than 100 miles per hour. British gunners, from their training and practice, came to consider that as a near-maximum speed for launching. Japanese planes, however, could launch at speeds of 150 to 190 miles per hour, and British gunners found it difficult to adjust to this unusually high speed. Consequently, as accompanying diagrams indicate, torpedoes were responsible for most of the ship damage.

Of 15 torpedoes launched against *Prince of Wales*, 7 found their mark, for a ratio of 46.7 per cent. Against *Repulse*, hits were scored by 14 out of 34 torpedoes fired, for a hitting rate of 41.2 per cent. Both scores were better than any achieved in practice. *Prince of Wales* was hit by two out of seven bombs aimed at her, *Repulse* by one out of fourteen.

High-speed battleship *Repulse* sank at 1420. Her final stur-

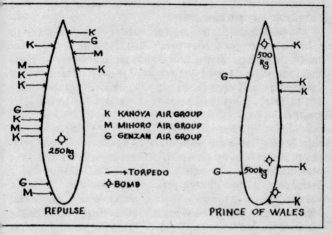

Diagram of Torpedo and Bomb Hits in *Repulse* and *Prince of Wales*.

diness was a tribute to the quality of her construction. Despite her twenty-five years, it took fourteen direct torpedo hits to finish her off.

Prince of Wales, the first "unsinkable battleship" to come to Singapore, was much more powerful than *Repulse*. But she was hit in vulnerable spots by five out of seven torpedoes launched in the early attacks, with the result that her speed was slowed to six knots. Next assailed by three 500-kilogram bombs (two direct hits, and a near miss which did some damage), one of her powder magazines exploded, dooming the ship. She sank at 1445.

News that this famous battleship had fallen victim to aerial attack caused a great stir in naval circles throughout the world, and resulted in the revamping of strategy and tactics. There was criticism of Vice Admiral Sir Tom Phillips for having taken his force into a zone where control of the air was in enemy hands. Phillips was well aware of the danger, as evidenced by his repeated requests for fighter-plane protection.

Headquarters at Singapore maintained that no planes were available for such missions.

Admiral Phillips' reasons for withdrawing his ships from the Singapore naval base were sound. He wanted to prevent their defenseless destruction within the harbor, as at Pearl Harbor. He had hoped that a show of strength by his powerful warships would deter the admittedly inferior Japanese surface ships in the vicinity. These considerations led to his final battle.

Admiral Phillips was one of the most able flag officers in the British Navy, and an outstanding authority on naval aviation. As his flagship sank staff officers urged him to abandon the bridge and try for safety. Their entreaties were met with a terse refusal, and Phillips perished with his ship. He was a strong believer in the importance of air power in modern naval warfare, and had he survived it is likely that he would have praised the brilliant and daring performance of the Japanese Navy's land-based planes.

3. Dutch Indies and Indian Ocean Operations

In the early days of the Pacific War the main strength of the Japanese Army was deployed in China and Manchuria. Only eleven divisions and some seven hundred planes were allocated for southern operations, to which almost four million tons of shipping had been assigned. These were second-line naval forces, to be sure, since Admiral Yamamoto's First Fleet was anchored at Hiroshima and Vice Admiral Nagumo's Carrier Striking Force was engaged in attacking Pearl Harbor. Yet, with these comparatively inferior forces, Japan enjoyed unprecedented victories. Within 50 days after the beginning of hostilities she succeeded in occupying the Philippine Islands. Malaya fell in 100 days, and the Dutch East Indies in 150 days. Almost everything went according to plan.

In the southern areas the primary function of the Navy was to support and assist the landing operatons of the expeditionary forces. Any consideration of a decisive battle with enemy naval units was purely secondary.

The naval force assigned to the southern operations was under the command of Vice Admiral Nobutake Kondo. It consisted of 2 battleships (*Kongo, Haruna*), 13 heavy cruisers (*Atago, Takao, Chokai, Kumano, Suzuya, Mikuma, Mogami, Myoko, Haguro, Nachi, Ashigara, Maya, Kuma*), 6 light cruisers (*Sendai, Kinu, Jintsu, Nagara, Naka, Yura*), 40 destroyers, and 15 submarines. These were organized into nine operational units: a main body, the French Indochina Force, an escort group, four attack groups, an air attack group, and a mine group. In November 1941 this force was considered capable of dealing with all Far Eastern forces of the United States, Great Britain, the Netherlands, Australia, and New Zealand.

Japanese complacence on this score had been somewhat shaken in early December when Britain's *Prince of Wales* and *Repulse* appeared in the Far East. But the sinking of these two great ships in one day gave Japan renewed assurance of success. Her heavy cruisers would now be able to cope with any remaining naval forces in the southern area.

On 26 February 1942 heavy cruisers *Nachi* and *Haguro*, with 16 ships of Destroyer Squadrons 2 and 4, escorted a convoy of 41 transports toward Java. Enemy ships were sighted when this force reached a point 60 miles northeast of Surabaya. Salvoes were exchanged at maximum range and the Allied ships started to flee, but then turned to engage in earnest and by midnight the two forces were joined in a gun and torpedo duel.

This was the first surface-to-surface engagement of the Pacific War. It brought into action the proudest weapon of the Japanese Navy, the Type-91, oxygen-fueled torpedo. At a speed of 32 knots it had a range of 40,000 meters—five times that of any British or American torpedo. At its maximum speed of 50 knots the oxygen torpedo had a range of 20,000 meters; and this formidable weapon left no telltale surface track.

Within a matter of hours, on 27 February, these remarkable

torpedoes spelled the doom of Dutch light cruisers *De Ruyter* and *Java*, destroyer *Kortenaer*, and British destroyer *Electra*. Other Allied ships in the vicinity, assuming that the sinkings had been caused by mines, were astounded to see Japanese warships steam through the same waters without damage. Not until after the war did the enemy learn that all of these sinkings had been caused by long-range torpedoes. Japanese crews, well beyond the range of ship-borne guns, swarmed on deck to observe enemy ships go down in bursts of flame and smoke. It was like watching a fireworks display. This action, which is known as the Battle of the Java Sea, might well have been called the Battle of the Oxygen Torpedoes.

On the following day Cruiser Division 7 (heavy cruisers *Kumano, Suzuya, Mikuma, Mogami*) and Destroyer Squadron 5 were escorting a convoy of 56 transports. They met, engaged with gunfire, and sank three cruisers—U.S.S. *Houston*, H.M.A.S. *Perth*, and H.N.M.S. *Evertsen*—in the Battle of Sunda Strait. Japanese gunnery in this action was at its best.

News of the Java Sea and Sunda Strait battles was received in Japan with great jubilation, while the action continued in the Dutch East Indies.

Fifth Fleet was engaged in a screening mission off the coast of Java on 1 March when it met a British force consisting of cruiser *Exeter* and destroyers *Pope* and *Encounter*. The Fifth Fleet ships, soon joined by Third Fleet cruisers *Ashigara* and *Myoko* surrounded the hapless British warships and sank all three by gunfire.

With these battles Japan gained control of the sea in the Southwest Pacific. A few American destroyers and other Allied ships managed to escape the Japanese onslaught by slipping through Bali Strait, and they were the only enemy warships to survive. Allied surface strength in the Far East had been wiped out in three months.

Vice Admiral Nagumo's task force followed its great success at Pearl Harbor by bombarding Port Darwin, Australia, on 19 February, and ended the month helping to clean up the Java area.

Colombo, Ceylon, was attacked 5 April. British cruisers
Dorsetshire and *Cornwall* attempted to flee, but were caught
by planes from Pearl Harbor veterans *Akagi* and *Kaga*. The
aerial force of 53 torpedo planes and 38 bombers, escorted by
36 fighters, sank *Dorsetshire* within eight minutes after the
first bomb fell, and *Cornwall* was finished half an hour later.
It was a startling demonstration of aerial marksmanship and
effectiveness.

The task force struck Trincomalee on 9 April and sank
several ships, including British aircraft carrier *Hermes*, which
suffered more than forty direct hits. Thus the Indian Ocean
operations ended with yet another sweeping victory for Japan.

As Japan climbed to victory after glorious victory in early
1942 it was inconceivable that she would lie broken and defeated in three and a half years.

The Japanese Navy, accepting its favorable tide of fortune,
decided to strike a blow at British shipping in the Indian
Ocean. Toward this end, Carrier Division 1 sortied from the
homeland on 9 March, escorted by the Second Fleet.

4. Battle of the Coral Sea

Scarcely pausing for breath, Japanese naval forces
sortied to invade the southwestern shore of Papua. This "*MO*
Operation" included the preliminary seizure of Nauru and
Ocean Islands and Tulagi as steppingstones toward Port
Moresby, a strategic point from which Australia was within
easy bombing range.

Rear Admiral Chuichi Hara commanded the *MO* Operation
task force. It consisted of carriers *Zuikaku* and *Shokaku*, 6
heavy cruisers, 3 light cruisers, 15 destroyers, numerous auxiliaries, and a convoy of 14 transports carrying landing troops
and a construction unit.

In confidential talks with ranking naval officers during the
early part of the war I had learned of plans for an outer defensive perimeter for Japan. It was amazing to see it actually tak-

ing form. I had never heard, however, that this defense line was to include Port Moresby. This optimistic extension was a product of Japan's amazing good fortune as the war began. The successes of the first five months produced in the Japanese mind what has been characterized as "victory disease," and an early symptom was the mistaken notion of invincibility. So firm was this conviction that even the failure to seize Port Moresby was interpreted as yet another great victory.

The *MO* Operation could have dealt a stunning blow to the Allies. Against this Japanese offensive the enemy had available one British battleship and the following United States warships: 2 carriers, 2 battleships, 4 heavy and 4 light cruisers, and 17 destroyers.

Scout planes from each side discovered ships of the enemy at dawn of 8 May, and there followed the first naval battle in history in which opposing ships did not exchange a shot. All offensive action was by carrier-based planes, and each side lost about thirty in combat.

Japanese planes sank carrier *Lexington*, fleet oiler *Neosho*, and destroyer *Sims*; and damaged carrier *Yorktown*. As against this, the Japanese Navy lost destroyer *Kikuzuki* and three auxiliary vessels in action, plus light carrier *Shoho*, which was sunk the previous day while escorting the convoy away from the battle zone. Numerically, Japan was winner in the Battle of the Coral Sea.

Against *Lexington* Japanese planes had dropped 19 bombs and scored 10 hits, for a score of 53 per cent. Of 14 torpedoes launched, 9 hit. The fire power of the U.S. ships in this battle was infinitely greater than that of the British fleet in the Indian Ocean; yet, once again, superior Japanese naval air strength had proved itself.

Despite a numerical victory at Coral Sea, Japan suffered her first setback of the war in failing to achieve her intended invasion of Port Moresby. The battle ended with the withdrawal of Japanese forces, and must be counted as one in which the Japanese commander quit too soon. Had Admiral Hara been more persistent and aggressive he could easily have destroyed the damaged *Yorktown* and enhanced his tally. What is more important, *Yorktown* would have been prevented from participating in the Battle of Midway a month later where, before she was sunk, her planes sealed the doom of Japanese carrier *Akagi*.

4
MIDWAY

聯合艦隊

1. Groundwork for Defeat

BY THE SPRING OF 1942 the Japanese people were intoxicated with the idea that their nation was invincible. The attack on Pearl Harbor had scored a telling blow against the United States, and succeeding operations from the Philippines to the Indian Ocean had continued victoriously. Unit after unit of Japan's fleet returned triumphant to home ports. It would have been fortunate for Japan if the war could have ended abruptly in the spring of 1942.

The United States, like Japan, had never been defeated in war. Both nations had suffered military setbacks but, no matter how dark the outlook, neither had ever been vanquished. A powerful Germany had started World War I with spectacular successes, only to be brought down in defeat within four years by the combined strength of Great Britain and the United States. This still-fresh memory caused certain Japanese leaders to oppose of idea of going to war against the United States and her Allies. In an Imperial Conference of 6 September 1941 Admiral Osami Nagano, Chief of the Naval General Staff, told the Emperor, "We can successfully oppose the United States in war for a period of two years. Any longer conflict would tend to be unprofitable for Japan."

This view was shared by all Japanese who knew the fighting strength of their own country and also understood the capability of their potential enemy. The first six months of war brought greater victories for Japan than anyone could possibly have imagined. The second half year was about to begin in May 1942. While the rest of the nation went wild with joy over Japan's early successes, such men as Admiral Isoroku Yamamoto were sober and reflective.

Yamamoto knew the value and importance of air power, and he could not forget the existence of the United States Navy's seven first-class aircraft carriers. None of them had been present at Pearl Harbor on the first day of the Pacific War, and by the end of the April 1942 not one of them had been damaged.[1] Japan's eastern defensive perimeter in the Pacific Ocean extended over a 3,000-mile line from north to south, and it was expected that this line would soon be breached by enemy task forces. The backbone of such task forces—aircraft carriers—had to be destroyed.

The enemy had already succeeded in attacking the Japanese homeland on 18 April 1942 with B-25s led from the deck of carrier *Hornet* by Lieutenant Colonel James Doolittle. This strike, though inconsequential in physical damage, was a terrible shock to the people of Japan, for it showed that the sacred homeland was *not* inviolate.

To minimize such threats Japan had extended her lookout posts some six hundred miles eastward from the home islands by means of a chain of small fishing craft equipped with radio transmitters. This early-warning system of picket boats,

---

[1] Except for *Saratoga* (CV-3) damaged by torpedo from submarine *I-6* on 11 Jan. 1942, in position 500 miles SW of Oahu; the *Enterprise* (CV-6) slightly damaged 1 Feb. 1942 by Japanese plane attempting a crash dive.

simple as it was, and ineffective as it proved to be against the B-25 raid, was Japan's sole substitute for her lack of adequate radar.

Neither the person of the Emperor nor his sacred soil was safe while enemy carriers ranged the seas. This was especially disturbing to Admiral Yamamoto, who felt a strong sense of responsibility for the Emperor's safety.

2. Hope for Compromise

Army leaders in Japan believed that the United States could be easily defeated. But Admirals Yamamoto and Nagano knew the temper, traits, and character of the American people, as well as the military history of the country, and they had no illusions of an easy victory for Japan.

Their hope was that Japan might quickly achieve such overwhelming successes that the United States would accept a compromise peace. There was risk involved, but Yamamoto decided in favor of decisive battle. The question then remained as to where the battle should be fought. The Naval General Staff hoped that it could be in the Solomons.

The Solomon Islands, stretching southeasterly from Rabaul to Guadalcanal, could provide valuable bases for the Japanese fleet. The General Staff figured that seizure of these islands would constitute such a threat to Allied lines of communications that the United States Navy would oppose their occupation, and could then be annihilated. This concept depended heavily on the enemy's rising to the bait. If the enemy shied from decisive battle in the Solomons, Japan would be faced with a long war.

Admiral Yamamoto, on the other hand, advocated Midway as the battleground. He reasoned that Japanese occupation of Midway and the Aleutians (all part of the same operation plan), would guarantee a challenge from the United States Navy. He felt that Americans could accept the fall of Guam and Wake, but that they would not tolerate Japan's advance beyond the 180th meridian. He also felt that his Midway plan had a better chance of success than the Solomons strategy.

The Midway strategy, however, involved a greater risk. The distance from Japan's Inland Sea to Midway is more than twice the distance from Pearl Harbor to Midway. Midway's comparative proximity to Pearl Harbor would make it extremely difficult, if not impossible, for Japan to support an island garrison. The chance was very great that the enemy could easily recapture the atoll.

But Admiral Yamamoto argued that the opportunity for a decisive battle must be expected to entail risk. Midway should be seized. If the enemy came out to regain the island, Japan's long-sought opportunity would be provided. A fleet-opposed action of Japan's choosing would lead the way to another "Pearl Harbor," in which, this time, enemy aircraft carriers could be destroyed. With the U.S. Navy's strength divided between the Atlantic and Pacific Oceans, Yamamoto felt that the Pacific half would fall easy victim to the concentrated Combined Fleet of Imperial Japan.

While these two plans were being discussed, a third suggestion was put forth by Yamamoto's chief of staff, Rear Admiral Ryunosuke Kusaka. He pointed out that the fleet had just finished a long series of operations in the South Pacific, and that pilots and crews were exhausted. Because ships and planes needed repair and refitting, Kusaka proposed a delay of forty or fifty days. During this time the pilots who had gained valuable combat experience in the early operations would be transferred to land bases, to train new fliers. Thereafter the freshly trained pilots could be used to augment the ranks of experienced aviators in decisive battle. Unfortunately, however, detailed plans for the Midway operation were developed without consideration of Admiral Kusaka's proposal.

Persuaded by Admiral Yamamoto's enthusiastic arguments, even the most reluctant members of the naval high command became convinced that Midway was a proper target for invasion.

3. Combined Fleet Committed

The strategic objective of early decisive battle was established by the Naval General Staff, but the method of achieving it was left to Commander in Chief Combined Fleet. Thus, although the opinion of the General Staff was taken into consideration, it was Admiral Yamamoto's decision that prevailed in final determination of the offensive plan, just as with the attack on Pearl Harbor.

Navy Order No. 18 was issued by Imperial General Headquarters on 5 May 1942. It directed Commander in Chief Combined Fleet to:

Invade and occupy Midway Island and key points in the western Aleutians in cooperation with the Army, in order to prevent enemy task forces from making attacks against the homeland.
Destroy all enemy forces that may oppose the invasion.

According to an Army-Navy "Central Agreement," which was issued at the same time, the Navy's tactical objective was to:

Attack Midway Island and destroy the enemy's land-based air forces prior to the invasion, and
Support the landing operations with the main strength of Combined Fleet.

According to these directives the primary objective was the seizure and occupation of Midway Island. But in Admiral Yamamoto's mind the main goal was to lure the enemy fleet into a decisive surface battle.

Early in May the date of 7 June was set for the invasion. There were to be neutralizing strikes in the Aleutians on 4 June by a Northern Force under Vice Admiral Moshiro Hosogaya, followed by landings at Adak and Kiska Islands on the 6th. Similarly, the Midway landings were to be preceded by a pre-invasion air strike on 5 June to knock out defensive installations. Beginning on 26 May, Japanese warships sortied from bases in the homeland and the Marianas for this grand offensive operation. The principal ships were organized as follows:

1. MAIN FORCE
Admiral Isoroku Yamamoto in *Yamato*

a. Main Body

Battleships *Yamato, Nagato, Mutsu*
Light carrier *Hosho* (8 Type-96 bombers)
Light cruiser *Sendai*
Nine destroyers
Seaplane carriers *Chiyoda, Nisshin* (carrying midget subs)

b. Guard (Aleutians Screening) Force

Vice Admiral Shiro Takasu in *Hyuga*
Battleships *Hyuga, Ise, Fuso, Yamashiro*
Light cruisers *Oi, Kitakami*
Twelve destroyers

2. FIRST CARRIER STRIKING FORCE
Vice Admiral Chuichi Nagumo in *Akagi*

a. Carrier Group

Cardiv 1 (Nagumo) *Akagi, Kaga* (42 fighters, 42 dive bombers, and 51 torpedo bombers)
Cardiv 2 (Rear Admiral Tamon Yamaguchi) *Hiryu, Soryu* (42 fighters, 42 dive bombers, 42 torpedo bombers)

b. Support Group

Rear Admiral Hiroaki Abe in *Tone*
Battleships *Haruna, Kirishima*

c. Screening Group

Rear Admiral Susumu Kimura in light cruiser *Nagara*
Eleven destroyers

3. MIDWAY INVASION FORCE
Vice Admiral Nobutake Kondo in *Atago*

a. Invasion Force Main Body (Kondo)

Battleships *Kongo, Hiei*
Light carrier *Zuiho* (12 fighters, 12 torpedo planes)
Heavy cruisers *Atago, Chokai, Myoko, Haguro*
Light cruiser *Yura*
Eight destroyers

b. Close Support Group

   Vice Admiral Takeo Kurita in *Kumano*
Heavy cruisers *Kumano, Suzuya, Mikuma, Mogami*
Two destroyers

c. Transport Group

   Rear Admiral Raizo Tanaka in light cruiser *Jintsu*
Twelve transports and three destroyer transports carrying 5,000
   troops of the Midway Landing Force
Ten destroyers

d. Seaplane Tender Group

   Rear Admiral Ruitaro Fujita
Seaplane carrier *Chitose* (16 float fighters, 4 scout planes)
Seaplane carrier *Kamikawa Maru* (8 float fighters, 4 scout planes)
One destroyer
One patrol boat

   4. NORTHERN (ALEUTIANS) FORCE
   Vice Admiral Moshiro Hosogaya in *Nachi*

a. Main Body

Heavy cruiser *Nachi*
Two destroyers

b. Second Carrier Striking Force

   Rear Admiral Kakuji Kakuta in *Ryujo*
Light carrier *Ryujo* (16 fighters, 21 torpedo bombers)
Carrier *Junyo* (24 fighters, 21 dive bombers)
Heavy cruisers *Maya, Takao*
Three destroyers

c. Attu Invasion Force

    Rear Admiral Sentaro Omori in *Abukuma*
Light cruiser *Abukuma*
Four destroyers
One transport (carrying Army Landing Force of 1,200 troops)

d. Kiska Invasion Force

    Captain Takeji Ono in *Kiso*
Light cruisers *Kiso, Tama*
Auxiliary cruiser *Asaka Maru*
Three destroyers
Two transports (carrying Naval Landing Force of 1,250 troops)

In addition to the 133 warships and transports of Combined
Fleet there were a number of auxiliaries and submarines,
bringing the total to well over 150 Japanese ships involved in
this operation, plus some 200 land-based planes.

As Admiral Yamamoto's Main Force debouched from
Bungo Strait on 29 May it was notified of a nearby enemy submarine. All ships were ordered to antisubmarine alert, and a
second submarine was detected, but the force passed safely
from homeland waters.

Sightings of four enemy submarines were reported the next
day, and the interception of radio messages along the way
made it clear that a dozen or more shadowing submarines were
keeping track of our fleet's progress. These submarines must
have been under instruction to report our warships' movements, but not to attack.

Combined Fleet, full of confidence, followed a zigzag
course and proceeded along its plotted route. Admiral Yamamoto apparently failed to realize that the mere presence of
submarines meant that the enemy had *some* foreknowledge of
the movement toward Midway.

As a matter of fact, Commander in Chief United States
Pacific Fleet, Admiral Chester W. Nimitz, knew of Japan's
intention to capture Midway Island a full month before the
landing was to have taken place. This advance knowledge
enabled him to strengthen the island's defenses and assemble

all his available naval forces to oppose the Japanese onslaught.

4. Negligence Born of Conceit

United States awareness of the Midway operation was
the result of brilliant intelligence work and the amazing success of American experts in breaking Japanese communication
codes. It was the same remarkable success that six months
earlier had given indication that Japan was about to go to war,
and then in months to come would account for the death of
Admiral Yamamoto.

It is no exaggeration to say that the American high command was almost as well informed of the plans for Midway as
was the Japanese Imperial General Staff. Blame for the defeat
at Midway, and for the tragic loss of Admiral Yamamoto's
life in April 1943, must be placed directly on Japan's relaxed
security measures. This relaxation of security was attributable
directly to the fantastic victories Japan had enjoyed early in
the war.

Admiral Nagumo's First Carrier Striking Force was confident as it sortied from Japan and sailed eastward on 27 May.
The weather held good until 2 June, which turned into a day
of densest fog. Formed in a single column, each ship trailed a
marker buoy for the next in line to follow; but the fog was so
thick that even this was of little use. Since a delay of even a
few hours would disrupt invasion plans it became necessary,
despite an order for radio silence to the contrary, to resort to
broadcast signals. At 1030 on 3 June (Japanese time and date),
change-of-course orders were sent by short-range transmission, with the firm conviction and hope that they would not
reach beyond the area covered by the task force.

It was later learned that this transmission had been picked
up by flagship *Yamato*, 400 miles to the rear. From this it is
obvious that any enemy receiver within 400 miles of the carriers might also have heard the signals.

By next morning the fog had lifted and the sun rose brightly in a clear sky. Pearl Harbor veterans *Akagi, Kaga, Hiryu*, and *Soryu*, the world's foremost aircraft carriers, sped on their way. Radio signals from an enemy plane were reported in mid-morning, and cruiser *Tone* sent out a reconnaissance plane. A lookout in *Akagi* reported an enemy plane in the afternoon, and a fighter plane was launched from *Akagi*'s deck to investigate. Both search planes returned with negative results, and the "sightings" were dismissed as erroneous.

In evaluating Japanese command decisions at Midway it is important to consider a pre-battle statement by Admiral Nagumo, the task force commander: "Although the enemy is lacking in fighting spirit, he will probably come out to attack as our invasion proceeds." In view of the agressiveness shown by the enemy at the Battle of the Coral Sea, this assertion is difficult to understand. Perhaps with these words Nagumo was trying to bolster the courage of his men and himself. As a matter of fact, the enemy, eager to engage the Japanese fleet at any opportune moment, was full of fighting spirit. It may be unfair to point out, from the vantage of hindsight, that the conceit expressed by Nagumo's words was probably a strong contributing factor to the fiasco of Midway.

On the morning of battle he said further, "The enemy is unaware of our presence in this area and will so remain until after our initial attacks on the island." This kind of thinking was more than over-optimistic; it was disastrous.

Even without knowing that Japanese codes had been broken, and the enemy was thus fully aware of the intended attack on Midway, there were several obvious indications that the enemy was aware of the offensive move. Some enemy submarines were in position to observe the sortie from the homeland, and there may have been unknown others. Yet even after two enemy planes were reported during the approach, Nagumo's estimate of the situation included the naive remark: "It is assumed that there are no enemy carriers in the waters adjacent to Midway."

This astounding conclusion was entirely without basis. From the time of sortie until the morning of battle, the task force had not sent up a single scout plane to search for enemy ships. Such was the Japanese bland confidence that there was nothing to fear. It was not until the Midway attack squadrons were launched that the first aerial search was made, and it was entirely perfunctory. Clearly, no pre-invasion attack by enemy carrier planes was seriously considered.

It is hard to believe that the same men who had done the careful intelligence work for the Pearl Harbor attack could have done the haphazard job of the Midway operation. As we now know, the intelligence by the carrier force staff was so bad that one wonders if they were functioning at all. Every estimate was bad, every guess was wrong.

Imperial General Headquarters was no better in their long-range forecasts. They had estimated, for example, that the island would be guarded by about 750 troops and some 60 planes. It was figured that 2,800 Japanese landing troops and almost 300 ship-based planes should find little resistance there. Actually the enemy had 285 planes and more than 5,000 troops at Midway. Considering, in addition, the number of planes on the enemy's alerted carriers, there was little, if any, advantage to the Japanese force in numbers of planes. If the Japanese landing forces had tried to invade the island they would have been annihilated.

Two final pre-battle evaluations by Admiral Nagumo show how wrong he was in estimating the situation: "If the enemy fleet counterattacks we will be able to destroy it. . . . We are capable of annihilating any land-based planes that may attack our forces."

It is to be expected that a highly successful fighting machine, such as the Japanese Navy had been for six months, would tend to be confident. But excessive arrogance totally blinded it to even the possibility of strength and preparedness on the part of its enemy.

5. Faulty Planning Brings Disaster

At 0430 hours on the 4th of June,[2] half an hour before
the sun rose on Midway, the Japanese Navy's First Carrier
Striking Force arrived at a point 230 nautical miles northwest
of the island. Fifteen minutes later the first wave of attack
planes had been launched and was winging toward its target.
This group, commanded by Lieutenant Joichi Tomonaga,
consisted of 36 fighters, 36 level bombers, and 36 dive
bombers.

These planes assembled in perfect formation over the carriers before dawn and disappeared into broken clouds. Most
of the pilots were veterans of the Pearl Harbor attack. They
were experienced and confident, and there was no doubt that
they would be successful. This mission was not a war-opening
surprise attack, but merely a neutralizing assault preliminary
to an invasion in force.

Halfway to the target they were sighted by a scouting PBY,
which reported its findings to Midway. Search radar on the
island picked up the Japanese planes half an hour later and all
operable planes were put into the air—fighters to engage the
approaching enemy, bombers and patrol planes to get out of
harm's way.

A second high-flying PBY scout sighted the Japanese planes
and followed them to within 30 miles of the island, where it set
off a flare to alert the defenders. Some 26 Marine fighters
came out to engage. Combat was brief but fierce. The outnumbered and outclassed Marine planes were no match for the
Zero fighters. The Japanese shot down 17 planes and damaged
another 7 at a cost of only six of their own.

All bombers reached the island intact and dropped their
loads on air strips, storage facilities, barracks, and sand. Not
particularly worthy prizes, but with all American planes gone
that was all there was. Lieutenant Tomonaga radioed back to
the flagship and reported the need for another attack. This

---

[2] Local (Midway Island) Zone plus 12 time, West Longitude date.

need of a second strike was the result of poor planning. The enemy was fully prepared.

Although Admiral Nagumo had conjectured that there would be no enemy carriers in the vicinity of Midway, he nevertheless sent out an air search. Ordinarily such a search was a matter of great diligence and concern. This one, however, was so casual—indeed haphazard—as to betray the careless attention devoted to the whole Midway operation.

Reconnaissance flights were scheduled for launching as soon as the attrack group had taken off. Only seven planes were assigned to search the sector from north northeast to due south of the flagship. A plane from *Akagi* was to fly south a distance of 300 miles, dogleg 60 miles to the east and return; a *Kaga* plane to fly southeast the same distance and pattern; two planes from heavy cruiser *Tone* to fly east southeast and east respectively, and two from heavy cruiser *Chikuma* to fly east northeast and northeast. All of these were to fly out a distance of 300 miles, dogleg to the left 60 miles and return. The last plane, from battleship *Haruna*, was to fly north northeast only 150 miles and then 40 to the left and return.

This plan was thin enough; it was rendered even thinner when catapult trouble delayed the start of the *Tone* planes, and a balky engine delayed one from *Chikuma*. *Chikuma*'s late plane ran into bad weather halfway out, and turned back without completing its search pattern. The real grief of the Nagumo force, however, was occasioned by the belated send-off of the two search planes from *Tone*.

After launching the first Midway strike at daybreak, Admiral Nagumo readied a second attack wave on the decks of his carriers. This group—36 fighters, 36 bombers, and 36 torpedo planes—was to stand by in case the scouting planes discovered an enemy surface force. These plans and preparations were proper and would have been adequate but for the failure of the *Tone* and *Chikuma* search planes. If these scouts had taken off on schedule, instead of half an hour late, the situation would have been quite different. Or, indeed, if a second group of search planes had been sent out to dovetail their effort with the first (the usual procedure) the enemy fleet would have been discovered in time to make effective plans for the second attack wave.

This, however, is what happened. One of the *Tone* pilots, on his northern dogleg, first sighted the enemy at 0720 after reaching the limit of his 300-mile line from the cruiser. His vague report—"ten ships" which "appear to be enemy"—did not accurately identify the composition of the force. And he did not make clear until 0825 that one of the ships was an aircraft carrier!

Meanwhile, as the enemy force closed, 108 planes stood on Japanese flight decks awaiting orders. The PBYs, after discovering the Japanese carriers at 0530, had followed them more or less continuously, reporting their movements. From this point on, the United States Navy had the upper hand.

Lieutenant Tomonaga's request for a second strike was received by Admiral Nagumo at 0710. Minutes later an unsuccessful attack on the carriers by Midway-based bombers convinced the Admiral that Tomonaga's judgment was correct.

Admiral Nagumo died at Saipan in the summer of 1944, so there is no way of our knowing what was in his mind, but it is almost inevitable that his primary objective—occupation of Midway—was still uppermost. To pursue this objective it was necessary to replace the armament in his 72 torpedo and dive-bombing planes with land bombs. Nagumo made the decision to attack Midway again at 0715, and the re-arming began with great urgency. The job was almost completed an hour later when the second attack of Midway-based planes reached his carriers. These B-17s dropped their bombs ineffectively from 20,000 feet, and returned to base claiming four hits on two carriers. By skillful maneuvering the carriers completely avoided damage from this high-altitude attack.

Within a few minutes of 0830, three momentous events took place in Nagumo's carrier force: the unsuccessful B-17s ended their attack and departed; planes of the first Midway attack began to return to the carriers (having been shot at by "friendly" ships of the carriers' escort); and—frightful blow—a *Tone* scout plane reported the sighting of an enemy aircraft carrier!

To realize the impact of this last news on Nagumo and his staff it must be remembered that they had no suspicion that enemy carriers were anywhere in the vicinity of Midway. Cordons of Japanese submarines stationed between Hawaii and Midway were supposed to have warned of any sorties from Pearl Harbor; but, unfortunately, the submarines had reached their scouting positions only after the American carriers had passed to westward of those areas.

The Japanese carriers were like a family moving its possessions into a new home while a fire rages in the house next door. Uncomplaining, the crews, who had just replaced torpedoes with land bombs, now set to work replacing land bombs with torpedoes. At the same time, planes returning from the Midway strike had to be recovered. At 0855, as these two operations were drawing to a close, Admiral Nagumo sent a blinker signal ordering his ships to "proceed northward after recovering planes. We plan to engage and destroy the enemy task force."

He radioed to Admiral Yamamoto: "Enemy force of one carrier, five cruisers, and five destroyers sighted at 0800, bearming 010°, distant 240 miles from Midway. We will proceed to meet it."

It had taken almost two hours to rearm and ready the planes in Nagumo's carriers. At 0920, just as some of them—3 fighters and 27 torpedo planes each in *Akagi* and *Kaga*, and in *Hiryu* and *Soryu* 3 fighters and 18 torpedo planes apiece— were ready to be spotted on the decks for takeoff, screen ships reported the approach of enemy carrier planes!

Excitement and activity reached fever pitch as the torpedo-bearing attackers tried to score. So skillful and energetic were intercepting fighters that no more than a dozen torpedoes were actually launched at Nagumo's carriers; and thanks to excellent ship handling, none of these hit. The success of this defense does not detract in any way from the bravery and daring of the attacking pilots. They did their best and bore in to the last man. Their effort was greatly admired by Japanese witnesses who survived this day. Postwar accounts show that of 41 attacking torpedo planes from three enemy carriers only six returned safely.

In the meantime, our own planes were being readied for a counterattack against enemy ships. The preparations were so spurred on by the aerial battle that by 1020 Admiral Nagumo was able to give the order to launch when ready. Engines roared their warm-up as the four huge carriers turned into the wind. The lead planes were just starting to roll forward for takeoff, when enemy dive bombers suddenly came screaming out of clouds directly overhead to loose bombs at close range. Four direct hits on *Kaga*, three on *Soryu*, and two on *Akagi* knocked these three carriers out of action almost simultaneously.

Had the attack come ten minutes later, the flight decks would have been clear and the carriers might have survived these hits. But, their decks loaded with fully armed planes, and hazardously stowed bombs and torpedoes, all three ships were soon blazing infernos. They were shaken by numerous explosions which increased the fire destruction and killed many men.

Of the four carriers only *Hiryu* was able to continue the fight. At 1058 she launched 6 fighters and 18 bombers led by Lieutenant Kobayashi. They struck *Yorktown* about noon. Pilots of the three fighters and five bombers which got back from this attack were able to report that the American carrier had been damaged and left dead in the water. At 1300 Lieutenant Tomonaga led a flight of 6 fighters and 10 torpedo bombers from *Hiryu*'s deck, and he reported at 1445 that they had scored two torpedo hits on another carrier. Half of Tomonaga's planes failed to return.

Both of these attacks from *Hiryu* had struck the same target —*Yorktown*. She had been hit seriously by the first attack, but amazing damage control by her crew had the carrier operating and in action again within five hours. Thus it was that Tomonaga's planes reported they were attacking "another" carrier.

These final efforts by *Hiryu* were eclipsed at 1703 when 13

U.S. dive bombers singled her out for attack. Four bomb hits caused such fires and explosions that the great ship had to be abandoned early in the morning of 5 June. A few hours later, at 0700, a scout plane from light carrier *Hosho* sighted the smoldering and drifting *Hiryu*. Admiral Yamamoto ordered destroyer *Tanikaze* to her reported position, but at 1820—before *Tanikaze* could reach the scene—*Hiryu* sank.

Japan thus lost four fleet carriers in less than 24 hours! The magnitude of this defeat was beyond imagination. The commanding officer of *Hiryu* and *Soryu* chose to go down with their ships, as did Admiral Yamaguchi, the commander of Carrier Division 2, in *Hiryu*. Several other officers, including Admiral Nagumo, were also determined to take their lives out of shame for this defeat, but they were dissuaded by colleagues.

United States losses in this battle came to one aircraft carrier and one destroyer sunk, and 147 planes destroyed. The loss to the Japanese Navy was considerably greater: four carriers and one heavy cruiser sunk, a heavy cruiser and two destroyers moderately or heavily damaged, light damage to three other ships, and 332 planes failed to return.

American newspapers promptly reported this battle in headlines as big as were used at the time of Pearl Harbor, but this time the news was of victory. Papers in Japan, on the other hand, reported merely what Imperial General Headquarters authorized, which was that one American carrier had been sunk and one seriously damaged in a great naval battle, that Japan had won a great victory in invading the Aleutian Islands, and that there had been a naval action in the vicinity of Midway. News of the loss of the four fleet carriers was dribbled out to the homeland public over a period of a year following the battle.

In addition to Japan's loss of ships and planes there was the serious loss of men, especially of skilled pilots, who were thereafter in short supply for the remainder of the war. Survivors of sunken ships were held incommunicado until reassigned, and they were under strict injunction to keep silent about the terrible defeat Japan had suffered. Almost forty years earlier two capital ships of Admiral Togo's fleet were sunk by Russian mines off Port Arthur and the news was kept from the Japanese public for six months. The facts of the Midway battle were not divulged to the people of Japan until after the end of World War II.

All the strength of Admiral Yamamoto's mighty Combined Fleet went for naught in this critical battle. His own Main Force turned back to the homeland upon hearing reports of the carrier debacle. Vice Admiral Kondo's Invasion Force also withdrew, without an invasion effort. The carriers alone had engaged the enemy. They fought bravely and suffered mightily. So great was Japan's defeat in this one battle that the resourceful and skillful enemy must have been supported by the wrath of an avenging god.

There were many reasons for the defeat suffered at Midway. The ultimate blame, however, may be laid to Japan's unbelievable successes during the first six months of the war. These early successes gave rise to an arrogance—aptly characterized as "victory disease"—which engendered negligence and a lack of vigilance. As I see it, this fatal arrogance was terminated, so far as Japan's Navy was concerned, by the battle of Midway. Subsequent defeats had other causes.

The people of Japan have always attributed success in war to divine help and guidance. By this token they had to attribute the outcome of the Midway battle to the working of a super demon.

5

ATTRITION WAR
IN THE SOLOMONS

1. Guadalcanal—First U.S. Counteroffensive

ON 7 AUGUST 1942, the United States First Marine Division invaded Tulagi, Florida, and Guadalcanal at the southern end of the Solomon Islands chain. This was the first of a long series of Allied invasions in the Pacific which would end only with the defeat of Japan.

Not even the most far-seeing members of Imperial General Headquarters appreciated the full significance of these landings until long after the event. The Allies, having envisaged that the Pacific war would be long drawn, planned to advance on the homeland of Japan from the south, starting with the Solomon Islands and bypassing the strong points of Japan's defensive perimeter. It is surprising that Imperial Headquarters never expected this wisdom of the enemy and, instead, clung to the belief that a series of quick victories for Japan would make possible a negotiated peace. But then General Headquarters was still enthralled, if not intoxicated, with Japan's successes.

The loss of four carriers within twenty-four hours in the Battle of Midway had been quite a blow, but the situation was not desperate. If the war had ended within two years, as Admiral Nagano had estimated, the Midway loss would have been the only real setback in the first quarter of that period. There was a long way to go and the Japanese Navy still had carriers *Shokaku* and *Zuikaku*, scarcely six months old, and light carriers *Ryujo, Junyo, Hiyo* and *Zuiho*. Giant *Taiho* (32,000 tons, with her complement of 62 planes, plus 21 in reserve) would be in service within a year, and battleships *Ise* and *Hyuga* were being converted by the addition of plane platforms to their afterdecks. Super-carrier *Shinano* was scheduled for completion within two years.

Aside from the carriers, the surface forces of Admiral Isoroku Yamamoto's Combined Fleet were practically unscathed, and their strength was still almost double that of the United States Pacific Fleet. If these two navies were to meet in a mid-ocean engagement it seemed fairly certain that Japan would emerge victorious. Japanese naval strategists were eager that the engagement take place before their favorable balance of power was upset by the industrial capacity of the United States.

The Japanese Army, on the other hand, was completely absorbed with its occupation of the newly conquered territories of Southeast Asia. The staffs of the various army forces were busy exploiting resources, winning the cooperation of the populace, and conducting the administration of their territories. While the Army was concerned with these efforts, making sure that all newspapers under its control were giving them proper notice, the United States Marines landed on Guadalcanal. Thus while the Japanese Army concentrated on politics and economics, the growing military might of the United States was fighting a war.

Were it not for the bloody six-month struggle that took place between Japanese and American forces at Guadalcanal, beginning in August 1942, this remote island of the South Pacific would have remained unknown to the world. The first wartime occupation of the Solomon Islands had occurred three months before, in early May, when token Japanese forces landed on Tulagi and Guadalcanal. The peaceful and seldom used anchorage at Lunga Point on Guadalcanal received a small naval landing party commanded by Lieutenant Commander Okamura, whose principal arms consisted of two old howitzers and three machine guns. The force which landed at Tulagi boasted nothing more.

By any reasonable view, these Japanese efforts were unrealistic. As of the summer of 1942, these islands were vital, and their defense should have been taken up seriously and in strength. A rudimentary understanding of this principle should have called for the development of an airstrip and a supply of fighter planes to insure command of the air, as well as the maintenance of daily reconnaissance flights to guard against surprise. By early August, when Japanese planners took up these considerations, the enemy was already moving into the Solomons.

Imperial General Headquarters, incapable of properly evaluating enemy moves at this juncture, at first regarded the Guadalcanal landings as an isolated local operation of little consequence. The Army estimated that there would be no difficulty in driving the enemy forces from this island outpost. The Japanese Navy, less sanguine about the matter, realized that an enemy air base on Guadalcanal threatened the defensive perimeter which had been built up in the first eight months of the war, and saw that an enemy foothold in the Solomons could disrupt Japan's command of the South Pacific. This realization prompted Admiral Yamamoto to order his Second and Third Fleets and Tinian-based air forces to advance to Rabaul.

2. Daily Battles for Guadalcanal

Upon receiving news of the enemy landing at Guadalcanal, Vice Admiral Gunichi Mikawa, Commander of the Eighth Fleet, sortied from Rabaul with five heavy (*Chokai*,

Aoba, Kako, Kinugasa, Furutaka) and two light cruisers (*Tenryu, Yubari*), plus destroyer *Yunagi*, to strike at the invading forces. Mikawa's force was sighted late in the morning of 8 August, during its run south to Guadalcanal, by an Australian scout plane, but the pilot foolishly maintained radio silence and continued his search before returning to base to report. As a result, the Allied ships were caught completely off guard. The Battle of Savo Island, which the Japanese Navy called the First Naval Battle of the Solomons, began in the first hour of 9 August and was over by 0230. Four enemy cruisers were sunk, and one cruiser and two destroyers damaged in the brief one-sided battle which left Mikawa's force practically untouched.[1]

The glory of victory in this action was considerably dimmed in that the enemy transports, with priceless troops and supplies, remained intact. As Mikawa's ships withdrew he discussed with his staff the feasibility of making another attack. But fear of possible dawn air attacks from enemy carriers, known to be south of Guadalcanal, induced Mikawa to return to base.

With most of the protecting enemy warships sunk or damaged, Mikawa could easily have raised havoc with the transports. His failure to do so enabled the invaders to get a firm foothold on Guadalcanal, leading to their conquest of the entire Solomons. Dire as were the consequences of Admiral Mikawa's decision, he should not be held solely to blame, because it was traditional with the Japanese Navy that warships—not auxiliaries or transports—were the principal target. Mikawa was over-cautious about the danger of air attack; and, undoubtedly, he was also influenced by the recent debacle at Midway. But it would have been worth the sacrifice of his entire force if he had knocked out the enemy transports at Guadalcanal.

Another factor in Admiral Mikawa's decision was the attitude of the Japanese Army which, with but slight knowledge

---

[1] Allied losses were cruisers *Astoria, Quincy, Vincennes,* and (Australian) *Canberra* sunk; cruiser *Chicago* and destroyers *Ralph Talbot* and *Patterson* damaged.

of the United States, had always considered Soviet Russia its primary enemy. Little thought was given to the prospect of land fighting against American troops and, accordingly, there was little concern for their fighting ability. At Army Headquarters it was felt that the invaders of Guadalcanal could easily be driven from the island.

On 21 August occured the first decisive clash at Guadalcanal. The focal point of action was a Japanese airstrip which had been under construction for only a few weeks when the enemy struck. Most of the defending Ichiki Detachment was annihilated.

Four days later the rest of the Ichiki Regiment—the regiment which had been scheduled to invade Midway two months earlier—was sent to reinforce Guadalcanal, under protection of all available Japanese surface units. The Army High Command obviously was still confident that the reduction of the enemy in the Solomons would be a simple matter. The Imperial Navy, on the other hand, deeply concerned about the strength it might meet in supporting this landing operation, called to the task Vice Admiral Nobutake Kondo's Second Fleet and Vice Admiral Chuichi Nagumo's Third Fleet. On 24 August this combined force of two aircraft carriers, three battleships, and other warships, engaged U.S. Task Force 61, under Vice Admiral Frank Jack Fletcher, in the Battle of the Eastern Solomons. The action lasted into the next day and resulted in the loss of carrier *Enterprise* for the United States, and carrier *Ryujo* and one destroyer for the Japanese Navy. Most important, however, was that this second Japanese effort to reinforce Guadalcanal failed completely.

During September the enemy strengthened his position on the island and enlarged the airstrips. At the same time the situation became increasingly worse for Japan. One highlight in the generally disappointing war record of Japanese submarines came on 15 September, when torpedoes from *I-19* accounted for the sinking of carrier *Wasp* near Espiritu Santo.

There were many aspects to the Guadalcanal reinforcement effort. On 11–12 October the Japanese Navy lost heavy cruiser *Furutaka* and destroyer *Fubuki*, and the force commander,

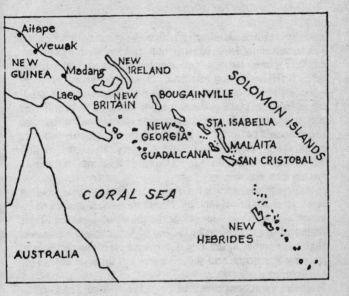

Solomon Islands Area

Rear Admiral Aritomo Goto, was killed when heavy cruiser *Aoba* was seriously damaged in the Battle of Cape Esperance. Two nights later battleships *Kongo* and *Haruna* gave a boost to Japanese morale when they bombarded Guadalcanal airfields and shore installations for an hour and a half with their 16-inch guns, inflicting great damage. Land fighting on Guadalcanal, which continued for nearly six months, was accompanied by almost daily naval actions resulting from the Japanese effort to reinforce the island.

3. Port Arthur of the Pacific

It is still astounding to realize the speed with which the Americans completed construction of an airstrip at Guadalcanal. Japanese troops had seen bulldozers at Wake Island when it fell in the first month of the war and were greatly impressed by their performance. When the Japanese commanding officer of Wake ordered a labor detail of three hundred men to repair the damaged airstrip, he was amazed to find that the job could be done by a handful of men in a matter of hours using the powerful American machinery. It is curious that Japan did not reproduce these captured machines in quantity for her own war use.

American planes were flying from Guadalcanal fields a week after the initial landing, and their number seemed to increase almost daily. Meanwhile the supply of Japanese planes dwindled so rapidly that by the end of August there were fewer than fifty planes in the area. Combined Fleet then brought in air reinforcements, and started a series of attrition battles for the Solomons.

The naval actions that took place for the island of Guadalcanal are well known to all readers of the Pacific War. To a degree these battles paralleled the actions of almost forty years earlier when the Japanese Navy undertook the siege of Port Arthur against the Russians. I wish to point out these parallels and emphasize the special features of the Guadalcanal actions that had grave implications for the later development of the war.

In 1904, during the Russo-Japanese War, Port Arthur with its well protected forts withstood two general offensives over a period of four months, at great cost to the Japanese Army. An Imperial rescript was issued to encourage the troops, and General Nogi announced that if the next attack failed he would himself, with drawn sword, lead a suicide unit. Ten years earlier, in the Sino-Japanese War, Port Arthur had fallen to the Japanese in one day, and there were many who thought it would be just as easy to take Port Arthur from the Russians. In fact, when the first general offensive began on 24

August 1904, news reporters stayed in the War Office all night, waiting minute by minute for word that Port Arthur had fallen. But it took four long months of bitter fighting, and cost Japan 59,000 officers and men, before Port Arthur was finally captured on New Year's Day of 1905.

The American landings at Guadalcanal, as we have seen, provoked immediate concern among officers of the Japanese Navy. The Army, on the other hand, pursued other operations, and it was not until 21 August that an Army detachment under Lieutenant Colonel Kiyonao Ichiki made the first attempt, intending to recapture the island in one day. The effort ended in miserable failure, as had the Port Arthur venture of 1904.

The Army attacked again a week later with a force of 7,000 men commanded by Major General Kiyotake Kawaguchi. Preparations were laid more carefully on this occasion and the effort was thorough. Defeat, however, was even more thorough, and further reminiscent of Port Arthur.

In Imperial General Headquarters the Army Section now realized for the first time that the strength and fighting spirit of the enemy at Guadalcanal were more than had been anticipated. A third general offensive was staged on 24 October with a division and a half built around the Second Sendai Division under Lieutenant General Masao Maruyama. The attack was supported by the full strength of the Second and Third Fleets. The troops were confident of victory, but this attack was also a debacle.

These repeated failures caused grave concern in Imperial General Headquarters. The wisdom of trying to wage a decisive battle over Guadalcanal was seriously reconsidered. The night-battle defeat of the famed Second Sendai Division had been a particularly heavy blow, because this was one of the best and toughest night-fighting divisions in Japan, having to its credit the successful night attack on Crescent Hill during the Russo-Japanese War.

It was decided to shift the emphasis from night attack to regular heavy artillery action in order to recapture the island. For this purpose the 38th and 59th Divisions were, starting at the end of October, organized into the Eighth Area Army under Lieutenant General Hitoshi Imamura, with headquarters at Rabaul. Preparations for the next big general offensive were well under way by the end of December. An Imperial Rescript was prepared for issuance in the new year to express concern for the military situation in the Solomons, as had been done thirty-nine years previously in regard to Port Arthur, but this time it was not issued.

The new year brought a change of plans in Imperial General Headquarters. It was clear that another major setback in the Solomons area would mean an unbearable loss of prestige for the Army, and defeat seemed almost certain. After nearly five months of trying to reinforce and recapture Guadalcanal, Japanese military leaders realized that it would be foolhardy to transport thousands of troops into a theater of action where the enemy had complete command of the air. Thus on 4 January 1943 the decision was made to withdraw Japanese troops from Guadalcanal. This evacuation, which involved the removal of 11,000 troops, was completed on 8 February, whereupon organized resistance on the island came to an end. There too ends the parallel between the sieges for Port Arthur and Guadalcanal. Thirty-nine years earlier Japan had been victorious.

At the beginning of World War II Japan had successfully concentrated her military and naval strength on specific targets. Guadalcanal, like Midway, was an example of Japan's failure to concentrate and it, like Midway, ended in failure. If our military leaders had grasped the significance of the enemy landings at Guadalcanal early enough, and had concentrated a maximum effort at the proper time, they might have succeeded in driving the enemy from the island. When the Americans were able to reinforce the troops of the initial landings, Japan's cause there was lost.

4. A Win, Loss, and Draw
in the Southern Solomons

Meanwhile, GHQ had been prompting the Navy to take some action; and the Naval General Staff was urging an engagement of the enemy fleet, off Guadalcanal, to assist the Army in recapturing the island. Combined Fleet Headquarters issued a "desideratum" to Rabaul that the task force sortie for a decisive battle in Guadalcanal waters. A "desideratum" was sent rather than an "order" because of Admiral Yamamoto's aversion to commanding his forces into battle against unreasonable odds. The actual decision was left to Admiral Nagumo and his Chief of Staff, Rear Admiral Ryunosuke Kusaka. They considered the situation at Guadalcanal, the wishes of GHQ, and the opinion of the Combined Fleet. It was decided that Third Fleet should sortie to the south as screen for a reinforcement convoy under Rear Admiral Raizo Tanaka which left Rabaul on 19 August.

The task force made up of carriers *Shokaku*, *Zuikaku*, *Ryujo*; battleships *Hiei*, *Kirishima*; heavy cruisers *Kumano*, *Suzuya*, *Tone*, *Chikuma*; light cruiser *Nagara*; and 14 destroyers. Light carrier *Ryujo*, with *Tone* and two destroyers were detached to operate as a diversionary group. As such they received the brunt of the attacks and *Ryujo* was sunk. The main force was sighted on 24 August by an enemy scout plane which shadowed the warships for an hour and a half, and dropped a bomb from high altitude as it departed. The bomb fell between *Zuikaku* and *Shokaku*, but did no damage. The next scout plane appeared shortly and dropped a bomb on *Zuikaku*'s flight deck. Thereupon the task force withdrew to launch two waves of its own reconnaissance planes.

These planes found the enemy's carrier group 250 miles to the southeast. Thereupon the first attack group of 67 planes was launched, led by Lieutenant Commander Seki. It was followed by a second group of 48 planes commanded by Lieutenant Commander Murata.

These veteran pilots brought back reports that they had sunk or heavily damaged three carriers, one battleship, five heavy cruisers, and four destroyers of the enemy force. American announcements of this engagement mentioned merely that the enemy had inflicted "some" losses.

Carrier *Enterprise* was hit by bombs and caught fire, billowing a huge smoke column. Her attackers had reason to think she was mortally damaged. But her fires were brought under control and the huge ship survived the action. Japanese rejoiced at the thought that they had sunk carrier *Hornet*—flagship of the "Doolittle Raid"—and thus avenged the 18 April air strike on Tokyo. The thought was premature.

Japan's losses in this action were by no means slight. Light carrier *Ryujo* was sunk; *Shokaku*'s flight deck was damaged, and *Zuikaku* received minor injuries. In addition, 70 planes and their trained crews were lost. Most of all, the Japanese effort had failed.

In the Third Solomons Sea Battle the enemy scored a similar victory. At that time Japan's principal task force had returned to the Inland Sea, leaving Admiral Kondo's Second Fleet to cooperate with the Army forces fighting on Guadalcanal. On 12 November battleships *Hiei* and *Kirishima*, accompanied by a destroyer flotilla, were on a mission to bombard shore facilities at Lunga Point when they met and engaged an enemy surface force. In a fierce action, the Japanese lost battleship *Hiei* and destroyers *Akatsuki* and *Yudachi*, but managed to sink or damage a dozen enemy ships.[2]

On 14 November Admiral Kondo commanded a force of one battleship, two heavy and two light cruisers, and nine destroyers to escort the Army's 38th Division in a reinforcement effort for Guadalcanal. The enemy came out to meet this operation with a large fleet which included two new 16-inch battleships of the *Idaho* class. After several night clashes the battle ended with the sinking of three enemy ships,[3] and

[2] In the actions of 12–13 November U.S. Naval losses were:
Sunk:
    Light cruisers *Atlanta, Juneau*
    Destroyers *Cushing, Monssen, Laffey, Barton*
Damaged:
    Heavy cruisers *Portland, San Francisco*
    Light cruiser *Helena*
    Destroyers *Sterett, Buchanan, O'Bannon, Aaron Ward*
[3] Sunk in this action were destroyers *Preston, Walke,* and *Benham*.

Japanese loss of battleship *Kirishima* and destroyer *Ayanami*. The Mikawa Force, covering the troop transport convoy, was subjected to persistent aerial attacks which sank heavy cruiser *Kinugasa* and seven of the eleven transports.

This series of engagements, known as the Third Solomons Sea Battle, was another Japanese defeat and the fleet returned home. The enemy task force withdrew temporarily from the area, but his air bases on Guadalcanal were extended and his aerial activity was stepped up. Japan, on the other hand, had a mere 30 planes based in southern Bougainville, and they managed only infrequent air strikes against Guadalcanal. The enemy held command of the air at Guadalcanal from the time his first air base was set up there, and his area of control in the Solomons increased with each passing day.

5. Supporting Operations of Destroyers

A scouting flight by a Japanese seaplane at daybreak on 18 November revealed the presence of six enemy air strips on Guadalcanal, with hundreds of planes readied for operations. The build-up of enemy air strength had been much faster than we had anticipated. In addition, Admiral Halsey's task force in the area, augmented by several carriers, was in undisputed command of air and sea in the southern Solomons.

In November there were on Guadalcanal nearly 15,000 Japanese officers and men, thousands of whom were incapacitated by sickness—malaria, stomach disorder, malnutrition. All day they had to fight against steadily growing enemy land forces. At night they were engaged in receiving such food, ammunition, stores, and medical supplies as might be brought in by fast destroyers or submarines. These "grocery runs" were made at full speed, under cover of darkness on moonless nights.

In hope of avoiding air attacks, Japanese destroyers stayed by day at Shortland Bay in Bougainville. Yet even there they were subjected to bombing attacks by the far-ranging American planes. These regular bombings were dubbed *teikibin*, meaning scheduled runs.

When the air-raid alarm sounded, all ships would get underway and maneuver violently, swinging their bows hard left or right to dodge the falling bombs. These attacks came so frequently and regularly that the destroyer skippers began to look forward to them as a chance for practicing evasive tactics. Admiral Tomiji Koyanagi, commander of the destroyer squadrons, nicknamed these evasive maneuvers the *"Bon* Dance" because of their left and right swinging movements, so reminiscent of the dancing in the annual *Bon* Festival of Lanterns. The dance of the destroyers was laughable, if one could ignore the deadly consequences of a misstep.

By night, various means were employed to bring provisions to Guadalcanal. The most effective method was to have the supplies loaded in metal drums strung together with rope and hung from the gunwales of destroyers. Around midnight a ship would run at high speed toward a designated point on the beach. As it approached shoal water the string of drums was cut loose and the destroyer went into a sharp turn, dumping its cargo and heading back for Bougainville. Parties from shore, swimming or in small boats, secured a lead line to the chain of provisions and hauled it to the beach where, tug-of-war fashion, the precious supplies were pulled from the water. This procedure had to be completed before daybreak, when enemy planes or patrol craft would detect the operation and machine-gun the working parties.

For the troops ashore and the destroyer crews the risk involved was extremely great, but there was no question of hazard pay. The men carried out this precarious program, daring the enemy's blockade by sea and air, sustained by their loyalty to Emperor and comrades in arms.

The futile effort to reinforce Guadalcanal continued for six months. At the end of January 1943 the Japanese high command finally decided that the island should be abandoned and evacuation of the island was begun by destroyers on the night of 1 February.

That evacuation was an amazing success in itself. It took a

total of sixty sorties to remove the Japanese garrison from Guadalcanal. The transport destroyers used for this purpose had to operate under heavy aerial attacks by the enemy. Combined Fleet Headquarters had anticipated that half of them would be lost, yet not one ship was damaged during the operation. This good fortune was due in part to the fact that a destroyer is small and fast, and therefore a poor target; but, in addition, during the supply runs, which lasted for two and a half months, the officers and crews achieved mastery of the problems of navigation and evasion. Hence the withdrawal of the Japanese garrison from Guadalcanal was one of the great tactical successes of World War II.

The Naval High Command was greatly concerned, however, at having to use destroyers for such supply operations, in which a number of them had been lost. Even more important than the losses was the detrimental effect that "taxi" operations would have on crews in the future. The undignified use of destroyers as supply ships was demoralizing to sailors who had been trained for traditional combat operations. With this in mind, it was proposed to develop a special transport destroyer, to be used exclusively for supply and transport operations, leaving regular destroyers and their crews to proper combat duties. Long before the proposal was put into effect, however, Guadalcanal was evacuated, and so the plan for transport destroyers was abandoned.

6. Submarine Transports

Deplorable as was this destroyer situation, the story of misused submarines is even sorrier.

When first-line submarines were employed almost exclusively in the demeaning task of supply operations, the war for Japan took on a gloomy aspect despite many great naval victories.

Early in the effort of supplying Guadalcanal by surface ship, it was realized that nocturnal destroyer runs could not bring in enough material. Accordingly, submarines were detailed to the same task. As need for supplies increased, more submarines were assigned until, by January 1943, thirty-eight submarines were eventually involved. This "submerged freight service" cost Japan the loss of 20 submarines and their seasoned crews. During this period another four submarines were sunk in the Solomons area while on regular patrol. The loss of 24 submarines in a few short months was bad enough, but it was especially painful that 20 of these aggressive fighting machines should be lost in the course of nonaggressive operations for which they were never intended.

Submarines assigned to this duty were stripped of all torpedoes, shells, and guns to make room for supplies. Crews were dejected when informed of their mission, even though they realized the importance of bringing needed materials to Guadalcanal. It was a further blow to morale when the crews witnessed enemy submarines, on proper offensive missions in the same area, attacking our ships and disrupting our supply lines.

Quite naturally our submariners felt that their proper and primary task was to cut off the line of supply between the mainland of the United States and Guadalcanal, or to attack the line of communication between Guadalcanal and Australia. Disruption of the enemy's line of communication to Guadalcanal—so much more extended than that of Japan—would have been far easier for Japanese submarines had they been allowed to pursue their proper function. And it would also have been far more profitable to the Japanese war effort.

With only three Japanese submarines engaged in offensive operations around Guadalcanal, it is to their great credit that they succeeded in sinking the enemy aircraft carrier *Wasp*. The poor showing of Japanese submarines in World War II, as compared with those of Germany and the United States, must be attributed in major part to their unwise employment in late 1942 and early 1943.

If the thirty-odd Japanese submarines available in the Solomons had been mobilized offensively to the east and south of Guadalcanal they could have seriously disrupted enemy convoys and been a great threat to the supply strategy of the United States. When Japanese submarines were finally released from logistic support operations and resumed regular offensive tasks, there was a marked increase in their effectiveness against enemy ships.

Losses at Guadalcanal, if dragged on long enough, would have led to certain defeat for Japan. Therefore, on the last day of 1942, the naval staff urged the evacuation of the island. When the decision was announced by General Headquarters it was referred to as an "advance by turning."

In a wartime lecture at Keio University I used the phrase "strategic retreat" to describe the situation, and was promptly cautioned by the security police. Military leaders, extremely sensitive about the operations at Guadalcanal, insisted on the use of their own phraseology. It had seemed to me that the phrase "advance by turning" was a logical impossibility, for Japan lies to the north, and to turn northward was to turn backward, not to advance. Thus the chosen phrase was itself a denial of logic, which could have fooled no one who bothered to study a map.

Japanese withdrawal from the island was completed by mid-February 1943, and Army and Navy forces were finally released from a bitter, bloody, and costly struggle. The release proved to be of short duration, as the enemy maintained his offensive tempo. With accelerated zeal and fighting spirit he pushed up the Solomons chain and pursued the series of "attrition battles" which sapped the blood and energy of Japan's hitherto indomitable fighting machine.

7. Shocking Air Losses

Japan lost 893 planes and 2,362 airmen in the half year which ended with the withdrawal from Guadalcanal. During the following year, 1943, Japan lost 6,203 planes and 4,824 men. The staggering total of 7,096 planes lost was three times more than the number of planes Japan had boasted at the beginning of the Pacific War. Factories accelerated their production of planes, but never caught up with the losses. Moreover, training of new plane crews could not be achieved in short order, and the loss of the experienced veterans of Pearl Harbor, the Indian Ocean, and Midway was irreparable. The enormity of Japan's plane losses in this period is detailed as follows:

PLANE TYPES	NO. OF PLANES	MEN
Fighters	3,264	1,581
Carrier-based bombers and attack	1,119	1,292
Land-based bombers and attack	1,087	3,115
Float fighters	557	568
Flying boats	113	385
Others	956	245
Total	7,096	7,186

United States plans in the Solomons battles probably did not have as their specific purpose the destruction of Japan's air power. It just happened that way. The American strategic objective was simply to advance northward for eventual battle on the Japanese homeland. The leapfrog strategy, which was so effective in Europe was used also in the Pacific. First, the target area was repeatedly bombed, then shelled by warships to reduce further the enemy's resistance before landing. With the occupation of the target area, airstrips were immediately built and air superiority was extended toward the capture of the next target area. At the end of the war the United States had 40,893 first-line planes, and 60 aircraft carriers. Japan's Navy was overwhelmed from the sky. Japan fought well at the Solomons; but when the ratio of strength was 100 to 30, the results were foreordained.

As a poor farmer is often himself forced to consume what he produces for sale, and finally ends up in debt, so Japan was using up planes faster than she could build them. The United States reaped the double harvest of geographical advance and dissipation of Japan's air strength. Japanese military spokesmen eventually began to mention "the enemy's material superiority." Yet that superiority had been obvious since long before the war began.

Japan advanced too far beyond her strength, or, to use a military term, had exceeded the offensive terminal point. When an advancing army crosses a certain point, its strength diminishes. Supply lines lengthen, the territory of the advance becomes increasingly hostile and uncooperative, and troops reach a point of fatigue which even the thrill of victory cannot surmount.

All of these elements reduce the fighting capability of the offensive army, and they inevitably give a counteroffensive advantage to the defending force. When the resulting counterattack succeeds, the initiative is taken by the defenders and the invading army loses ground at an accelerating speed. The offensive terminal point lies one step before the line at which the tide of battle turns. It is the ideal point for the offensive force to hold, rest, and strengthen its lines of communication, supply, and reinforcements before taking the next forward step.

In May 1942 I wrote a series of articles for the *Chubu Nihon Shimbun* of Nagoya, entitled "The Offensive Terminal Point." My intention was to oppose indirectly the further southward advances. An influential businessman of Osaka, who read an early installment in the series, wrote a letter saying, "Your article confirmed my concern and anxiety. I would like to read all of the series." On the other hand, long afterward an Army acquaintance, Colonel Tanihagi (who later rose to Lieutenant General) advised me not to write my ideas so explicitly lest the sensitive Army officials take action against me.

8. Overextending the Offensive

In theory, and with benefit of hindsight, it is easy to establish the offensive terminal point of a military offensive operation. In practice, and on the battle line, it is difficult not only to determine when an offensive effort has reached its optimum point but also, when it is properly determined, to do anything about it. This is true of any nation and of any war. A military leader on the offensive tends to push onward, and it is almost impossible for the rear area headquarters to check the aggressive commander, even after it is realized that his aggression is unwise. Efforts at restraint come too late.

To the average observer or participant the optimum point of an offensive effort is hidden. It can be realized only by a superior commanding officer, who must be able to discern when he has reached the point where he must consolidate his forces and lines for the next offensive. That point between the successful terminus of the first offensive and the beginning of the next offensive is known as the strategic interval. The strategic interval cannot be determined unilaterally. An enemy counteroffensive may disrupt or completely destroy the most careful plans for the strategic interval. Therefore a commander, to know his real strength, must be able to visualize his offensive terminal point and estimate properly the strategic interval before beginning his next offensive.

During the Russo-Japanese War of 1904–05 an interval of two months was allowed to consolidate lines of advance as the Japanese Army moved from Te-li-ssu to Liao-yang, and then to Sha-ho, and finally to Mukden, which was considered to be the terminal point for the offensive advance.

In the Pacific War, such a strategic interval was not possible for the Japanese. After the withdrawal from Guadalcanal, Japan had hoped for a one-year strategic interval in which to build up air strength impoverished during the second half of the Solomons campaign. The enemy, however, was unobliging. The United States not only did not slacken its pace, but, on the contrary, stepped up its offensive and began air attacks on the Marianas before Japan was even half prepared. The strategic interval for the United States was extremely brief and its offensive terminal point deeply advanced.

The offensive terminal point for any army is related to its strength, supply requirements, and the speed with which the supplies can be delivered. The terminal point for the United States lay far distant from its homeland, while Japan was forced to fix her terminal point comparatively close to home bases. Japan had to advance to the south to get oil, without which she could not pursue the war. Japan had started the war knowing that she did not have enough tankers to carry oil from the south seas to the mainland, but she had counted on capturing tankers to supplement those of her own fleet. Therefore, in the initial stages of the war, when the Navy was sinking enemy merchant ships, Imperial Naval Headquarters ordered that an effort be made to capture them instead.

Once begun, the war had to be fought through. It is now clear, however, that Japan went to war totally ignoring from the outset the offensive terminal point.

Imperial Headquarters should have fixed the offensive terminal point in time to maintain forces within the maximum areas of battle required to secure oil fields and maintain lines of supply. Extended pursuit of the enemy invites the danger that he will sever supply lines.

It was feared by some that even Rabaul was beyond the offensive terminal point. Islands differ strategically from land masses, and it was inevitable that the advance would continue from one island to another. But the Japanese advance should have stopped at Rabaul, at the northern end of the Solomons. Our admirals and generals on the front lines lacked jurisdiction over such matters, and it was probably too much to expect the necessary insight and courage from Imperial Headquarters, whose poor judgment was actually to blame for the defeat in the Solomons.

9. Indecisive War

Between August 1942 and February 1944 the Pacific War was focused around Guadalcanal and the northern adjoining islands of the Solomon Archipelago. During that year and a half the Pacific Ocean elsewhere saw no naval engagements of note. In December 1943 the United States learned of the presence of a Japanese airstrip on Kwajalein in the Marshalls. Until then the stage for decisive battle had remained in the south, far removed from Japan. Now it drew closer to the homeland.

Meanwhile, as the United States counteroffensive advanced northward from Tulagi and Guadalcanal, the character of naval warfare changed from traditional surface engagements between great fleets to landing operations and their various supporting actions. The war goal of the United States was to advance along the road to Tokyo. On 2 July 1942 the U.S. Joint Chiefs of Staff adopted "Operation Watchtower," for the purpose of capturing Tulagi and adjacent strategic points, with Admiral Nimitz as naval commander. And General MacArthur had as his immediate goal the occupation of Papua, as the first step toward garnering the rest of New Guinea in his northward march.

It was a strange spectacle to see the United States Army and Navy divided in operations toward the same goal in the same area. The Navy and its Marine Corps were attacking Tulagi and Guadalcanal, while the Army was striking at Bougainville and Rabaul. It seemed, therefore, that Japan could have won the battles of Guadalcanal and the Solomons if she had taken advantage of this divided effort. Major General Anderson has said about Guadalcanal, "If the Japanese Army had thrown into the second general offensive what they used in the third attack—one and a half divisions—probably the Americans would have had to withdraw in defeat."

Interservice rivalry existed in Tokyo, to be sure, but on the fighting front both services cooperated fully, as was evident in Malaya where General Tomoyuki Yamashita and Admiral Jisaburo Ozawa displayed perfect teamwork. In the Guadalcanal operations, also, the Japanese Army and Navy cooperated.

The Americans at the front, however, did not yield to each other. One conspicuous example of this occurred when an emergency policy conference was held on 4 September 1942 at Noumea to discuss the Japanese counteroffensive, which was endangering the American forward lines. Present at the conference were Admiral Nimitz, CINCPAC; General Arnold, Air Force Chief of Staff; Admiral Ghormley, Commander in Chief, South Pacific; General Sutherland, Chief of Staff, Far Eastern Army; and General Turner, Commandant of Marine Corps. General MacArthur refused to come to the meeting. When Admiral Nimitz asked General MacArthur for 10,000 soldiers as reinforcements, MacArthur turned down the request, saying that he could not divert a single man from the New Guinea operations—even though he then had 55,000 men under his command. When MacArthur in turn asked Admiral Nimitz for a fleet with two carriers, one Marine division, and a squadron of large bombers for his northward operations, Nimitz refused and explained that operations at Guadalcanal would not permit such a diversion of his forces.

When the situation at Guadalcanal became critical for the United States, President Roosevelt finally took direct measures to dissolve the interservice rivalry. On 24 October 1942 he sent an emergency order, as Commander in Chief of the Armed Forces, directing the immediate reinforcement of Guadalcanal.

Until early 1943 the Allied Powers regarded Europe as the primary theater of operations, and eighty-five per cent of all Allied forces were employed there. The Pacific was secondary. At the Casablanca Conference in January, 1943, the main aim of the United States was to increase the allocation of forces in the Pacific to at least 30 per cent of the total effort. With Pacific forces thus doubled, the United States hoped to conquer Japan and Germany at the same time.

At Casablanca, President Roosevelt drew a good deal of attention by proposing increased use of submarines, pointing out that they could most economically defeat Japan by sinking her ships. He also stressed the need for enlarging aerial activity against Japan by operating from bases in China. In keeping with these proposals, General Marshall and Admiral King emphasized the need for greater strength in the Pacific to secure the initiative.

10.　Two Roads to Tokyo

Even after the Japanese withdrawal from Guadalcanal the United States did not think in terms of a decisive fleet surface engagement with Japan, but concentrated on invading the Japanese homeland. This was the theme of the meeting between Roosevelt and Churchill in Washington on 12 May 1943, and again at the Quebec Conference in August. The following routes were adopted as the logical roads to Tokyo:

A.　Marshalls-Truk-Marianas-Iwo-Japan
B.　New Guinea-Mindanao-Luzon-Formosa-Okinawa-Japan

A bitter rivalry developed later between Admiral Nimitz (Route A) and General MacArthur (Route B), but both felt that more forces were necessary in the war against Japan, and they agreed on the general tactics of leapfrogging through the islands, using carrier-based air power, and bypassing the strong points. At the Cairo Conference in early December 1943, the same two-route strategy was confirmed, and the objectives for 1944 were determined as follows:

1.　The primary objective is to capture advance bases and force Japan into unconditional surrender.
2.　Blockade Japan by submarine and air force, and destroy Japanese fleet units whenever possible.
3.　Offensive action on Route B should be taken in conjunction with offensive action along Route A.
4.　Establish B-29 bases on Saipan, Guam, and Tinian for strategic bombing of the Japanese mainland.

At this time Admiral King stated his conviction that the United States Navy would be strong enough to destroy the Japanese fleet before the spring of 1945. This appraisal, from a man who had a reputation for never exaggerating, deeply impressed all commanders of the United States armed forces.

On 28 December 1943, the Joint Chiefs of Staff issued directives to Admiral Nimitz and General MacArthur to launch offensives along the prescribed routes as soon as possible. General MacArthur, not content with the strategy of this two-pronged offensive, sent his chief of staff, Lieutenant General R. K. Sutherland, to Washington in January to register his dissent. He firmly believed that Route B was the proper highway to Tokyo, and that Route A was secondary. Admiral Nimitz, not to be outmaneuvered, sent his chief of staff, Rear Admiral Forrest Sherman, to refute MacArthur's contention. At the time MacArthur had four United States and six Australian divisions. Nimitz had two Army and six Marine divisions.

In Washington, Vice Admiral Russell Wilson, Army Lieutenant General Stanley D. Embick, and Air Force Major General Muir S. Fairchild, of the Joint Strategic Survey Committee, tried to smooth out the differences. They recommended the elimination of Truk from Route A, and of Mindanao from Route B. They emphasized the importance of Saipan, and recommended that losses be kept to a minimum. Still the rivalry persisted between MacArthur and Nimitz. President Roosevelt finally invited the two commanders to a conference in Hawaii. It took place 27–28 July, and the meeting effected a reconciliation between the two men and their ideas. It was decided that Nimitz should dispatch his carrier task forces to help MacArthur, and that MacArthur should bypass Formosa.

Turning to Japan, we see a different kind of rivalry. The battle of the Solomons was fought mainly by the Naval Air Force. Plane losses ran to the staggering total of 7,000. The nation's total capacity for plane production should have been mobilized to replenish these losses. The Army, however, insisted on one half of all aircraft production for its own use. Since the Army Air Force had sustained no losses in the

Solomons, it should have relinquished its quota to the Navy, but it did not. Two decades earlier, when the Navy under Admiral Tomosaburo Kato was feverishly trying to build its 8-8 Fleet, the Minister of War, General Giichi Tanaka, offered to divert part of his appropriations to assist the Navy's expansion. Such understanding and cooperation, however, could not be expected from the Army leadership of General Tojo. The Navy's antipathy toward Tojo was extreme, and men in the Navy Ministry were correspondingly disturbed by their weak leadership in Admiral Shigetaro Shimada. In the United States, harmony prevailed at the highest level of command, while discord erupted between field commanders. In Japan, on the other hand, there was harmony among field commanders of both various services, but disunity and friction at General Headquarters.

Meanwhile, the scheduled offensives were launched by Admiral Nimitz in the Gilberts and the Marshalls, and by General MacArthur in New Guinea. Japan had no way of knowing which was the main offensive line. She abandoned the Solomons operations, gave up her outer perimeters, and was forced to withdraw to an inner defensive line along the Marianas and the Philippines. This forced withdrawal left Japan with makeshift lines which were indefensible. If she had been content with these inner defensive lines in the first place, and had devoted her efforts to establishing strong positions along these lines, she would have given a much better account of herself.

聯合艦隊

6

MARIANAS
SEA BATTLE

1. First Mobile Fleet Expectations

THE JAPANESE NAVY had to wait two full years after Midway for a decisive surface engagement with the United States Fleet. In the meantime, attrition battles in the Solomons caused the weakened Navy to hope that the decisive action might be delayed until the spring of 1945, so that Japan could regain some of her lost strength. In December 1943, however, the enemy laid plans for the invasion of Saipan which precipitated decisive battle at a time and place of the enemy's choosing.

During this two-year interval the Japanese Combined Fleet lost two commanders in chief. The first of these tragedies occurred on 18 April 1943, when Admiral Isoroku Yamamoto and his staff flew in two transport planes from Rabaul to visit Buka Airfield at the southern tip of Bougainville, to boost the morale of his forces in the Solomons. With their escort of six

fighter planes the two transports were only minutes from landing when they were attacked and shot down by a flight of
sixteen P-38 Lightning fighter planes from Guadalcanal.
Yamamoto was killed when his plane crashed in the jungle.
This tragic loss resulted from the American military's interception of coded messages giving Admiral Yamamoto's flight
schedule. His death shocked and demoralized the entire nation.

Yamamoto's successor as Commander in Chief, Admiral
Mineichi Koga, did a fine job of raising naval morale in succeeding months, and twice led the fleet to the Marshalls, at the
edge of Japan's defensive perimeter, in hope of engaging the
enemy. The enemy avoided battle, however, while continuing
to make successful advances with his fast carrier task forces.
Accordingly, Admiral Koga withdrew to an inner defense line
which followed along the Marianas, Western Carolines, Philippines, and Northern Australia; by taking advantage of this
geographical situation he determined to personally lead his
forces in a decisive battle.

On 27 March 1944, a Navy scout plane reported the sighting
of an enemy task force heading westward along the northern
end of New Guinea. At the same time General Headquarters
reported that a large convoy of enemy transports was moving
to the north in the same area. Thereupon Admiral Koga and
his staff embarked in two flying boats to transfer their headquarters from Palau to Davao. In flight the planes encountered a storm which caused both to crash, and Koga was
killed. A year earlier, Admiral Yamamoto had been in the lead
plane when he was killed, while his chief of staff, Ugaki, in the
second plane, survived. Admiral Koga had also been flying in
the lead plane, and his chief of staff, Vice Admiral Shigeru
Fukudome, in the second plane, survived. It seemed like a bad
omen.

Admiral Koga, with full grasp of the war situation, had
believed that the time for decisive battle was not far off and,
accordingly, on 1 March 1944, he had made the following
policy decisions:

1. Execute a reorganization of Combined Fleet, with the mobile fleet as the Main Body,
2. Expand land-based naval air forces, in the Inner South Seas, with Tinian as their main base, and have them cooperate with the surface forces,
3. Move Combined Fleet Headquarters to Saipan, where it will fight to the bitter end.

Had Admiral Koga lived, Saipan would probably not have fallen so easily to the enemy. Thinking back on these events, with misfortune after misfortune, one must conclude that the God of War had abandoned Japan.

The enemy could not have predicated his plans on Koga's death but, beginning in April 1944, the tempo of the enemy offensive was greatly accelerated. On 1 April, Truk was twice attacked by air; Hollandia was invaded on the 3rd and fell to the enemy on the 27th. On the first day of May, Truk received its third air attack, and strategic Biak Island was invaded on the 27th. There was no way of knowing where the enemy would concentrate his offensive efforts. Would it be north of Australia and in the Philippines (because of the Biak division)? In the Inner South Seas and Saipan (because of the attacks on Truk)? Or in the middle, at Palau? It was the enemy's strategy to keep us guessing, and in this he was successful. Japan had to try to be prepared in all of these sectors.

On 2 May, Combined Fleet issued advance notice of Operation "A" (pronounced "AH"). "All forces are to be prepared to meet the enemy in the area of his main offensive and, with one blow, destroy the enemy fleet and thus thwart his offensive plans." This effort to insure "certain victory" showed that the Japanese Navy was far more aggressive and realistic than it had been at the time of Midway. If this battle should be lost we knew that it would be an act of fate and not because of a lack of preparation and caution.

The first and most important consideration was the reorganization of First Mobile Fleet as planned by the late Admiral Koga. It was assembled in Tawi Tawi, at the northeastern tip of Borneo, awaiting orders. Operation "A" was the only engagement of the war in which Japanese surface and carrier forces united as one body to oppose the enemy. Battleships were to serve as escorts to the aircraft carriers whose planes would be the main offensive weapon. The new organization of the Fleet, completely different in concept from that of Admiral Yamamoto, was as follows:

First Mobile Fleet (*Vice Admiral Jisaburo Ozawa in* Taiho)

Third Fleet (Vice Admiral Ozawa)

Cardiv 1: (Vice Admiral Ozawa)
 Taiho, Zuikaku, Shokaku
Cardiv 2: (Rear Admiral Takaji Joshima)
 Junyo, Hiyo, Ryuho
Cardiv 3: (Rear Admiral Sueo Obayashi)
 Chitose, Chiyoda, Zuiho
Desron 10:
 CLs *Yahagi, Agano,* and 15 DDs

Second Fleet (Vice Admiral Takeo Kurita in *Atago*)

Batdiv 1: (Vice Admiral Matome Ugaki)
 Yamato, Musashi, Nagato
Batdiv 2:
 Kongo, Haruna
Crudiv 4:
 Atago, Takao, Maya, Chokai
Crudiv 5:
 Myoko, Haguro
Crudiv 7:
 Kumano, Suzuya, Tone, Chikuma
Desron 2:
 CL *Noshiro* and 14 DDs

2. Land-based Air Forces in Decisive Battle

In addition to the organization of Admiral Ozawa's Mobile Fleet, another strategic preparation was the expansion of land-based air forces. In February 1944, land planes were hurriedly disposed to Tinian and other bases of the Inner South Seas. The First Air Fleet at Tinian was placed under the direct command of Naval General Headquarters, and Vice Admiral Kakuji Kakuta, a veteran naval aviator, was appointed as its commander in chief. A total of 1,644 planes were to be distributed on Tinian, Guam, Saipan, Rota, Iwo Jima, Yap, and Palau. Their mission was to attack enemy invasion operations within the Inner South Seas, and at the time to give powerful support to Admiral Ozawa's Mobile Fleet (with its own 455 planes). It was expected that they would provide even more fighting strength than Japan's carrier-based planes.

If everything went according to plan the sea battle of the Marianas was to be a great victory, and American forces attempting to invade Saipan would be annihilated. Unfortunately, the plan met with various obstacles. The planes, instead of being properly crated and shipped in groups, had to be flown singly to their destinations as quickly as they came from the assembly lines. Not knowing where the enemy would strike next, Admiral Kakuta at Tinian kept shifting the planes from one base to another. From the southern Philippines to the area north of Australia, from Biak to Palau, then to Halmahera, to Tinian, to Saipan, they were constantly on the move. Hopping from base to base was a simple and welcome operation for skilled crews, but it was a disastrous routine for pilots who lacked proper training and practice—and it was fatal for 80 per cent of the planes involved.

The Navy, having lost many skilled pilots and air crewmen at the Battle of Midway—and many more in the attrition war in the Solomons—made serious efforts to replenish these losses. Time, however, was lacking. General Headquarters had planned to have the land-based air forces organized within one year. The press of war demanded that this reorganization be completed even sooner, but impoverished Japan could not meet the demand.

The plan for reorganization had been conceived in July 1943, but the program did not get underway until six months later. The assembly lines then began to turn out fighter planes even more powerful than the Zero—so feared by American pilots early in the war—as well as bombers and torpedo bombers which were a match for their American and British counterparts. With properly trained crews these planes could have been put to good account, but there was no time.

In March 1944, Combined Fleet ships were moved to the southern regions where fuel was available. The planes and crews moved with the carriers but, because of enemy air and submarine activities, there was little chance for exercise maneuvers. After May 1944, all drill flights were suspended for more than a month, with the result that the new pilots had no chance to train and the veteran pilots no chance for practice. Had there been time, there might have been a way to correct this situation, but the enemy was moving everywhere six months ahead of Japanese expectations.

3. Misjudged Decisive Battle Area

As of 1 June 1944, the Japanese High Command had the following facts as a basis for judgment in preparing for a defensive operation: the enemy had invaded Biak Island; he was attacking Saipan, Tinian, and Iwo Jima; and he had based at Majuro in the Marshall Islands a tremendous concentration of forces (discovered by Lieutenant Takehiko Chihaya in an extraordinary aerial reconnaissance). From these facts Japan could conclude only that the enemy's main offensive effort would be either north of Australia, at Saipan, or at Palau. Accordingly, for Operation "A" the main battle area was designated as being "from the Central Pacific to the Philippines and north of Australia."

In other words, not knowing where the enemy would strike,

Japan had to be ready for action in any of three possible areas—an impossible task. It reflects seriously on Combined Fleet Headquarters that they were unable to designate a single main area of battle.

Guesswork and debate regarding the enemy's main offensive front had raged hot and heavy on board flagship *Oyodo* as she lay at anchor in Tokyo Bay. Half of the staff had decided that the main front would be the Palau area, and most of the others settled on the area north of Australia. One lone member, Commander Chikataka Nakajima, the staff Intelligence Officer, estimated that it would be Saipan. It was eventually concluded that the most important place at the moment was Biak Island, where the enemy had already landed. If an airfield was established on this island, the southern Philippines as well as Palau would fall within range of American B-24s. Therefore, if Japan could recapture Biak, the Palaus and the southern Philippines might be saved; and, in support of the strategically important island of Biak, the enemy task forces would sortie and provide an opportunity for decisive battle.

On 3 June, accordingly, orders were issued for Operation *"Kon,"* the recapture of Biak Island. These orders called for the assembly of Ozawa's carrier fleet and Kurita's battleship fleet at Tawi Tawi, equidistant from Biak and Palau. In addition, some fleet planes and 480 land-based planes from Tinian were to assemble at Halmahera Island, also equidistant from Palau and Biak. In the week that followed, two futile attempts were made to recapture the island.

While the main strength of the Japanese Navy was engaged in Operation *"Kon,"* the main strength of American task forces appeared unopposed in waters 170 miles to the east of Guam. On 11 June, the enemy launched simultaneous air strikes on Saipan, Tinian, Guam, and Rota; followed the next day by more severe attacks at the same targets, and enormous damage was inflicted on our land-based air forces. Actual numbers are not known, but no fewer than 500 planes were destroyed. Before passing judgment on the ineffectiveness of Kakuta's land-based air forces, the misjudgments of the

High Command must again be taken into consideration. As it turned out, Commander Nakajima was correct in his estimate that Saipan would be the main battle area.

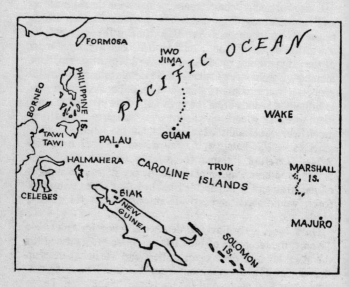

Operation A

The enemy's intention to invade Saipan became entirely clear on 13 June with his ship bombardment of that island, and Operation *"Kon"* was cancelled. An urgent radio message directed Ozawa's fleet to proceed at full speed for Saipan —2,000 miles distant. At the same time, Tinian-based planes were ordered into immediate action. Only a handful, however, had survived the air attacks of the past two days, so it was up to the Saipan garrison alone to resist until the arrival of Ozawa's fleet and additional land-based planes.

Saipan was the northernmost extremity of Japan's lifeline. Its first line of defenses crumpled under siege of a seven-hour bombardment by the enemy, who landed easily despite all-out resistance by the defenders. The island fell within three weeks. For the ineffective resistance at Saipan, the Army must assume some blame since Chief of Army General Staff Hideki Tojo had declared that he would personally be responsible for the defense of the island. But the Navy is also culpable for having concentrated its main fighting strength against Biak, thus leaving Saipan relatively defenseless. In any event, the defensive works of earth and wood on Saipan were crude and inadequate. Even if they had been well constructed they could not have withstood the enemy bombardment. I recall the words of one Army officer who said, "If the enemy would only come to Saipan, that is what we want." Again our Army completely underestimated the opponent.

The invasion of Saipan had been proposed at the meeting of the Allied Combined Chiefs of Staff at Casablanca in January 1943. It was settled upon at Quebec in August, and on 25 October of the same year it was settled that the invasion would take place in July 1944 and that B-29 bases on the island would be completed by the following October. United States forces were almost precisely on schedule in carrying out these plans which had been laid a full year and a half in advance.

4. The Enemy's Material Strength

Admiral Ozawa's fleet, after loading 10,800 tons of fuel at Guimaras during the night of 13 June, proceeded northward followed by seven tankers. On the way the fleet was joined by *Musashi, Yamato,* and other warships from Operation *"Kon."* Twice they were successful in eluding contacts with enemy submarines and, at 1500 on 18 June, they arrived in position five hundred miles west of Saipan. This was quite an accomplishment for a fleet which suffered severe fuel shortages, and it was a terrific challenge for a fleet whose commanding officers regarded Saipan as the least likely of three possible battle areas.

Ozawa immediately dispatched scout planes over wide areas. Unlike the inadequate job of scouting done by Admiral Nagumo at the Battle of Midway, Ozawa sent out 16 seaplanes, 13 carrier attack planes, and 13 bombers. Scout planes reported the sighting of four groups of United States naval forces in the vicinity of Saipan:

Group 1: 2 carriers, 15 other warships including battleships
Group 2: 3 carriers, at least 20 other warships
Group 3: 2 carriers, 16 other warships
Group 4: 4 carriers, more than 30 other warships
(Group 4 was discovered farther to the south by land-based air forces.)

According to past experience, the presence of seven fleet carriers close to Saipan meant that there probably were also some eight light carriers and perhaps ten escort carriers nearby. And the total of at least 80 other warships in the area indicated that the United States Navy was prepared to engage in decisive battle. The actual strength of the enemy armada assembled in the Marianas was 7 fleet carriers, 8 light carriers, 14 escort carriers, 14 battleships, 10 heavy cruisers, 11 light cruisers, 4 antiaircraft cruisers, and 86 destroyers—a total of 154 warships!

Japanese reconnaissance planes had sighted only the advance, or first-line, strength of the enemy. Half again as many ships waited a hundred miles to the rear as a reserve force, to be used in the event that a second engagement was necessary. The enemy had amassed a naval strength three times greater than that of Japan. Here was another example of the enemy's tremendous industrial capacity which so threatened Japan in a prolonged war.

The battle situation in the Marianas proved to be for the Americans what Japan had hoped for at the time of the Battle of Midway. By invading the strategic island of Saipan the

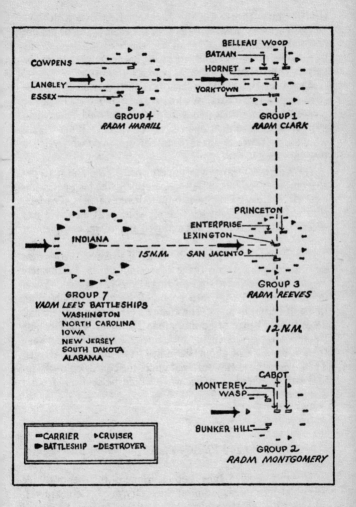

Task Force 58 Formations, 19 June 1944

United States fleet lured the Japanese fleet into a decisive battle. The odds were all in favor of the enemy, and he did not make the mistakes that Japan had made at Midway. While learning by experience and increasing his material strength, he had waited patiently for the propitious moment.

Where the United States had 19 aircraft carriers of various sizes, Japan had a total of nine. Against Japan's 430 carrier planes—of which only 380 were operational—the enemy had 891. What chance did Japan have for victory? What chance would a *sumo* wrestler have against an opponent who weighed twice as much?

Yet Admiral Ozawa was unperturbed. He planned to destroy most of the enemy flattops, especially the big ones, without serious loss of his own outnumbered carriers. Fearless, careful, and thorough, his fighting spirit was high. He had determined the tactics to be employed and he was confident of success.

Ozawa's plan was to launch his aerial strike before his own task force came within range of enemy planes. Fortunately Japan had succeeded in building Type-92 fighters, *Suisei* bombers, and *Tenzan* torpedo bombers, all of which could range at least 400 miles. The enemy's Grumman fighters had an estimated range of no more than 280 miles. The Japanese would outrange the enemy by launching a first attack wave from a distance of about 380 miles from the enemy targets. Then, while the enemy suffered under the confusion of the initial strike, a second attack wave would be sent out from a distance of 200–250 miles.

5. *Premature Victory Plans*

At 1530 on 18 June, upon learning of the enemy's three carrier groups, Rear Admiral Sueo Obayashi, Comcardiv 3, advocated launching an immediate attack. In fact, he alerted his planes and several actually took off from carrier *Chiyoda*. Admiral Ozawa, however, forestalled this hasty action and made it clear that the all-out attack would not begin until dawn the next day. His reasoning was that a 1530 attack would necessitate night-time recovery of returning planes, with some having to land at Guam, thus reducing the carrier strength available for the following day.

Ozawa's cool and deliberate attitude befitted an admiral in command of a great fleet. While he maintained readiness for an all-out attack, he kept in mind the tactics planned for the next day, and restrained his impatient men so that their fighting spirit could be used to fullest advantage.

Experience had taught the enemy to expect an attack within two hours after scout planes were sighted, and he braced for a dusk attack on 18 June. When an all-out attack did not materialize that evening, the enemy must have concluded that the Japanese fleet had been dissuaded by the three-to-one superiority of the American forces and had withdrawn temporarily. The only place of retirement for the Japanese was Guam. An early morning air strike on that island would destroy Japanese air bases and, at the same time, locate the

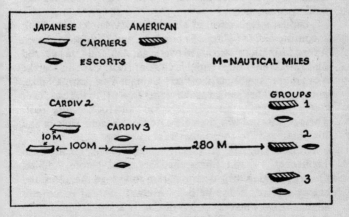

Outranging Tactics in the Marianas Naval Battle, June 1944

Imperial Fleet. With this in mind, the American surface forces stood 200 miles west of Saipan during the night.

As the sun rose on 19 June the sea was pelted by occasional squalls from dark, low-hanging clouds. The day was not ideal for battle, but it was not entirely without hope. Ozawa first launched a group of 16 scout seaplanes about an hour before daybreak. A second group, of 14 planes, and a third, of 11 *Suisei* bombers and 2 seaplanes, were launched within the next hour. These last were to search out a distance of 580 miles.

A plane of the first scout group reported an enemy force of five fleet carriers, four battleships, and ten other warships in position bearing 264 degrees, 160 miles distant from Saipan. The next sighting, by a plane of the second scouting force, was of another large group of enemy warships; details and location were not included. The third sighting was of three fleet carriers, five battleships, and ten other ships 70 miles west of Saipan.

The nearest reported enemy ships were 300 miles from Cardiv 3, the Japanese vanguard, and 400 miles from Ozawa's main force. While we had sighted the enemy, he did not seem to have sighted us. Admiral Ozawa's plan proceeded according to schedule.

The first attack wave, of 129 planes, was launched at 0730. It consisted of 48 fighters, 54 bombers, and 27 torpedo planes. As the formations assembled overhead, Admiral Ozawa stood on the flagship bridge with his chief of staff, Captain Matake Yoshimura, senior staff officer, Captain Toshikazu Ohmae, and others. They smiled as the planes flew off to the east, confident that at long last the time was at hand for a victory toast. Their confidence was shared by Admiral Soemu Toyoda and his Combined Fleet headquarters at Kisarazu.

Before taking off, the Cardiv 1 flight leaders, among them Lieutenant Takashi Ebata, had appeared before Admiral Ozawa pledging their determination to avenge the losses and shame suffered at the Battle of Midway. Similar procedures were underway on the carriers of Cardiv 2, which launched 16 fighters, 7 bombers, and 26 attack planes; and Cardiv 3, which sent off 14 fighters, 8 bombers, and 46 attack planes. Everything went smoothly at the outset.

Ozawa and his staff became concerned when three hours had elapsed and there was no report from the attack group. Watches were consulted with increasing frequency. The radio should have been crackling with reports of strike runs on enemy ships. Instead there was silence.

Perhaps the distance of 380 miles was too great for the plane crews with their limited experience. The Pearl Harbor and Midway attacks had each been launched from a distance of about 230 miles, but those pilots had been well trained.

Perhaps the weather had become critical. Or the enemy's radar-controlled guns had prevented our planes from making a successful attack. Even so, the 50 per cent greater range which our planes enjoyed was an advantage we had to exploit. It was our only hope in scoring a sound victory over the numerically superior forces of the enemy. The strategy was right, the tactic was not wrong. The silence was mystifying and disturbing.

6. *Dark Clouds Shroud the Battle Area*

Despite the great anxiety that prevailed at fleet headquarters, the attack plan had to continue. At 1000 Admiral Ozawa had launched from Cardiv 2 a second group consisting of 20 fighters, 36 bombers, and 26 attack planes. A second unit from Cardiv 1 was also to have sortied at this time, but it was delayed by an accident on flagship *Taiho* and did not get off until 1230, when 4 torpedo planes, 4 bombers, and 10 attack planes headed for the third group of enemy ships. At the same time a few planes from the first sortie returned to their carriers.

The pilots, somewhat dejected, reported that the battle area was covered with heavy clouds and—what was worse—with numerous enemy fighters, in the air and waiting some 30 miles in front of the target ships. These reports indicated that most of the 246 planes of our confident first attack waves had been destroyed even before they had had a chance to strike. If these reports were true, it was obvious that the enemy had enough knowledge of our plans to spread a net of interceptors properly timed to defeat our far-ranging planes. It also meant that the enemy had far outranged us in terms of tactics.

Postwar information reveals that the enemy was not as omniscient as he appeared at the time. The Japanese planes were destroyed by American planes, but not in ambush. Actually, enemy planes had been sent out at 0800 to attack Guam, about 100 miles away. When American radar detected the approaching attackers, the U.S. planes which had been speeding toward Guam were diverted to intercept, and half of our planes were destroyed.

This was not the first time that the enemy had caught our attack planes far in advance of the target area. It had happened at Midway. The Marianas action, however, proved to us the keen efficiency of the enemy radar systems which could detect planes at a distance of 150 miles! No wonder the interceptors were ready and waiting for our attack force.

7. End of Battle and Withdrawal

Ozawa's 32,000-ton flagship *Taiho*, commissioned only the month before and considered to be practically unsinkable, was hit by a torpedo from submarine *Albacore* at 0810 on 19 June, just after her planes had taken off for an attack on the enemy fleet. One of the last planes launched was piloted by Warrant Officer Sakio Komatsu who saw an *Albacore* torpedo heading for a sure hit on the carrier. With lightning decision and determination Komatsu crash-dived his plane into the torpedo. This brilliant display of courage and precision was observed by Ozawa and his staff from the bridge of the flagship. Immediately thereafter they saw the track of another approaching torpedo. A sharp turn was ordered, but it was too late. The second torpedo hit and scored.

Under ordinary circumstances, one, two, or three torpedoes would never have been enough to sink this fine new carrier. But, from the time of this hit, everything went wrong for *Taiho*. A damaged elevator jammed closed, gas from a defective fuel tank seeped into the elevator spaces and, at 1432, an electric spark ignited the accumulated gas causing a tremendous explosion which sealed the ship's doom. Six hours later, at 1828, *Taiho* heeled to port, turned over and sank, 500 miles west of Saipan.

In the afternoon of 15 June, submarine *Flying Fish* discovered Ozawa's fleet as it moved out of San Bernardino Strait into the Philippine Sea. That same evening Ugaki's battleship detachment was spotted by U.S.S. *Seahorse*. And on 17 June submarine *Cavalla* sighted an enemy tanker train in the morning, and a group of fifteen or more large warships that night.

All of these submarines cruised in the vicinity of the Marianas on 19 and 20 June, waiting for targets of opportunity. Their job was well done and thorough. On the 19th at 1120 carrier *Shokaku* was torpedoed by *Cavalla* and set afire. Flames engulfed the ship, and she sank at 1400. Of Japan's three fleet carriers in the Marianas battle, only *Zuikaku* remained afloat.

When flagship *Taiho* sank, Admiral Ozawa transferred to heavy cruiser *Haguro*. He had determined to launch a third attack wave, but was forced to abandon the idea. There were no more than 100 carrier planes then available to him, and the approaching darkness greatly reduced his chances of success.

In the meantime the second attack group, after failing to locate the enemy, ordered 50 of the Cardiv 2 planes to Guam at 1511. They encountered a large group of enemy fighters which shot down 33 planes; the remaining 17 crash-landed at Guam and were so severely damaged that they were out of commission. In this one day of battle the carrier-based plane losses of the Japanese Navy reached the staggering total of 280.

That night Combined Fleet Headquarters ordered a withdrawal, and Admiral Ozawa complied. The fleet refueled early in the morning of 20 June and set course for Nakagusuku Bay, Okinawa. At 1710 a reconnaissance plane reported the sighting of two enemy carriers accompanied by ten other warships, some 200 miles to the rear of the Japanese force. Hoping for a break, at 1900 Ozawa ordered Kurita's Second Fleet to prepare to engage in night battle. Before that order could be carried out, however, enemy planes came sweeping down on the Mobile Fleet to score direct hits on carriers *Zuikaku, Junyo, Ryuho,* and *Chiyoda;* and carrier *Hiyo*, still adrift after its torpedoing by an enemy submarine, was sunk by aerial bombs.

Admiral Kurita, meanwhile, after launching ten reconnaissance planes, turned in pursuit. Two hours later, at 2100, Kurita was ordered to retire, without having caught a glimpse of the enemy, and without having fired a single shot from the mighty 18.1-inch guns of *Yamato* and *Musashi*. On 24 June the Mobile Fleet returned to Hashirajima anchorage in the Inland Sea to nurse its many wounds.

Thus the Japanese Navy's last real opportunity to destroy the enemy fleet ended in tragic defeat. With two out of three fleet carriers and one of three light carriers lost, together with the destruction of nearly 400 carrier planes, it would be almost impossible to reconstitute the Mobile Fleet. At least six months would be needed to prepare properly for surface action.

In contrast to Japan's tremendous losses in this two-day naval battle, the United States Navy suffered damage to battleships *South Dakota* and *Indiana*, carriers *Bunker Hill* and *Wasp*, and heavy cruiser *Minneapolis*, and lost slightly more than 100 planes.

8. The Defeat in Retrospect

No one on the staff of Ozawa's Mobile Fleet nor in Combined Fleet Headquarters dreamed that the "A" operation could have ended in such humiliating defeat. The facts of what happened and the reasons for the failure of this operation have been noted above. The most important factors were Japan's waning strength and, as some people were beginning to feel, her abandonment by the God of War.

The tactical plan of using our planes to outrange the enemy's had been a long shot, predicated on his three-to-one strength advantage. The hope had been to destroy the enemy fleet without having to sacrifice any of our few ships. Behind that great naval strength was a material and productive capacity which Japan could not hope to match.

By the summer of 1944 Japan's stocks were low in every commodity, and especially in the supplies of war. This weakness was compounded by a poor system of distribution. The veteran air personnel of Cardiv 2 were furnished with old Type-99 bombers, while the new *Suisei* bombers were allotted to the inexperienced crews of Cardiv 1. Thus Japan's most modern bombers, which should have struck the heaviest blow in this engagement, were reduced in strength when the green crews recklessly flew low over their own advance ships and lost several of their number to "friendly" antiaircraft fire.

Radar was an important element in this battle. Japan's radar research was well advanced, but production was limited and there were too few instruments in the fleet. The United States, on the other hand, had plenty of efficient radar sets in its ships and used them to good advantage to obtain early warning of the approach of our attack planes.

The employment of Japanese submarines in Operation "A" requires explanation. Under Combined Fleet all submarines were organized into the Sixth Fleet (Vice Admiral Takeo Takagi) which deployed 21 boats—almost its entire strength —for this operation. Admiral Takagi moved his fleet headquarters from Kure to Saipan in the spring of 1944 to assume command of all land, sea, and air forces there. But at Saipan there were no repair facilities for his out-dated submarines, and by the summer of 1944 the boats and their crews were exhausted after months of operating without proper upkeep and maintenance. Lack of modern gear made the boats extremely vulnerable to enemy attack; conversely, American antisubmarine warfare (A/SW) tactics and methods were excellent and effective. The enemy used his well-equipped destroyers and frigates in conjunction with A/SW planes to good purpose. These planes with their modern detection equipment, and the ships with hedgehog and depthcharge launchers, made a deadly combination against Japanese submarines. Thirteen fell victim to enemy attack during the operation, and Admiral Takagi perished on the island of Saipan.

With the defeat of the Japanese fleet in the Marianas, Saipan became untenable. No matter how strong the land defenses, they could not have held out for long once the supply lines were severed.

The debacle of the Marianas sea battle left the Combined Fleet so discouraged that no ideas worthy of consideration were immediately forthcoming. Then, out of desperation, it was proposed to send battleships *Fuso* and *Yamashiro* into the area with their big guns blazing, in order to throw the enemy off balance and give the hard-pressed island garrison a chance to counterattack. This reckless proposal was a first manifestation of the "bulldozer tactics," which were to characterize most of Japan's subsequent efforts. In this instance Admiral Soemu Toyoda vetoed the idea, knowing that it would have spelled certain doom for both of the ships and every man on board.

The bloom of these "bulldozer tactics" was to come to full fruition with the kamikaze suicide attacks, beginning in October at Leyte Gulf. The very concept was futility itself, and it bespoke the desperation of Japan and her fighting forces.

The contemplated use of *Fuso* and *Yamashiro* at Saipan was prophetic. Both battleships finally ended their career at Leyte Gulf in an endeavor that was little different from the one considered for them at Saipan.

After the battle of the Marianas the Mobile Fleet was in sad need of rebuilding. Warship production in Japan was so inadequate that there was no hope of providing new ships to replace losses. *Zuikaku,* the lone remaining fleet carrier, was joined with hermaphrodite carrier-battleships *Ise* and *Hyuga,* light carriers *Junyo, Zuiho,* and *Ryuho,* and converted carriers *Chiyoda* and *Chitose.* The surface fleet of Admiral Kurita was separated from this remainder of the Mobile Fleet, and sent south to Lingga Roads because there was not enough fuel for them and the carriers in Japan.

While the carriers were still in the home islands, every effort was made to supply them with replacements of planes and crews. There were, however, never enough planes to restock even the few carriers that remained. And Japan's few new planes were deployed to land bases in the south.

7

聯合艦隊

THE BATTLES FOR LEYTE: PHASE ONE

1. The "Bulldozer Fleet"

THE JAPANESE NAVY'S effort to repulse enemy landings at Leyte Gulf, in October 1944, led to the final sea battle of the Pacific War. It was a decisive battle, but not the one which Japan had longed for during the two years since its defeat at Midway. Instead of bringing victory, the naval actions at Leyte spelled the finish of the Japanese Navy as a fighting force. The entire battle, from the time of the Combined Fleet sortie until its retirement in defeat, covered a period of six days and involved surface actions in four separate arenas of combat.

The official Japanese name for this venture was Operation *"Sho"* (Victory), but it came to be known as the "bulldozer operation." The purpose of the plan, conceived in the early fall of 1944 when Japan was being forced from all sides, was to defend the homeland and its immediately adjacent regions, which were divided into four areas: *Sho* 1, the Philippines;

Sho 2, Formosa and the Ryukyus; *Sho* 3, Honshu, Kyushu, and Shikoku; and *Sho* 4, Hokkaido and the Kuriles.

Japanese planners had calculated that they could recover from the defeat in the Marianas and be ready for battle again by the early spring of 1945. The enemy, however, not heeding Japanese plans and aspirations, moved into the Philippines months in advance of Japanese readiness.

On 17 October 1944, United States forces commanded by General Douglas MacArthur landed on Suluan Island at the mouth of Leyte Gulf. This forward jump was typical of the enemy, who for many months had been leapfrogging across the Pacific, bypassing Japan's strong points in surprise attacks on more advanced targets. An example of this strategy was seen when the enemy avoided Truk, which was braced and ready, and struck instead at Saipan and the rest of the Marianas.

The order to activate Operation *Sho* 1 was given on the night of 17 October, following verification of the enemy's landing on Suluan. With proper reconnaissance Japan might have detected the assembling of enemy forces at Hollandia and activated *Sho* 1 as early as 10 October, or at least by 14 October, when the giant U.S. Naval force sortied. As it was, the enemy was already landing in Leyte Gulf before the order was issued.

2. *No Hiding Place*

After three years of fighting, Japan was showing signs not only of fatigue, but of decay as well, and nowhere was this more apparent than in the fields of communications and intelligence. The Japanese Navy was hampered by inferior radio communications, radar, and intelligence from the time of Midway until the end of the war. Japanese naval movements were frequently known to the enemy sooner and with more accuracy than in Japanese headquarters. Our weakness, further accentuated by the enemy's great strength and continued successes, became painfully evident at the Marianas battle.

On 19 June 1944, as Kurita's force was retreating from the battle area, a lone enemy plane appeared. It reported the fleet's movements in plain-language radio messages which were intercepted by the battleships:

> Enemy force of twenty ships including battleships *Yamato* and *Musashi* heading southward. Location, X miles west of Tinian.
> A carrier five miles to port is on fire.
> Two destroyers are rescuing survivors from the water.
> Following ten miles behind the main force are three *Takao*-class cruisers.

It was exasperating that this enemy plane, from its point of vantage and safety high above the fleet, had a better view and knowledge of the situation than did the Japanese fleet commander. Worse still, the fleet had not a single plane to send in pursuit of this brazen intruder.

Our increasingly "deaf and blind" Navy was also losing its best offensive weapon—airplanes. Japan's brilliant victories at the beginning of the war had been directly attributable to her superior planes which had easily out-maneuvered and out-fought the enemy at Pearl Harbor, Singapore, and in the Indian Ocean. But, by the fall of 1944, Japan's supply of planes had dwindled pitifully while the enemy's supply had increased prodigiously.

Had there been enough Japanese fighter planes, the battles of 1944 might have turned out quite differently; the B-29s could not have dropped their incendiaries so freely over the homeland, and there would have been some opposition to the atomic bombings of Hiroshima and Nagasaki. It was Japan's lack of fighter planes which laid the homeland open to the methodical and practically unopposed attack by enemy bombers which began in late 1944. By that time the Combined Fleet had been suffering devastating air attacks for almost a year.

The Combined Fleet was anchored at Truk when the enemy chose that island as a target on 17–18 February 1944. The bombing and torpedo tactics introduced by the Japanese Naval Air Force at Pearl Harbor were used by the United States on this occasion with great success. The Japanese Navy lost 2 cruisers, 4 destroyers, and 325 precious planes.

Truk, which had been the headquarters of Combined Fleet since early 1943, was no longer tenable for this purpose and Admiral Mineichi Koga had to move. He chose Palau, in the Carolines, for his new base, and it was promptly discovered by enemy scout planes. On 30–31 March 1944 the Carolines were hit by 1,200 planes. In these two days Japan lost 80,000 tons of shipping in the harbor, and more than 200 planes. Admiral Koga flew from Palau on 31 March to move his headquarters to Davao. He was killed, however, when his plane crashed in a severe storm near the Island of Cebu.

Vice Admiral Takeo Kurita led the Combined Fleet from Palau to Davao, but this was no haven for the harassed ships. The only way to escape aerial attack was to find a base out of range of American planes, and that was no easy task by the spring of 1944. So it was that Combined Fleet came to be based at Tawi Tawi and Lingga Roads, and operated exclusively in the waters of Borneo and Sumatra.

3. Radar, Oil, Fighting Spirit

As we have seen, the Ozawa and Kurita fleets had returned to Hiroshima Bay after their defeat in the Marianas. During the few days that they remained in the homeland, all ships of cruiser size and larger were equipped with radar. Japan was two years behind the United States in installing these vital instruments of naval warfare; nevertheless, radar production was a singular achievement for the Japanese Army and Navy because in this instance they cooperated completely. When Imperial General Headquarters became aware of and concerned about the enemy's use of this electronic device and Japan's lack of it, a "Radar Headquarters" was established to expedite its development and production. Technicians and materials were liberally allocated to the project. This was one of the few occasions during the war when the Army, recognizing the importance of radar to the Navy, did not slow the effort by insisting on an equal share of all the required materials.

Technically the Japanese Navy's most serious shortcoming during the Pacific War was lack of radar. Night battle tactics had long been traditional with the Navy in theory, training, and practice. Excellence in night combat had led to a saying that dark Japanese eyes were superior to the fair eyes of the enemy for night engagements. Any validity this might have had vanished on the night of 11 October 1942, when three heavy cruisers of Rear Admiral Aritomo Goto's Cruiser Division 6 moved in to bombard Guadalcanal. In a completely surprise action the enemy's radar-controlled gunfire sank *Furutaka* and severely damaged flagship *Aoba*, in which Admiral Goto was killed. *Kinugasa* alone escaped damage. This Battle of Cape Esperance deprived the Imperial Navy of its vaunted ascendancy in night battle tactics.

On the heels of this setback a surface force which included battleships *Kongo* and *Haruna* was sent to Guadalcanal two nights later and caught the enemy off guard. For an hour and a half the island was bombarded by guns of all sizes, including the 12-inch guns of the battleships which fired mammoth incendiary shells. This assault set extensive fires on the airfield, in the barracks, ammunition depots, and quartermaster depots. If landing troops had been available and ready, the island of Guadalcanal could have been recaptured at that time.

The enemy, however, repaired damage, strengthened defenses, and doubled the radar network—for both gunfire control and advance warning—so that all such subsequent attempts were thwarted. Thereafter Japanese ships intent on night bombardment were detected long before they got within gun range of Guadalcanal, and were turned back. The enemy's radar had played a decisive part in Japan's loss of Guadalcanal.

The crews were overjoyed in late June 1944 to have radar installed in all major warships. Kure harbor resounded with banzais when the news was announced.

Then, after only one week in home waters, the Combined Fleet headed southward. The fuel shortage in Japan had become so critical that the ships had to move promptly to a source of fuel or be immobilized. With enemy occupation of the Marianas, the line of supply to the oil-rich lands of the south was broken.

For all its apparent strength the fleet suffered from many weaknesses. There were no aircraft carriers, and there were shortages of ships, planes, men, fuel, and ammunition. Radar could not compensate for these deficiencies. Practically speaking, the only commodity which was not in short supply was fighting spirit. Throughout all the demoralizing movements and shifting of bases that ensued, there was no defeatism among the men of Combined Fleet. Their burning fighting spirit must be appreciated if one is to understand the "fleet turnabout" at Leyte in the latter part of the following October, which is probably one of the most controversial subjects in the annals of naval warfare.

4. Training at Lingga

Lingga Roads, just across the strait from Singapore, was the southern base for Combined Fleet. There the tropical summer sun turns the sea water tepid, and sandy areas surrounding the anchorage are often too hot for strolling. The flat terrain is sparsely dotted with coconut trees, and that is all.

The men of Combined Fleet spent most of the daylight hours at rest. The slightly less torrid nights were devoted to frenzied training and practice. The pace of training in the Japanese Navy had always been thorough and rigorous, but training at Lingga in the summer of 1944 broke all records. There were no recreation facilities, but then there was no time for recreation.

In a typical practice operation the fleet would be divided into equal forces. Force A, with *Yamato* as flagship, would try to storm the anchorage while Force B, with *Musashi* as flagship, tried to defend it. Such maneuvers went on day after day and week after week.

Many of the officers and men at Lingga, including Admiral Kurita, were veterans of the protracted fight for Guadalcanal two years earlier. They remembered bitterly the loss of that island, resulting in part from a lack of Japanese radar equipment. Now their own ships were equipped with radar, and they went about their preparations with new confidence.

This time the Combined Fleet—or what remained of it—hoped to engage the enemy in a decisive surface action. The idea of a traditional fleet-opposed surface engagement was out of the question. Not only had carrier-based planes made that concept obsolete, but, unfortunately, there were no carriers and planes at Lingga. Japan's remaining carriers were in the homeland awaiting planes.

All manner of tactics were practiced—including swift interception, gunnery, long-range torpedo firing—with emphasis still on night battle. It was felt that with radar available to both sides, Japan's pre-radar advantage had been restored. The 18.1-inch guns of *Yamato* and *Musashi* fired by radar control would be tremendously effective in night actions. It was conceded that the enemy would have control of the air in any battles before the spring of 1945. Until that time Japan had to be prepared to fight with what she had, relying on stealth, deception, and diversion to achieve surprise, and relying on surprise to compensate for her lack of air power.

5. *The Naked Fleet*

Following the defeat in the Marianas in mid-June 1944, Japanese planners had estimated that it would take eight months for the Navy to be back in fighting trim. In just half that time Combined Fleet was obliged to sortie with all available forces. It was shattering to naval staff men when Operation *Sho* 1 had to be activated so precipitously on 18 October, after scarcely three months of training at Lingga. Yet, had they stopped to think of it, in view of the amazingly rapid advances the enemy had made in this third year of the war, the Japanese Navy was fortunate to have had even that long for a breathing spell.

Operation *Sho* 1 was designed to counter any enemy attempt to invade the Philippine Islands. Its tasks may be summarized as follows:

1. Land-based naval air forces were to meet the enemy invading forces at a distance of 700 miles from the islands; to reduce his strength by means of aerial attack with bombs and torpedoes; and, in cooperation with the Army Air Force, to annihilate the remainder of the enemy force at the invasion point.

2. Combined Fleet was to assemble at Brunei Bay, north of Borneo; and, at an opportune time, sortie to intercept the enemy's convoys and escorts.

3. Once the enemy had begun landing operations, Combined Fleet was to storm the invasion point with full strength and annihilate the invading forces.

4. Vice Admiral Ozawa's carrier division was to assist by coming south from Japan to lure the enemy task force northward.

Task 1 was assigned to the Fifth Base Air Force, in the Philippines under Vice Admiral Takejiro Ohnishi, and to Vice Admiral Shigeru Fukudome's Sixth Base Air Force in Formosa. Tasks 2 and 3 were assigned to all ships of Combined Fleet—aircraft carriers excepted—under Vice Admiral Takeo Kurita.

In the meantime, however, enemy air attacks hit Formosa, beginning 12 October, and depleted the strength of the Sixth Base Air Force. These air battles were reported at home as great victories for Japan, but nothing could have been further from the truth. Fukudome's air strength suffered such losses in these enemy attacks on Formosa that it was rendered useless for the *Sho* operation. I shall dwell on this in detail in discussing the defeat of Ozawa's carrier fleet. Here let us consider what Japanese air strength was available for Operation *Sho* 1.

When Admiral Ohnishi took command in the Philippines, on 17 October, the Fifth Base Air Force consisted of no more than 150 operable planes of limited capability. Japan had just suffered the loss of 325 planes at Truk and 203 at Palau.

Ohnishi, Japan's leading authority on naval aviation, had been Admiral Yamamoto's foremost adviser in this field. He realized at once that his command could not fulfill its *Sho* 1 assignment by ordinary means. He decided that the only chance of profitably expending his few remaining planes was by organized aerial suicide attacks. Admiral Ohnishi thereupon established the Kamikaze Special Attack Corps.

Critics of Ohnishi's decision may rightly point out that the Kamikaze Corps was not effective in the naval battles for Leyte Gulf. But it must be remembered that the small number of planes in the Philippines in October 1944 could not have achieved anything by conventional attack methods. If suicide attacks could have disabled the flight decks of enemy carriers, there was a chance that Kurita's fleet might have been able to engage the enemy in a decisive surface engagement. Had conditions been favorable, the plan might have worked. But the suicide effort failed at Leyte, and Japanese surface ships, without air support, had to fight against overwhelmingly superior naval forces possessed of tremendous aerial support.

Japanese aerial deficiencies at Leyte Gulf were almost too numerous to mention. The Philippine-based planes were incapable of ranging 700 miles from their airfields, for either scouting or attack purposes. Accordingly, all of Kurita's float planes, some 32 in number, were transferred from his battleships and cruisers to a field at San José on the island of Mindoro. It had been agreed, however, that Admiral Kurita could recall these planes to his command and control at any time.

It is clear now that it would have been better if these planes had stayed with the ships, to scout and keep the fleet advised of the enemy's location. In that way Combined Fleet might have been aware of the most propitious moment for attack, and might have been better informed about the composition and disposition of enemy forces.

There were, however, further considerations in the decision to send the battleship and cruiser scout planes to land bases. Admiral Ohnishi had requested them because of the limited range of his own planes in the Philippines. Also, the planes, had they remained with the fleet, would have been in jeopardy, since their mother ships could not have retrieved them from the submarine-infested waters between Brunei and Leyte which the fleet had to traverse.

There was endless bitterness and complaint about the disposition of Japan's naval planes for this operation. It was folly for a fleet to sortie without adequate aerial cover. As the ships' planes were sent off to Mindoro, one staff officer remarked in disgust, "I'd hate to be responsible for this decision when enemy submarines attack."

His statement was prophetic, for the fleet was not far from Brunei in its sortie when flagship *Atago* was hit by submarine torpedoes and sank in twenty minutes. Then in rapid succession cruiser *Maya* was torpedoed, sinking in four minutes, and *Takao* was so badly damaged that she had to return to base. These initial losses were directly attributable to the fleet's lack of aerial scouting and cover.

6. Discontent with Operation Sho

The concept of Task 1 in Operation *Sho* was well conceived, even though Japan's aerial weakness made satisfactory performance impossible. The plan for Task 2 was also perfectly logical and reasonable since the interception of an enemy fleet was a proper function of the main surface force. The fleet had been training specifically for this purpose, and for surprise dashes into enemy-held harbors *by night*. In such an operation the 18.1-inch guns of *Yamato* and *Musashi* could inflict much damage with a few quick salvoes and, with their training and practice, have a fair chance of escaping unscathed. Task 4, too, was of reasonable design as a supporting operation, and it proved to be of considerable assistance to Kurita's main force.

The order for Task 3, however, caused great discontent in Combined Fleet. The fleet was to storm into Leyte Gulf in broad daylight to attack and destroy enemy ships in the harbor. In the battles for Guadalcanal two years earlier, Japanese ships had on occasion dashed into enemy-held areas during the night; but the idea of entering an enemy-occupied harbor with surface ships in the broad light of day was absolutely without precedent. In twenty years of training prior to World War II, the emphasis had been on gunnery practice for the capital ships, and hit-and-run tactics for destroyers. The larger ships strove for increased fire power and range, the smaller ones for speed and maneuverability. Night-time approaches toward enemy harbors for the purpose of long-range bombardment were considered a proper occupation for the heavy ships; but daylight attacks on enemy harbors had been reserved as the special province of destroyers or submarines. Attacks on enemy convoys were also considered a task for destroyers and submarines, not cruisers or battleships.

Clearly, Operation *Sho* 1 was to be a final, all-out effort for a decisive fleet engagement, and it was so accepted by the men of the fleet. Yet they had expected that the tactics to be employed would be within the scope of their experience, training, and practice. Accordingly, when the word went out that the objective of this operation was to make a daylight attack on the enemy at Leyte Gulf, it is not surprising that men who had spent so many days in conventional training in the tropics should feel anger at learning of the impossible course they were expected to pursue.

7. Kurita Quiets Discontent

The alert order for Operation *Sho* 1 was issued at 0809 hours on 17 October. The fleet in Lingga weighed anchor at 0100 on 18 October and arrived at Brunei at noon of the 20th. From there it sortied on the 22nd at 0800, with no chance of reaching Leyte Gulf before 25 October.

In the meantime, United States Army forces under General MacArthur had made initial landings on Leyte Island in the evening of 17 October and within twenty-four hours had broken through the Japanese Army's first line of defense. It was clear that the unloading of the enemy's hundreds of transports would be virtually completed by 22 or 23 October at the latest. Thereafter most of the prime targets would be gone from Leyte Gulf, and there would remain only cargo and munition ships.

What was the point of exposing *Yamato* and *Musashi* for the sake of a few auxiliary transports? Admiral Kurita's desk was piled high with memoranda and notes protesting the use of the fleet for such an assignment. The tenor of these protests was as follows:

We do not mind death, but we are very concerned for the honor of the Japanese Navy. If the final effort of our great Navy should be spent in engaging a group of empty cargo ships, surely Admirals Togo and Gonnohyoe Yamamoto would weep in their graves.

Many men came to protest in person, until the situation became so involved that Admiral Kurita called a conference of his division commanders and their staffs on board flagship *Atago*. The meeting was held on the eve of their sortie, and the Admiral spoke movingly to the group:

I know that many of you are strongly opposed to this assignment. But the war situation is far more critical than any of you can possibly know. Would it not be a shame to have the fleet remain intact while our nation perishes? I believe that Imperial

General Headquarters is giving us a glorious opportunity. Because I realize how very serious the war situation actually is, I am willing to accept even this ultimate assignment to storm into Leyte Gulf.

You must all remember that there are such things as miracles. What man can say that there is no chance for our fleet to turn the tide of war in a decisive battle? We shall have a chance to meet our enemies. We shall engage his task forces. I hope that you will not carry your responsibilities lightly. I know that you will act faithfully and well.

As Kurita concluded these stirring remarks the assembled officers leaped to their feet and, inspired by the Admiral's determination, filled the room with resounding shouts of "Banzai!"

THE END OF THE IMPERIAL JAPANESE NAVY

Admiral Isoroku Yamamoto, Commander in Chief Combined Fleet, 1939–1943. Opposed to the war he felt Japan could not win, Yamamoto planned and ordered the attack on Pearl Harbor. He was brilliant, sound, and inspiring. His dramatic death was a blow and a great loss to the Imperial Navy.

The Battle of Midway. Heavy cruiser *Mogami* after aerial attack.

Vice Admiral Chuichi Nagumo, Commander First Carrier Striking Force. He led the Japanese carriers into the Battle of Midway. Charged with negligence born of conceit, after the defeat Nagumo wrote, "... we participated in this operation with meager training and without knowledge of the enemy."

The Battle of Santa Cruz, 26 October 1942. A Japanese bomb splashes astern of a United States carrier; above are antiaircraft bursts. On the horizon a battleship and destroyer are firing.

Admiral Mineichi Koga, Commander in Chief Combined Fleet 1943–1944. He planned a reorganization of Combined Fleet—with carrier forces as the Main Body. It was too late; the tide of battle had turned. He was killed when his flying boat crashed in a storm off the Philippines.

Unlike American carriers, the Japanese sometimes had no island super structure. They were conned from a bridge forward, just beneath the overhanging flight deck.

Admiral Soemu Toyoda, Commander in Chief Combined Fleet, 1944–1945. He ordered the Navy's last all-out, and in the long run pointless, attack—at Leyte Gulf—and thus presided over the death of the Imperial Navy.

Hangar deck afire, a *Zuiho*-class carrier maneuvers to avoid further damage. Note camouflage to resemble a battleship.

An "Ohka" piloted bomb—product of desperation.

The carriers were gone, the trained pilots dead. What remained was the Kamikaze attack, the "divine wind," in which a pilot perished with glory after flying a bomb-laden plane into an enemy ship. Here a suicide squadron receives its sortie orders.

A *Zero,* bomb in place, takes off for a Kamikaze attack.

Vice Admiral Takeo Kurita, commander of the Second Fleet at the Battles for Leyte Gulf. On the eve of their sortie for Operation *Sho* he reassured his officers by saying: "You must all remember that there are such things as miracles. What man can say that there is no chance for our fleet to turn the tide of war in a decisive battle?"

A doomed twin-engine "Frances" passes close above U.S. escort carrier *Ommaney Bay* in the Sulu Sea, May 1945.

The final instant. A suicide plane dives on battleship *Missouri*.

USS *Essex* on fire after being hit by a suicide plane. The Kamikazes did dreadful damage to carriers, destroyers, and destroyer escorts. Had they not concentrated on the picket ships during the Okinawa landings, they might have wrecked the transport fleet and delayed the invasion.

The symbolic finish. Battleship *Yamato*, largest in the world and carrying the largest naval guns in history, explodes after attack by aircraft in April 1945.

Vice Admiral Jisaburo Ozawa, Commander, First Mobile Fleet at the battle of Leyte Gulf. In May 1945 he became Commander in Chief of a fleet that no longer existed. "With no ships to command, he could do little more than stand and look at the waning moon."

8
THE BATTLES FOR LEYTE: PHASE TWO

聯合艦隊

1. The Still-Great Fleet

ON THE EVE of its final sortie the Japanese Fleet still presented a magnificent spectacle as it lay at anchor in Brunei Bay. The sight of these massed ships was enough to encourage a belief of great naval strength, despite the fleet's lack of air power. There was reason to hope that the tide of war might once again be swung in Japan's favor by this great surface force:

Second Fleet[1] (*Vice Admiral Takeo Kurita*)

Batdiv	1	(*Yamato, Musashi, Nagato*)
Batdiv	3	(*Kongo, Haruna*)
Crudiv	4	(CA *Atago, Takao, Maya, Chokai*)
Crudiv	5	(CA *Myoko, Haguro*)

[1] First Fleet was abolished when Combined Fleet Headquarters was moved ashore to Hiyoshidai in mid-September 1944.

Crudiv 7 (CA *Kumano, Suzuya, Tone, Chikuma*)
Desron 2 (CL *Yahagi, Noshiro,* and 15 DD)

Fifth Fleet (Vice Admiral Kiyohide Shima)

Crudiv 21 (CA *Ashigara, Nachi*)
Desron   1 (CL *Abukuma* and 4 DD)

Nishimura Force (Vice Admiral Shoji Nishimura)

Batdiv   2 *(Yamashiro, Fuso)*
Desdiv   4 (CA *Mogami* and 4 DD)

Third (Mobil) Fleet[2] (Vice Admiral Jisaburo Ozawa)

Cardiv   3 *(Zuikaku, Zuiho, Chitose, Chiyoda)*
Cardiv   4 *(Ise, Htuga)*
Desron 10 (CL *Isuzu, Oyodo, Tama* and 8 DD)

The fleet departed Brunei at 0800 on 22 October—divided into two groups spaced six kilometers apart—and steamed northward at 18 knots on a zigzag course. With the next dawn these ships were greeted by submarine attacks off Palawan Island, where flagship *Atago* and two other cruisers fell victim to torpedo hits.

Kurita shifted his flag to battleship *Yamato*, and continued on his northern course. Before dawn on 24 October the ships veered to the east, just south of Mindoro Island, and entered the Sibuyan Sea. This body of water divides the Philippines into two approximately equal parts—north and south. The plan was for Kurita's ships to transit these waters, debouche through San Bernardino Strait, and turn southward for the run to Leyte Gulf. It was a long way to go, and the Sibuyan Sea, with its numerous irregular islands, was an ideal stalking ground for enemy submarines, but this was the only route by

---

[2] The actions of Ozawa's Mobile Fleet, which joined from the homeland, will be described in a later section.

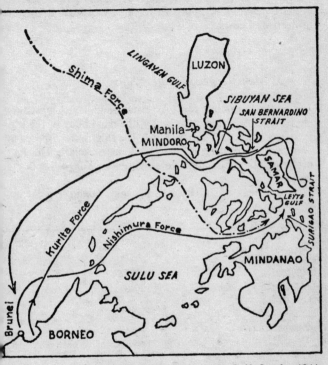

Tracks of Main Japanese Forces, Battles for Leyte Gulf, October 1944

which Kurita's main force could hope to reach Leyte Gulf for a surprise attack.

Another approach to Leyte Gulf for ships coming from Brunei was by way of the Sulu Sea, north of Borneo, through the Mindanao Sea and Surigao Strait. This shorter passage was the one selected for Nishimura's ships, which were slower than Kurita's.

In a direct line Kurita's route was about 1,000 miles. What

with zigzagging and evasive courses to avoid enemy submarines it must have come to nearly 1,500 miles. In any event, it was a mighty long approach for a surface force devoid of protective air cover.

2. Main Targets: Capital Ships

After steaming for two exhausting days, constantly alerted against enemy submarines, the main body of the surface fleet entered the Sibuyan Sea. The ships were disposed in two circular formations, twelve kilometers apart. The first group had battleship *Yamato* at its center; *Kongo* was in the center of the second.

At daybreak of 24 October, flagship *Yamato*'s radar de-

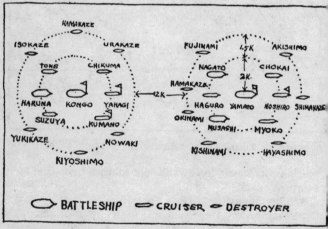

Combined Fleet Formation Heading East in Sibuyan Sea at 0800, 24 October 1944

tected enemy planes high in the eastern sky. General Quarters was sounded and all hands went to battle stations. A few of the more fortunate men had just started to eat breakfast, others had no time for food.

Yamato bristled with 150 AA machine guns, and the escorting cruisers each carried 100. In an antiaircraft alert these huge ships, with all gun barrels aimed skyward, resembled giant porcupines.

The first wave of enemy planes included about 25 dive- and torpedo-bombers.[3] They came within range at 1040, and all ships' guns opened up with concentrated fire, sending up a veritable wall of shells. Any plane flying into such a curtain would inevitably be destroyed or seriously damaged. This pattern of gunfire was effective while ships could maintain formation, but futile when they had to scatter under aerial attack.

The ensuing action lasted about an hour, and several planes were shot down. Fifth Fleet flagship *Myoko* was damaged so severely by torpedoes that she had to retire to Brunei. *Yamato* and *Musashi* were, of course, the enemy's main targets, but bombs literally bounced off their sturdy decks and plating, causing no material damage. One torpedo hit in each ship did not slow them and they steamed on. A second torpedo hit on *Musashi*, followed by several bomb hits near her bridge section, knocked out the main battery synchronizers. Even then the mountainous battleship continued to plow the sea at 27 knots.

The fleet had just reformed at noon, after the first strike, when a second attack wave appeared. This one consisted of 24 heavy torpedo planes. The men had fought without breakfast, and now they were going to miss their lunch as well. Twelve attack planes concentrated on *Yamato* and *Musashi* while twelve turned their attention to the other ships.

[3] From carriers *Intrepid* and *Cabot*.

3. *Death of* Musashi

The carrier-based planes which attacked battleship *Musashi* on 24 October revealed the U.S. Navy's indomitable spirit which made it such a worthy opponent. During the war the Cabinet Information Bureau spread propaganda about the United States, and anyone who praised the enemy in any way was branded a traitor. No writer could expect publication if his material mentioned the enemy in a favorable light. Navy men who engaged the Americans, however, were quick to admire their combat spirit and performance.

On the morning after the fleet's sortie for Leyte, flagship *Atago*'s detection gear had just picked up the first sign of an enemy submarine when four undetected torpedoes hit and sank the cruiser. Also hit in rapid succession by submarine torpedoes were cruisers *Takao* (damaged) and *Maya* (sunk).[4] Despite the shock of this surprise blow, Japanese staff officers were much impressed by the brilliant work of the enemy and remarked, "It's too bad our own subs can't pull off an attack like that."

By 1944 there was great admiration, too, for the skill and daring of the enemy's dive bombing and aerial torpedo attacks. American pilots in the Philippines were compared favorably with the Japanese fliers who sank *Prince of Wales* and *Repulse* off Malaya in 1941. And witnesses of an American aerial attack were always impressed that, no matter how heavy the antiaircraft fire, pilots never broke off the attack until all bombs and torpedoes had been dropped.

At 1325 the third attack wave came in.[5] Its 29 planes gave their undivided attention to *Musashi*. The huge ship was enveloped by towering water spouts from near misses. It seemed impossible that she could withstand this onslaught, but when the bombing ended, *Musashi* still moved majestically through the waves, apparently unperturbed.

Three torpedoes had found their mark, however, in the star-

---

[4] *Atago* and *Takao* were targets of USS *Darter* (Cdr. David H. McClintock), and *Maya* was sunk by USS *Dace* (Cdr. Bladen D. Claggett).
[5] From carriers *Essex* and *Lexington*.

board bow of this giant. These ripped outward the heavy steel plating of *Musashi*'s protective sheathing so that she cut plow-like into the sea, raising a cataract of water which inevitably slowed her speed. In answer to a query from the flagship, *Musashi* replied that she could still make 22 knots. Admiral Kurita ordered fleet speed reduced from 25 knots so that the crippled battleship could keep up, and notified Imperial Headquarters and the Fifth Base Air Force:

> The First Striking Force is engaged in hard fight in Sibuyan Sea. Enemy air attacks are expected to increase. Request land-based air forces and Mobile Force to make prompt attacks on enemy carrier force estimated to be at Lamon Bay.

This calm message represented the anger and anguish of every man in the Kurita Force. Throughout five hours of desperate fighting they had not received a report from any friendly headquarters. Nor was it evident that Japanese planes were making any effort against the enemy task forces, which thus roamed with free hand, striking at will against Kurita's ships. Where were the 32 long-range scout planes which had been removed from the ships and sent to land bases? The Navy had put these planes ashore with the understanding that they would be used for sea reconnaissance. With the fleet now engaged in a life-and-death struggle it was hopeless to be without air support. It seemed to the men of the fleet that their ships were being offered to the enemy for target practice.

The three torpedo hits which bent *Musashi*'s bow plates were disastrous. Other hits had damaged her, but not vitally. Counterflooding, to compensate for the starboard bow hits and keep the ship on an even keel, lowered her bow in the water and further slowed her. Despite the reduced fleet speed, she soon fell behind the formation. Anxiety for her safety mounted when the fourth attack wave of some 50 planes approached at 1430.[6]

More than 30 planes made straight for *Musashi*, now out of formation and losing speed. Her bows were awash but persis-

---

[6] From carriers *Essex* and *Enterprise*.

tent antiaircraft batteries still fired at the attackers. Two large torpedo bombers fell in streaks of black smoke, both hitting the water near destroyer *Kiyoshimo*. Additional torpedo hits reduced *Musashi's* speed to 12 knots, and at 1500 Admiral Kurita ordered her to leave the battle area, escorted by *Kiyoshimo* and *Hamakaze*.

Men of the fleet stood sadly at attention in farewell to the fatally wounded super-dreadnaught. They could not but think that she represented the fate in store for them, and possibly the nation.

At 1510 came the fifth attack wave, including more than 100 fighters and bombers.[7] They screamed down on the battle-weary fleet in repeated daring thrusts, selecting one damaged ship after another.

Musashi also came in for her share of these blows. By this time she had neither the strength nor means to fight back. Ten additional torpedo hits slowed her to 6 knots, with only two of four screws functioning. Captain Inoguchi ran for the nearest shore in an attempt to ground the sinking battleship, but her bows were now so low in the water that any effort to change heading would undoubtedly have caused *Musashi* to capsize. The bows sank lower; she began listing. Three of her four engine rooms had to be flooded to keep the keel as even as possible. On the remaining engine she was barely able to move.

In an effort to counter the list, every movable object was shifted to the port side. By 1850 the bows were submerged, leaving the two forward main turrets thrust above the surface of the water like islands, and then the remaining engine went dead.

Captain Toshihira Inoguchi assembled his officers, handed the "Exec" his last report, and ordered Abandon Ship. He remained alone on the bridge, to share the fate of his giant charge.

At 1935 mighty *Musashi* rolled suddenly to port and disappeared beneath the waves, with half of her 2,200-man crew.

[7] From carriers *Intrepid, Cabot, Essex, Franklin,* and *Enterprise.*

As she did so a monstrous pillar of smoke rose from the site, as if in final farewell to the fleet.

Inoguchi, a veteran gunnery officer, had been a staunch believer in big ships and big guns. In his last report he conceded the error of those beliefs and apologized to the Emperor and the nation for his mistakes.

4. Did Kurita Abandon the Sortie?

Battleship *Yamato*, sister to *Musashi*, also received direct hits in the fifth aerial attack of the day, but these did not impair her fighting efficiency. Battleship *Nagato*'s two torpedo hits slowed her to 20 knots, and light cruiser *Yahagi* was damaged so that she could do no better than 22 knots. There was damage to other ships as well, with the result that speed had to be reduced to 18 knots—the fleet speed of half a century earlier! It was difficult to see how these ships could possibly hope to thread the hazardous San Bernardino Strait at so slow a pace.

At 1530 Kurita's staff concluded that the enemy could send three more attack waves before sundown. Nevertheless, the fleet continued its eastward course, approaching the narrow passage at the eastern end of the Sibuyan Sea.

Ships' crews, who had been fighting all day without rest, worked feverishly repairing damage and making preparations for the next attack. A reported periscope sighting sent destroyer *Akishimo* rushing to depthcharge the indicated position. And the rumor of a submarine in the vicinity gave rise to numerous "sightings" of torpedo tracks. The memory was still fresh of the battering this force had taken just a few hours after sortieing, when torpedoes from submarines had scored on 10,000-ton cruisers *Atago, Maya,* and *Takao*. It was likely that enemy submarines lurked behind any of the numerous islands in these waters. United States submarines in the Sibuyan Sea could have had a field day, picking off cripples in the Kurita Force.

At this time, with nerves frayed yet tense, and every man alerted and on the lookout for submarines, a message was received from Combined Fleet Headquarters:

> Probability is great that enemy will employ submarines in the approaches to San Bernardino Strait.
> Be alert.

Under other circumstances this message might have been humorous, instead it was ludicrous and infuriating.

The difficulties of the search for enemy submarines were compounded because the water was littered with debris from the afternoon's engagements. Of 15 destroyers that had sortied with Kurita, there remained only 11 available for antisubmarine operations. *Asashimo* and *Naganami* had been used to tow badly damaged cruiser *Takao*. *Kiyoshimo* and *Hamakaze* had stayed behind to stand by crippled *Musashi*. The slow fleet speed of 18 knots made every ship a sitting duck for torpedo attack. Recklessness alone kept the fleet on its course.

Through it all, Admiral Kurita remained calm. At 1555, just as the ships were about to enter the narrowest passage of the strait, and when the enemy's sixth aerial attack was expected at any moment, Kurita suddenly ordered a reversal of course. His reasoning in this move was explained in a message sent to Combined Fleet Headquarters at Hiyoshidai:

> As a result of five aerial attacks from 0630 to 1530, our damages are not light. The frequency and numerical strength of these enemy attacks is increasing. If we continue our present course our losses will increase incalculably, with little hope of success for our mission.
> Therefore, have decided to withdraw outside the range of enemy air attack for the time being, and to resume our sortie in coordination with successful attacks on the enemy by our air forces.

As Kurita's fleet headed westward once more he again requested Base Air Force to initiate attacks on the enemy.

Combined Fleet Headquarters later regarded this first turn as improper, but American Admirals considered it a wise move. Kurita's reasoning has been stated above, but there was still another cause for the change of course. The original plan had been for Kurita and Nishimura to strike Leyte Gulf simultaneously. Enemy attacks, however, had delayed Kurita by six hours. Since he could not now join with Nishimura, it was essential that his own force, making the approach alone, be as strong as possible. If Kurita had continued on his forward course he would have exposed his ships to further attack and piecemeal destruction. The turn-around offered the possibility of avoiding these decimating assaults. The final evaluation of Kurita's decision must be left to naval strategists and tacticians. The turn-around itself was such a surprise to the enemy that, from this standpoint alone, it was a tactical success.

The enemy's fifth air attack of the day ended at 1535, but one plane remained behind to keep an eye on Kurita's ships. That plane turned eastward around 1620, and did not show again. Thus ended a day-long series of brutal aerial strikes.

This severance of aerial contact resulted unexpectedly in the abandonment of the enemy's best possible opportunity for annihilating Kurita's fleet. If Japan had been victorious in the Battles for Leyte Gulf Admiral Halsey would have been taken to task for ending his aerial attacks so soon. The premature termination of aerial surveillance of Kurita's ships was an error on the part of Admiral Halsey, and the reasons for this act are worth considering.

In the first place, Admiral Jisaburo Ozawa's Mobile Force, the so-called "Decoy Fleet," succeeded in its mission of luring the enemy to the north, and thus relieved Kurita from the continued pressure of enemy air attacks. Coming out from Japan's Inland Sea, Ozawa's carriers reached a point 150 miles north of Luzon on 24 October, and there Ozawa sent out radio messages to engage the enemy's attention. Admiral Halsey was anxious to destroy the Japanese carriers as quickly as possible. Engagement with this carrier force meant certain victory for Halsey, whose strength was three times that of Ozawa's. However, if the Ozawa carriers could have joined with Kurita's force, Halsey's chances of destroying them would have been greatly reduced. Thus when Halsey received word that Kurita's force had turned about, without further investigation or checking, he headed abruptly to the north.

Secondly, the decision was the result of over-confidence and logic. The battle of the Sibuyan Sea had been a great one-sided victory for the United States Navy. Japan had lost one battleship, four heavy cruisers, and four destroyers. The high point for the enemy had been the destruction of *Musashi*, which halved Japan's strength in super-battleships. The enemy had not witnessed her sinking, but he knew that she had dropped out of battle.

Exhilarated by victory, the enemy witnessed Kurita's withdrawal. The Sibuyan Sea was quiet and, logically, after such a defeat Kurita would not return. Therefore, the guard force at San Bernardino Strait was called off, and Halsey lost the chance of a lifetime.

5. *The Turn Again to Battle*

Meanwhile the Kurita Fleet, with no knowledge of enemy movements, turned about and resumed its original course toward San Bernardino Strait. Admiral Kurita fully believed that on the other side of San Bernardino Strait his chance for decisive battle was every bit as good as it would have been at Leyte Gulf. He expected to find enemy submarines waiting north and south of the exit, backed up by battleship groups with their guns trained and ready. Beyond the battleships he envisaged at least ten carriers with a thousand or more planes poised for takeoff against his surface ships.

Before his sortie Admiral Kurita had anticipated three likely areas of engagement with the enemy: Sibuyan Sea, San Bernardino Strait, and Leyte Gulf. He was entering the second of these areas, where enemy forces surely lay in wait, ready to jump on his weakened and weary fleet. It was for this reason that Kurita asked so repeatedly and insistently for air support. He felt that if land-based planes could attack the enemy's carriers and keep them occupied, his own destroyers could carry out antisubmarine actions, while his capital ships with their superior guns could take care of the enemy's large ships, and then make good a dash to Leyte Gulf.

Up until 1630 of the previous day the situation at the mouth of San Bernardino Strait had been almost precisely as Kurita had anticipated. But, as related above, at 1630 on the 24th the enemy mobile force had moved northward and his submarines had returned to Leyte Gulf. Thus when Kurita's ships exited from the strait at dawn on the 25th, they were first astonished at and then suspicious of the quiet sea, completely devoid of any sign of the enemy. This was indeed a case of divine help for the Japanese.

As has been discussed, after absorbing punishment from five aerial attack waves on the 24th, Admiral Kurita had concluded that any further attacks would be disastrous. Hence the turn-around, which the lone enemy scout plane had reported as a retreat. When an hour and a half had passed with no sign of a sixth attack wave, or even another scout plane, Kurita decided that the enemy's offensive had ended for the day. It

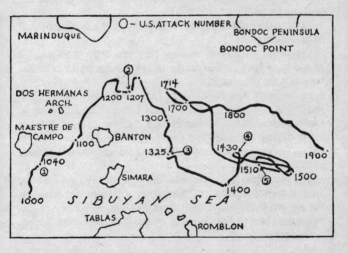

Sibuyan Sea Battle, 24 October 1944. Kurita Fleet Track

was at this point that he had ordered the turn again to the east. An astonished staff officer reminded him that there had as yet been no Headquarters reply to his 1600 message requesting the assistance of land-based planes and the Mobile Force.

"That's all right. Let's go!" was Kurita's only response, with no explanation given for his decision. The fleet made two right-angle turns and resumed its eastward course in the Sibuyan Sea. Leyte Gulf had been clearly defined as the objective for Operation *Sho* 1. It was Kurita's unswerving determination to proceed to that goal no matter how hazardous the journey. The time of his eastward turn was 1715 on 24 October.

Two hours later Kurita received from Imperial General Headquarters the reply which has since become famous: "Believing in divine help, resume the attack!"

For many months this message was thought to have inspired Kurita's resumption of the attack, until it became known that Kurita had ordered the course reversal a full two hours before receiving the Headquarters message. Kurita's staff greeted the tardy order with jeering remarks:

"Leave the fighting to us. Not even a god can direct naval battles from shore."

"Ignorant of enemy attacks, they can order anything. It would have been more realistic to say, 'Believing in annihilation, resume the attack!' "

In his book *The Japanese at Leyte Gulf*, Mr. James Field showed that he knew Kurita's fleet better than did Imperial General Headquarters when he said: "In this case, as in other cases during the war, the Japanese Navy demonstrated its characteristic courage and its ability to overcome a desperate situation."

The Headquarters order was followed shortly by a message from Admiral Nishimura. "Our force will storm the center of the eastern shore of Leyte Gulf at 0400 on the 25th." At this point the planned simultaneous attack with Nishimura was utterly impossible.

6. *Nishimura Heads Toward Death*

Vice Admiral Nishimura's relatively small force consisted of battleships *Fuso* and *Yamashiro;* heavy cruiser *Mogami*, and old destroyers *Mitsushio, Asagumo, Yamagumo,* and *Shigure. Fuso* and *Yamashiro*, more than thirty years old, were the first two dreadnaughts of the Japanese Navy. Their 14-inch main batteries were powerful, but the ships were slow and extremely limited in endurance and armament. Since the beginning of the war they had been used exclusively for training purposes in the Inland Sea. The very presence of these venerable warships in a combat area indicated the weakness in concept of Operation *Sho* 1. Both ships had, of course, been somewhat modernized, but they were beyond rejuvenation.

If mobility had been a prerequisite for participation in the *Sho* Operation, Nishimura's ships would have been disqualified at the outset. Their sole utility was that they might reach Leyte Gulf and fire some of their 14-inch shells before being sunk.

It was for this reason that Admiral Kurita detached Nishimura's ships from the swifter Main Body, and ordered each to take a separate approach route. Realizing that the presence of his ships would have been a handicap to the Main Fleet, Nishimura accepted Kurita's plan without explanation and undertook the suicidal approach toward Leyte Gulf.

Nishimura, who had risen to Vice Admiral without ever having served a tour of duty in the Navy Ministry, was a typical sea-going officer. Appointed to this second- or third-rate command only one month before the decisive battle, he did not complain or grumble. When ordered to join in the Leyte Battle, he responded as readily as a samurai who has found his appropriate place to die. He brought his ships to Lingga Anchorage on 10 October, just twelve days before the sortie.

The Admiral had lost his beloved only son, Teiji, in the Philippines. Although he never betrayed his feelings at the death of this young man, who had graduated from the Naval Academy at the top of his class, Nishimura was probably glad to have an assignment which would permit him to die nobly and join his son.

On the eve of the sortie from Lingga, Nishimura exchanged toasts and greetings with the commanders of each ship and squadron. Although he gave no hint that he was anticipating death, Admiral Kurita and his chief of staff, Koyanagi, saw the determination which lay within him. When critics comment on the recklessness of Nishimura's sortie they do so without understanding his situation and the particular circumstances of his assignment. Such criticism of a valiant man is grossly unfair.

Nishimura's force arrived at the western entrance of the Mindanao Sea in the early morning of 24 October. Enemy scout planes discovered it and summoned a high-level attack by 20 Grummans. They succeeded in damaging but one plane and a catapult on battleship *Fuso*. As compared with the assault suffered by Kurita's ships in the Sibuyan Sea two hours later, the attack was only nominal. This demonstrates the wisdom of the enemy strategy. Attacks by his carrier planes were concentrated on the superior Kurita Force, while the much weaker Nishimura Force was left to the enemy torpedo boats. Following the attack by the Grummans, Nishimura's ships continued eastward almost without incident—at 1400 they skirmished with a few torpedo boats—and arrived three hours ahead of schedule at a point four hours' cruising distance from Leyte Gulf. Kurita's Main Body was then six hours behind schedule as a result of enemy attacks in the Sibuyan Sea. Accordingly, Nishimura reduced speed to 13 knots, which merely invited enemy torpedo attacks.

It is not known whether Nishimura received Admiral Kurita's three messages: 1) requesting action by land-based air forces, 2) notifying of the temporary retirement of the Main Body, and 3) reporting the resumption of the attack course. There is no indication that Nishimura adjusted his movements as a result of receiving these messages; and his force, with the exception of destroyer *Shigure*, was annihilated.

On this point I have interrogated admirals who were well acquainted with Nishimura. They were agreed that Nishimura had determined to push toward Leyte Gulf at all cost in order to lessen the pressure the enemy could bring to bear on Kurita. This is in complete opposition to the conclusion reached by Mr. James Field who asserts that Nishimura's action was a strategic error, based on arbitrariness.

A fleet rendezvous in the presence of the enemy is always a complicated maneuver. It is understandable that Nishimura's force, which was relatively unencumbered in its approach, and Kurita's force, which suffered enemy attacks throughout the day, failed to effect a rendezvous which had been scheduled before any ships had even sortied from Brunei Bay. At the appointed time, Kurita's force still had to transit the narrow waters of San Bernardino Strait, with its treacherous 7- to 9-knot current, in blackout condition—an almost impossible task under any circumstances—after a day-long running battle against unopposed aerial attacks.

There was nothing for Nishimura to do but to proceed resolutely into Leyte Gulf alone.

7. *Death at Leyte Gulf*

While Admiral Nishimura sortied for Leyte Gulf with a foreboding of doom, he did not rush headlong to his death. In truth, his approach to Leyte Gulf was more cautious than any of the other three Japanese forces involved in the *Sho* Operation.

When Nishimura arrived at the entrance of the Mindanao Sea in the morning of 24 October, he launched the only plane in his force—from cruiser *Mogami*—to reconnoiter Leyte Gulf. This scout reached the gulf at 0650 and radioed: "Sighted four battleships and two cruisers to the south of the bay. There are also about 80 transports off the landing area. There are four destroyers and several torpedo boats near Surigao Strait. In addition there are 12 carriers and 10 destroyers in position 40 miles southeast of Leyte."

This was the first intelligence report received that day by

any Japanese forces concerning the situation at Leyte Gulf. It reached the Kurita Force about 1410. Admiral Koyanagi, Kurita's chief of staff, later confirmed that this was the only report about the enemy received by the Kurita Force throughout the entire action.

The enemy's force in Leyte Gulf was actually composed of 6 battleships, 6 cruisers, and 30-odd destroyers. Nishimura's search plane, though observing from high altitude, was able to confirm that the enemy fleet was present in strength at Leyte Gulf and that the main carrier force was standing by within two hours' steaming distance.

Admiral Nishimura was thus aware that enemy forces within the Gulf were three times greater than his own. It is impossible to know how he felt about his chances against so formidable an array; we know only that he did not retreat.

At 2030 on 24 October, Nishimura sent to Admiral Kurita: "It is my plan to charge into Leyte Gulf at 0400 hours on the 25th."

Kurita replied at 2145: "Kurita Main Body plans to dash into Leyte Gulf at 1100 on the 25th. You are to proceed according to plan, rendezvous with my force ten miles northeast of Suluan Island at 0900."

It is not known when Nishimura received this message, but he was unable to alter his schedule. Enemy torpedo boats attacked him with increasing frequency and ferocity, and at 0220 on the 25th destroyers *Yamagumo* and *Mitsushio* were attacked, hit, and sunk. Destroyer *Asagumo* was badly damaged and forced to withdraw. Still undaunted, Nishimura continued to approach with his four remaining ships in single column and, at 0320, ordered them to make the dash into the gulf.

From the flagship bridge Admiral Nishimura regarded the dark sky to the east. His radar presently warned of approaching ships, and at 0323 he radioed: "We have sighted what appear to be enemy ships."

Seven minutes later he radioed again: "Enemy destroyers and torpedo boats on both sides of north entrance to Surigao

Strait. Our destroyers have been torpedoed. *Yamashiro* hit by one torpedo but able to procede.''

This was the last message from Nishimura to Admiral Kurita. A second torpedo found its mark in *Yamashiro* with telling effect, and Nishimura signaled the rest of his ships: "We have been torpedoed. Proceed independently to the attack."

These words epitomize the fighting character of this valiant man. Almost with their utterance, *Yamashiro* received a third torpedo which hit her magazines, and she dissolved in the waters of Surigao Strait at 0340.

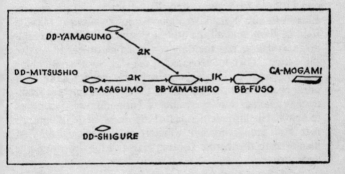

Formation of Nishimura Force Approaching Leyte Gulf

Fuso's skipper, Rear Admiral Masami Ban, took charge of the force and continued on, firing guns by radar control. Enemy shells fell like a torrential rain. *Mogami* was hit and set afire. *Fuso* took many more direct hits, and her fires raged uncontrolled. Nevertheless, through the billowing smoke which engulfed her superstructure, *Fuso* continued to blaze away with her 14-inch guns until she rolled over and sank at 0410.

Wreathed in flames, *Mogami* pulled away to the south, where she was sunk by gunfire from a friendly ship. The destruction of this force was achieved by bombardment from ships of the enemy's Seventh Fleet under Rear Admiral J. B. Oldendorf. These were the battleships which had been "sunk" in the attack on Pearl Harbor. It was one of the Japanese Navy's great surprises of the war to learn that these ships were still in action at Leyte Gulf.

Thus Nishimura's entire force—with the exception of destroyer *Shigure*, which limped back to Brunei on 27 October—perished. Who was responsible for this debacle? It is clear from his actions that Admiral Nishimura never raised that question.

The death of Nishimura was not just the demise of one man. An entire fleet perished in this action. It is regrettable that no one survived to recount the valiant fighting of such men as Rear Admirals Katsukiyo Shinoda, in *Yamashiro*, Masami Ban, of *Fuso*, and all the others. Commander Shigeru Nishino, of *Shigure*, was the only commanding officer to survive this action. When interrogated by the U.S. Strategic Bombing Survey, he disclosed that, in preparing his men for action, Admiral Nishimura had emphasized the need for spiritual readiness as much as combat readiness. Nishimura was reconciled to death. His attitude permeated the ranks, and Nishimura's men went along with him willingly on this suicidal duty. A memorial to this heroic fighting man and his fleet would be appropriate.

8. The Stepchild Fleet

Strangely, then, another fleet appeared where the Nishimura Fleet had just perished. Sole survivor *Shigure* signaled in desperation and learned that these were the ships of Vice Admiral Kiyohide Shima, whose flag flew in heavy cruiser *Nachi*. The time was 0430.

Why had these two fleets approached Leyte Gulf separately? Was there no agreement about their approach? Allied historians have ridiculed this situation as a gross example of command disunity. When the facts are known, however, one can see the matter differently.

Admiral Shima's force was composed of heavy cruiser *Nachi* and *Ashigara*, light cruiser *Abukuma*, destroyers *Akebono, Kasumi, Ushio,* and *Shiranuhi.* From the standpoint of ship types and numbers, the composition of this fleet was peculiar. It should not have been used in an operation of this kind, and an explanation is in order.

Shima's force was not under Admiral Kurita, nor was it a part of Admiral Ozawa's Mobile Force. Its orders came directly from Combined Fleet Headquarters, but for all tactical purposes in the Leyte operation it operated independently. Organizationally it had been made a part of Vice Admiral Mikawa's Southwest Area Fleet, just five days before the forces sortied.

The ships of this fleet had been so shifted and shunted about from command to command and from area to area that Admiral Shima would have been justified if he had complained of being treated like a stepchild. Originally his fleet was the main force for the defense of the northeastern part of the homeland. With the fleet reorganization of August, 1944, after the defeat at Saipan, he was assigned to Admiral Ozawa's First Mobile Fleet. Shima's ships had trained with that fleet in the Inland Sea until mid-October.

Complications began in mid-October with the attacks on Formosa by Admiral Halsey's fast carrier striking forces. The air battles off Formosa, according to the reports of surviving Japanese pilots, were a great victory for Japan. The cumulative results of these reports indicated that one dozen capital ships of the enemy had been sunk and another two dozen heavily damaged. On the basis of these reports, it was judged that the enemy would not soon return. In reality, only two enemy cruisers had been damaged, while Japan suffered the loss of 174 planes. These air battles were, in fact, a great victory for the enemy.

On the basis of erroneous reports, Admiral Shima's fleet was ordered out to pursue the fleeing enemy south of Formosa, and to rescue downed pilots. Shima's ships were selected because of their high speed and mobility. The men approached the mission with light hearts, on the assumption that mopping-up operations after a great victory would be an easy task. As Shima approached the scene of his intended "mopping-up operation," however, he was astounded to find two gigantic naval forces, in perfect battle order. His ships could not last five minutes against such an enemy. Admiral Shima wisely ordered a course reversal for his cruisers and destroyers and, at flank speed of 34½ knots, headed for Amami Oshima and comparative safety.

On 18 October these harried ships received their next assignment, as the main body of a surface mobile counterattack force, that is, a counterlanding force. (Staff officers have told me that this assignment was a cover-up for the high command error of having sent these unfortunate ships on the "mopping-up" operation five days earlier.) They were assigned to the Southwest Area Fleet (Admiral Mikawa) and sent to Mako in the Pescadores to await further orders.

There were, however, no orders from Vice Admiral Mikawa. This was understandable. The purpose of counterlanding operations is to recover territory previously taken by the enemy. In mid-October the Japanese Navy was much too busy defending itself against new enemy landings to consider the retaking of any enemy-held positions.

Admiral Junichi Mikawa's Southwest Area Fleet included Vice Admiral Ohnishi's Fifth Land-based Air Force (First Air Fleet) and Vice Admiral Fukudome's Sixth Land-based Air Force (Second Air Fleet). It was a powerful organization, but as a surface fleet it was weak, in that its main strength consisted entirely of Shima's ships. At noon on 21 October, Shima received the following Combined Fleet message as relayed by Admiral Mikawa's headquarters:

> It is deemed advisable for Second Striking Force (Shima) to storm into Leyte Gulf from the south through Surigao Strait, and cooperate with the First Striking Force.

The words "It is deemed advisable" must be stressed. Three distinct changes of orders within the space of one week! It was as though the fleet were a plaything. The patience of Admiral Shima and his staff was sorely tried. Considering, however, the all-out character of the Leyte operation, this was no time to let personal feelings become involved. That morning, on 21 October, the fleet had diverted *Wakaba, Hatsuharu,* and *Hatsushimo* to duty as transports between Takao and Manila, thereby giving up three of its seven destroyers. At 1600 the rest of the Shima Force hurriedly departed Mako for Coron Bay, on the other side of Mindoro Island. Admiral Shima then, and for the first time, received information about the operational plans for the forces of Nishimura and Kurita.

Thus from the confused planning by General Headquarters, the orders for the Nishimura Force were also transmitted to the Shima Force. Without any pre-battle conference, without specific orders from either Nishimura or Kurita, without knowing the suicidal nature of the operation, and with only the general idea that he was to serve as rear guard for the Nishimura Force, Admiral Shima led his ships into the Mindanao Sea at 2200 on 24 October.

From the standpoint of chain of command or seniority, there was no reason for Shima to be taking orders from Nishimura. Also, since Nishimura commanded the main force driving into Surigao Strait, and since Shima arrived on the scene unannounced, there was no reason for him to be taking orders from Shima. Thus, and again because of the confusion in Combined Fleet Headquarters, these two commands were thrown into the same battle area with no senior commander in over-all charge. As a consequence, Nishimura proceeded independently and Shima, with equal independence, decided to follow one hour behind.

Soon after 2200, Shima intercepted Kurita's message to Nishimura ordering the rendezvous ten miles southeast of Samar Island for 1000 hours on the 25th. Accordingly, Shima decided to join in this rendezvous and boosted speed in his ships so as to arrive at Leyte Gulf at 0400. In consequence he arrived at the scene of battle just after the annihilation of the Nishimura Force.

Admiral Shima's ships had not undergone rigorous training at Lingga Anchorage. They were few in number and light in fire power, so their only real capability was to hit and run. That is exactly what they did in the ensuing battle. Light cruiser *Abukuma* was attacked by PTs and torpedoed at the entrance of the Strait and had to be left behind. *Nachi* and *Ashigara* pushed forward at 30 knots. At 0430 they discovered the enemy fleet about eight miles ahead, and sighted burning *Mogami* to starboard. All ships then veered right to launch torpedoes, which took about five minutes. While in this turn, *Nachi* collided with crippled *Mogami*, putting a hole in her port side. *Mogami*'s distraught crew wondered that the fully operative *Nachi* could not avoid their flaming ship. The consensus was that the fault for the collision lay with *Nachi*.

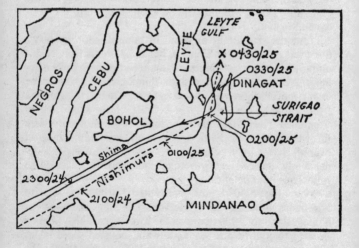

Nishimura and Shima Tracks for Penetration of Leyte Gulf

At the end of the five-minute action Shima's force withdrew under cover of a smoke screen. American reporters called this battle a rout. It was, rather, an ineffective hit-and-run action. The idea of ordering the Shima Force to participate in this operation was wrong from the start. A staff officer who took part in the planning expressed the view to American investigators that the Shima Force was nothing but a useless supplement in this battle. To dismiss it thus as merely a supplement is outrageous. As a newspaperman, the unceremonious casting aside of even a supplement infuriates me, and my lengthy description of this action is intended as a protest on behalf of the Shima Fleet.

9. The Debacle-bound Fleet

While the Kurita, Nishimura, and Shima ships were suffering heavy damage, annihilation and rout, yet another force was also heading toward Leyte and defeat. This was Vice Admiral Jisaburo Ozawa's First Mobile Fleet, and with its destruction went the aerial striking power of the Imperial Japanese Navy, in name and in fact.

The mission of Ozawa's carrier division was "to assist the Kurita forces by coming south from Japan to lure the enemy task force northward." Appended to these orders was an instruction to engage and destroy the enemy at every opportunity. It would have been more realistic to have ordered Ozawa to *have his ships be engaged and destroyed by the enemy*. His force did not have one chance in a thousand against the mighty fleet of Admiral Halsey. After the war, when the truth about Ozawa's force became known, American admirals were moved to laughter at their own wartime overestimate.

Ozawa's actual strength was no greater than that of the totally inadequate force of Admiral Nishimura. And, like the Nishimura Force, its mission was suicidal. Yet it is a mistake to make light of Ozawa's defeat. It was a part of his mission to be defeated, and in being defeated he accomplished that mission. The whole affair is another example of the confused planning of the Leyte Operation.

Ozawa's carriers had become the main force of the Imperial Navy with the realization that the aircraft carrier had replaced the battleship as first-line ship of the fleet. As of early June, 1944, the strength of the Japanese Navy was as follows:

FIRST MOBILE FLEET
(Main Force for decisive surface battle)
Vice Admiral Ozawa

BB *Yamato, Musashi,* etc. (First Striking Force)
Third Fleet, Vice Admiral Ozawa
   3 fleet carriers, 5 converted carriers
Fifth Fleet, Vice Admiral Shima
   Nachi, Ashigara, etc. (Second Striking Force)

In July 1944, however, the Second Fleet was separated from the Main Force, and sent off to Lingga Anchorage. In October the Fifth Fleet was detached and assigned to the Southeast Area Fleet. Thus Ozawa suffered the loss of losing two of his supporting fleets. Then in mid-October came the air battles off Formosa, when the planes from Ozawa's carriers were consigned to land bases. In order to realize what a severe blow this was, let us take a look at the organization of the Ozawa Fleet as of mid-August 1944.

First Mobile Fleet
Vice Admiral Ozawa

Cardiv 1 (*Unryu, Amagi*—both under construction)
     601st Air Group (294 planes of various types)
Cardiv 3 (*Zuikaku, Zuiho, Chiyoda, Chitose*)
     653rd Air Group (182 planes of various types)
Cardiv 4 (*Ise, Hyuga, Junyo, Ryuho*)
     634th Air Group (130 planes of various types)

In this line-up both ships of Cardiv 1 were under construction and would not be completed before the end of 1944. Thus Cardivs 3 and 4 were the mainstay of Ozawa's fleet. When most of their planes were transferred to Formosa, the force was bereft of fighting capability. Jisaburo Ozawa was appointed to command the main fleet in March 1944 because of his bravery and his good judgment. With his feeble forces of October 1944, however, it was impossible for him—or any other commander—to play a positive role in the Leyte actions.

With *Unryu* and *Amagi* still under construction, the actual composition of Ozawa's force as he sortied for the Leyte battle was as follows:

Cardiv 3 (Vice Admiral Ozawa)
   Zuikaku, Zuiho, Chiyoda, Chitose
Cardiv 4 (Rear Admiral Chiaki Matsuda)
   BB *Ise, Hyuga*
Escort Squadron 31 (Rear Admiral Heitaro Edo)
   CL *Isuzu, Oyodo, Tama*
   DD *Sugi, Kiri, Maki, Kuwa, Shimotsuki, Akizuki, Hatsuzuki, Wakatsuki*

The poverty of this fleet was truly abject. There were no planes for assignment to his carriers. Admiral Ozawa made valiant efforts and he obtained some planes which had been reserved for *Amagi* and *Unryu* (601st Air Group). With remnants from Cardivs 3 and 4, he somehow assembled a carrier force composed as follows:

CARRIER	FIGHTERS	FIGHTER-BOMBERS	BOMBERS	ATTACK PLANES	TOTAL
Zuikaku	24	16	8	12	60
Zuiho	8	4	0	4	16
Chiyoda	8	4	0	4	16
Chitose	8	4	0	4	16
Total	48	28	8	24	108

A total of 4 carriers and 108 planes. *Ise* and *Hyuga* (shown on the previous table) had been converted to aircraft battleships by the removal of their main after turrets and the installation of a small hangar deck, each with a capacity of 24 planes. They became Cardiv 4 and claimed the versatility of having both surface and air striking power. But the vaunted versatility was never achieved. After the six stern guns had been removed from each ship and the hangar decks installed, no planes were available. The high command then insisted that *Ise* and *Hyuga* be used as battleships. Two other ships to be considered were light carriers *Junyo* and *Ryuho*, but since there were no planes available for them either, they were left behind in the Inland Sea. Thus, although the Ozawa Fleet had 8 carriers and 312 planes on paper, it actually had only 4 carriers with 108 planes—the complement of a single United States fleet carrier. To further compound its weakness, the air crews of this fleet were composed almost entirely of green recruits. It takes many months of rigorous training to teach a pilot how to make carrier take-offs and landings, and how to score hits with bombs and torpedoes. Such pilots were no longer available.

10. Gallant Sacrifice

"A decoy, that was our first and primary mission," are the words used by Vice Admiral Ozawa when he was interviewed by the United States Strategic Bombing Survey about the battles for Leyte Gulf. This was not merely a post-battle afterthought. In presenting his operation plan to Admiral Toyoda on 19 October, Ozawa had said, "I propose to maneuver my ships from the north in such a way that they will lure the enemy task force away from the battle area and thus reduce pressure on the Kurita Fleet. I shall disregard any damage which may be inflicted on my force in this operation." Toyoda approved.

According to Toyoda's original plan for Operation *Sho* 1,

Ozawa's ships were to have steamed into Leyte Gulf together with Kurita's fleet. Ozawa calculated, however, that the odds were greatly against his weak force if it attempted to enter the target area. He felt that since his ships were bound to be annihilated in this operation, they should be sacrificed in the most profitable manner. It was for this reason that he proposed the decoy tactics.

His battle plan was wise but tragic. Ozawa's part in this operation has been characterized in American history books as an "all-out sacrifice." It was exactly that. He intended to lure the enemy, even if this meant the total destruction of his fleet. In this instance the objective was not to attack, but to be attacked. Admiral Ozawa adopted this suicidal tactic knowing that his fleet would be destroyed, but calculated that by the time his ships were destroyed Kurita's ships would have had a chance to enter Leyte Gulf.

He could not disclose this plan to his men. His battle order was to lure the enemy task forces to the north of the Philippines and destroy them. It is difficult to believe that the men of his fleet, who knew the weakness of their own air power, had any illusion about their ability to destroy the enemy. They showed no hesitation, however, about accepting the battle order. Jisaburo Ozawa had the complete confidence of every man in his command. At the signal to sortie, all ships weighed anchor and the fleet passed through the Bungo Strait at 1730 on 20 October 1944.

In the early morning of the 21st, scout planes were dispatched to the southeast; three of them did not return. Inadequate training and poor communications were already taking their toll. The day passed without further event. On the 22nd, scout planes were again sent out. Another three failed to return. Admiral Ozawa became increasingly concerned about his chances of recovering planes after battle action, since they apparently could not manage to return safely after a routine scouting mission. He decided, accordingly, that if his ships engaged the enemy within flight range of Luzon Island, his planes should head for Clark Field instead of attempting to return to the carriers.

At 1115 on 24 October a scout plane reported an enemy force in position 160 miles southeast of Ozawa's ships. The Admiral immediately ordered an attack to be launched, and he added: "If the attacking planes deem it difficult to return to the carriers because of the weather, they are to proceed to land bases and notify the fleet at once upon their arrival."

If the planes proceeded to land bases, Ozawa's fleet would be devoid of air striking power. Nevertheless, if Ozawa could lure the enemy north to attack in force, his mission would be fulfilled.

At 1145 a flight of 30 fighter planes, 19 fighter bombers, 4 torpedo planes, and 5 attack planes was launched. After seeing them off, Ozawa bowed his head and looked away. He knew that these 58 planes were a poorly integrated group. Some thirty different types of planes were represented, hastily collected from various units throughout the homeland. Where was the vaunted Japanese Naval Air Force which had once winged so effectively over Pearl Harbor? What results could be anticipated from this hodgepodge collection of old planes?

11. *The Enemy Leaps to the Lure*

The first group of planes to take off from *Zuiho, Chiyoda,* and *Chitose* engaged enemy Grummans near the target area and flew on to Clark Field without sighting any enemy ships. The second group, composed of 6 fighters, 11 fighter bombers, and 1 attack plane, took off from *Zuikaku* and did attack enemy ships. After setting fires in one fleet carrier and one light carrier, they also flew to Clark Field, except for three of the planes which became separated and returned to the fleet after sighting no enemy.

This pathetic action spelled the end of Japan's carrier-based air strength. Admiral Ozawa must have secretly anticipated this. The fighting spirit of the untrained men was high, but their performance was expectedly poor.

Still more serious, however, the reports of this engagement

with the enemy task force never reached Admiral Kurita. His ships were then being hit by the second enemy attack wave in the Sibuyan Sea. Kurita anxiously awaited the result of Ozawa's decoy tactic, but heard nothing because of radio failure in flagship *Zuikaku*. Ozawa knew of Kurita's bitter struggle, and realized that his assignment of luring the enemy to the north was not enough. He therefore ordered Rear Admiral Chiaki Matsuda to proceed with *Ise* and *Hyuga* for a night battle, while he sped toward Luzon with his remaining ships at maximum speed.

Admiral Ozawa believed that the enemy would engage his ships this day. At 0610, in order to save his few remaining planes with their inexperienced crews, he dispatched all except the fighters to Tuguegarao in the Philippines. This flight, consisting of 5 fighter bombers, 4 attack planes and 1 bomber, dipped their wings in farewell salute as they flew off to the west. This difficult decision reflects the real worth of Admiral Ozawa.

About 0815 as expected, 120 enemy planes in two groups came to attack the forces of Ozawa (*Zuikaku, Zuiho, Ise, Oyodo,* destroyers *Kuwa, Akizuki, Wakatsuki, Hatsuzuki*) and Matsuda (*Hyuga, Chiyoda, Chitose, Isuzu, Tama,* destroyers *Shimotsuki, Sugi, Kiri, Maki*). The 13 fighters that remained with the fleet rose to engage, and were all shot down by 0930. Thereafter the ships were completely at the mercy of the attacking enemy. As decoys they merely maneuvered to avoid bombs.

At this same time to the south the Kurita Force was engaging the escort carrier group of the enemy. Believing that he was surrounded by three or four groups of fleet carriers, Kurita was concerned about how to break the siege and make his charge into Leyte Gulf, 60 miles away.

Informed of the predicament of Kurita's force, Ozawa sent the following message: "The enemy fleet has been lured to the north and is attacking our ships with its entire force." He thus intended to inform Kurita that the decoy operation was succeeding.

This message never reached Admiral Kurita. Accordingly,

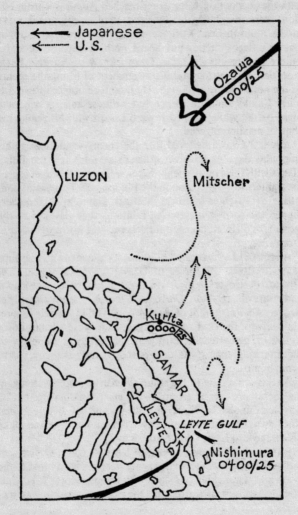

Ozawa's Track, 25 October 1944

Kurita judged that he was all alone and tried to break through on his own. It was unfortunate that he could not make use of Ozawa's sacrifice in his planning at this point.

The enemy aerial attack on Ozawa continued until 1500. The planes bombed the ships with impunity, staying out of antiaircraft gun range. Their aim was not good, but so many bombs were dropped that after hours of attack they succeeded in sinking all the carriers, light cruiser *Tama*, and destroyer *Hatsuzuki*. *Zuikaku* was the last remaining ship of those that had participated in the attack on Pearl Harbor. When it sank at 1415, Admiral Ozawa stubbornly refused to leave the bridge. It recalled the *Prince of Wales'* sinking at the beginning of the war, when Admiral Tom Philipps, Commander in Chief of Britain's Far Eastern Fleet, rejected the entreaties of his staff officers and went down with his ship. Admiral Ozawa was of the same frame of mind.

When staff officer Toshikazu Ohmae found that persuasion was useless, he had Admiral Ozawa forcibly removed from the ship to destroyer *Wakatsuki*, and later transferred the flag to light cruiser *Oyodo*, which led the remnants of this defeated fleet to the north. At 1900, however, Ozawa ordered his ships to turn around, intending to engage the enemy in night battle with the 14-inch guns of *Ise* and *Hyuga*. The fleet steamed southward for two and a half hours, but when Ozawa realized that he could not overtake the enemy, he ordered a return to base at Amami Oshima. Thus ended the decoy operation, which had succeeded in luring Admiral Halsey northward. It was the only Japanese part of the Leyte operation which was successful.

12. *Enemy Fleet on the Horizon*

In the meantime, the Kurita Force Main Body, with no word from any of its supporting forces, proceeded eastward in the Sibuyan Sea. At 1800 on the 24th Kurita informed Combined Fleet Headquarters: "This fleet intends to charge into

Leyte Gulf at 1100 on the 25th without regard for any damage we may suffer." At 2330 the fleet entered San Bernardino Strait in a single-column formation of 22 ships.

It was pitch dark. There were no lights ashore and none showed in the ships as they moved through the narrowest point of the strait against an eight-knot current. Night-battle training paid off and they debouched successfully from the strait at 0035 on 25 October. None but the most experienced of navigators could have accomplished this feat.

A crisis was passed, but there was no time to relax. Admiral Kurita fully expected a life-and-death battle as he came out of the strait. Enemy submarines and surface ships properly stationed could have caught the Japanese ships in the most vulnerable of all battle situations—a single-column formation exiting from a narrow strait. The situation was ideal for a T-crossing that would have been as devastating to Kurita's force as it was to Nishimura's three hours later when he came through Surigao Strait.

Suspicious of the ominous calm, Kurita led his ships 20 miles due eastward from the strait. Thence he turned south toward the target area. His ships were then in night scouting formation, the van consisting of Desron 10, Crudivs 7 and 5, and Desron 2 spaced five kilometers apart on a line of bearing east to west. Five kilometers to the rear were Batdivs 1 (*Yamato, Nagato*) and 3 (*Kongo, Haruna*). The fleet moved to the south at the most economic antisubmarine speed of 18 knots, standing some ten miles east of Samar Island. It was inconceivable that the American ships, with their powerful search and detection apparatus, were unaware that a great Japanese surface fleet was within 100 miles of and approaching the target area. Daylight of 25 October brought no sign of the enemy, but the Japanese anticipated aerial attacks on an even fiercer scale than those of the preceding day.

The sun rose at 0627. Clouds hung low and visibility was poor. There were occasional rain squalls, with only fleeting glimpses of blue sky. The wind speed of four meters (per second) raised white caps all around. The fleet was shifting into formation against air attack, with *Yamato* at the center, when suddenly at 0645 four masts were detected on the horizon to the southeast.

Excitement ran high when planes were seen taking off from ships' decks. These were the enemy task forces which from the Gilbert Islands onward had been taking Japanese-held territory with little or no opposition. Here were Halsey's carriers. The 100 days of rigorous training at Lingga had been aimed for this encounter. Admiral Kurita radioed to Combined Fleet Headquarters: "By Heaven-sent opportunity, we are dashing to attack the enemy carriers. Our first objective is to destroy the flight decks, then the task force." These ships were judged to be the southernmost group of the enemy's carrier forces, and this was a perfect opportunity to attack and destroy them one by one.

The fleet had to move quickly. Any delay to complete the change in battle formation might lose the opportunity for surprise. Kurita ordered full speed on an attack course of 110 degrees. Thus it happened that each ship approached the enemy independently, over a wide area, with no fixed formation.

It is not clear what Kurita meant by "destroy the flight decks." Did he mean to use the Type-3 incendiary shells, or the ordinary big shells of his battleships? It was clear, however, that Kurita's ships would have no chance against an all-out aerial attack by the enemy, so he had to concentrate on knocking out the enemy's aircraft carriers with his ships' guns. Carriers have little or no defensive armor against big guns and Kurita was anxious to take advantage of this.

This gun duel was the last ship-to-ship engagement in which the Imperial Japanese Navy would ever participate. It was in this battle that the Japanese Navy's unique 18.1-inch guns were fired for the first and last time against surface targets.

13. Battle Off Samar

Battleship *Yamato*'s nine 18.1-inch guns fired a full salvo at 0659 in the morning of 25 October 1944. A second salvo followed and the mast-top lookout reported "a pillar of fire!" Aircraft carrier *Gambier Bay* had been hit and it was thought at the time that the first salvo from *Yamato* was responsible. Actually, the carrier had come under fire from Japanese destroyers, cruisers and battleship *Kongo*, and it was the latter which delivered the *coup de grâce*. *Gambier Bay* broke in two, capsized and sank, the first victim of this action.

Occasional squalls obstructed visibility, and smokescreens from enemy destroyers skillfully shielded the enemy's carrier groups, so that *Yamato* and *Nagato* had difficulty in using their big guns. *Yamato* was within 22 kilometers of the enemy ships and closing when she sighted the wakes of six torpedoes approaching on her port quarter. *Yamato*'s skipper, Rear Admiral Nobuei Morishita, ordered a turn which evaded the torpedoes but put *Yamato* in the middle of their spread, heading away from the scene of conflict. The speed of both ship and torpedoes was 26 knots, and for ten minutes they sped along together, three torpedoes on each side of the huge battleship. After the torpedoes had run their course the battleship was again able to turn toward the enemy ships, but they were now 30 kilometers distant.

Kurita ordered a scout plane to be catapulted for gunnery observation and it reported that the enemy fleet was retreating southward. Accordingly, at 0820, Kurita sent his entire force in pursuit. *Yamato* joined the southward chase, firing her guns by radar control. A break in the enemy smokescreen yielded a view of what appeared to be a cruiser. Actually this was destroyer *Hoel*, which had bravely approached to launch torpedoes. She was promptly taken under fire of *Yamato*'s secondary batteries and sunk.

The disorganized Kurita fleet was spread out over a distance of 15 miles. Communications were understandably poor and it was most unfortunate that Kurita did not know that cruisers

Haguro and *Tone* had opened a path for the destroyers to attack the enemy.

It was difficult to close the enemy ships, which were taking
advantage of their position by fleeing on the arc of an inner
circle while Kurita pursued on an outer arc. The enemy destroyers showed great skill and courage in laying smokescreens
to shield the carriers and, at the same time, launching torpedo
attacks. Then there came a fierce enemy air strike. Heavy
cruisers *Chikuma* and *Chokai* were forced out of the pursuit
because of damage inflicted by the attacking planes. Destroyer

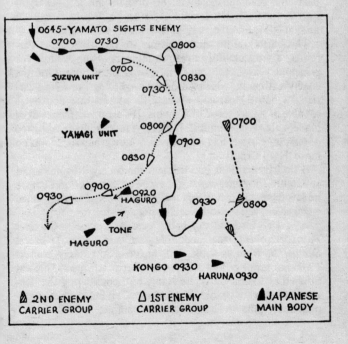

Track of Forces in Battle off Samar, 25 October 1944

Fujinami was assigned to *Chokai*, and *Nowaki* to *Chikuma*, for rescue purposes. It appeared that battle damage could easily continue to the point where there would not be enough Japanese destroyers for rescue work.

After 0830 the air attacks became more frequent and intense, and the planes seemed to be coming in regular waves. Our losses increased. The pursuit had now been going on for two hours, and, since Kurita's ships were running at full speed, he began to be concerned about their fuel supply. He wanted to destroy the enemy carriers but, judging their speed to be 30 knots, realized that continued pursuit would seriously delay the accomplishment of his primary mission—charging into Leyte Gulf. He decided therefore to turn toward Leyte and, at 0911, ordered all ships to assemble accordingly.

This battle was no shining victory for the Japanese. It was, rather, a most skillful retreat on the part of the enemy. The principal reason for our failure was misjudgment of the enemy's strength, which Kurita believed to be 5 or 6 fleet carriers, 2 battleships, and at least 10 cruisers and destroyers capable of a fleet speed of 30 knots. His error was the result of inadequate aerial scouting. The enemy force actually consisted of 6 *escort* carriers and 8 destroyers whose group speed was no more than 18 knots.

A decisive battle is impossible if the enemy does not stand and fight. The American ships, aware of Kurita's Force before he saw them on the horizon, had turned away. The unexpected engagement caught both fleets disorganized.

American losses in this battle were escort carrier *Gambier Bay*, destroyers *Hoel* and *Johnston*, and destroyer escort *Samuel B. Roberts* sunk. The Japanese lost heavy cruisers *Chikuma, Chokai,* and *Suzuya*, and three destroyers. This was no victory for the Japanese Navy, but, considering that Kurita's ships were devoid of air cover, Combined Fleet Headquarters felt that the battle was not a complete failure.

14. *The Great Controversy*

It took Kurita's ships two hours to reform after the action was broken off, and finally at 1120 they headed on a course of 225 degrees for the target area of Leyte Gulf. At the time of sortie from Brunei Bay, three days earlier, the fleet had consisted of 32 warships; now it was down to 15. There was, however, no diminution in the fighting spirit of this decimated force as it sped in ring formation toward Leyte Gulf. At 1140 Kurita spotted a *Pennsylvania*-class battleship and four destroyers which, having caught sight of the Japanese force, were fleeing southward. Kurita ignored them and continued toward his objective.

An hour later there occurred an incident which will always be a subject of controversy in the annals of naval warfare. At 1235 Admiral Kurita stopped the dash toward Leyte Gulf and reversed course.

At 1205 he had radioed to headquarters: "We are determined to execute the planned penetration of Leyte Gulf despite any enemy air attacks which may be encountered." What happened within that half hour that caused him to change his mind and head northward? In the past two days there had been at least eight severe aerial attacks which had whittled his fleet strength down to less than half of what it had been at the time of sortie. Yet he had continued stubbornly on. Now within 45 miles of the goal, Kurita suddenly turned away.

It is vitally important to find the reason for Kurita's decision—not just for the sake of one vice admiral, but for the sake of the entire Japanese Navy. This was the Combined Fleet's final battle. (Subsequent suicidal activities by Japanese ships cannot be dignified as battles.) The honor of the Japanese Navy was at stake. Admiral Togo, forty years earlier at Tsushima Strait, had made his famous two right-angle turns in the face of the enemy to go on to a great victory. Kurita, as commander of the Main Body at Leyte Gulf, had a responsibility to carry on the honor of the great Imperial Navy. Yet he made only one turn, and that was *away* from battle. For this he has been criticized from every quarter.

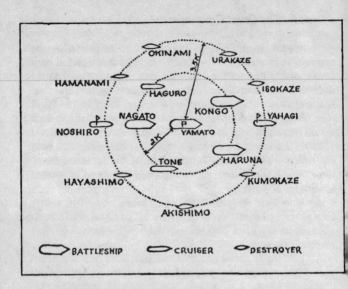

Kurita Fleet Formation Heading for Leyte

Let us examine the official records and study the movements of the Kurita Force. The fleet had arrived at a point only two hours from its goal. All guns and torpedoes were ready, battle stations manned, and men waiting for action. Then suddenly came the order for a turn to the north. While wondering what had happened the men saw signals from flagship *Yamato* saying, "We will seek out and engage the enemy task force which is in position bearing five degrees, distant 113 miles from Suluan Island lighthouse." The decision for this momentous turn was made by Admiral Kurita himself, and, according to his own statements, he consulted no one on the matter.

The superstructure of flagship *Yamato* includes a pagoda-like mast. On the upper level of this mast is the flag bridge, where the commanding officer stands. In the operations rooms below his staff assembles information which is passed on to the commander by his chief of staff. Admiral Kurita was a commanding officer who made decisions without much discussion. On this day, with the information he had at hand, Admiral Kurita spoke his decision for the northward turn to Chief of Staff Koyanagi, who relayed the order.

The change in course gave rise to shouts of "Banzai!" from the men, but these were not cries of relief that death in Leyte Gulf had been avoided. The men understood the order to mean that the enemy's mobile task force would first be attacked and destroyed. They knew full well that just as action in Leyte Gulf could wait, so too death was waiting at every turn.

15. No Suicide for Empty Transports

Kurita must have made his final decision only after careful consideration of several complicated elements. Otherwise this serious-minded and brave admiral would not have abandoned his orders from Imperial Headquarters just as the moment approached for carrying them out.

Let us first examine the information known to Admiral Kurita. That morning, while pursuing the enemy escort carriers, he had heard their call for help, as well as the reply that it would take two hours before help would be available to the small carriers. This was an important consideration for Kurita in making his estimate of the position of the other enemy forces. If help for the enemy were to arrive on schedule, one powerful task force would reach a point south of Samar shortly after noon.

A second consideration, derived from intercepted plain-language messages, was that planes from the small carriers which Kurita had attacked that morning had all gone to Tacloban airfield on Leyte (where the enemy had landed seven days earlier). From this nearby land base these planes could make devastating attacks against Kurita's ships.

Thirdly, the enemy Seventh Fleet was at sea and assembled somewhere nearby. Its six battleships were not to be ignored. (It will be remembered that one *Pennsylvania*-class battleship of the enemy had been sighted by Kurita shortly before noon.)

Lastly, as indicated above, Kurita was aware of an enemy task force off Suluan Island. These were the critical pieces of information available to Kurita at noon on 25 October.

It would have been simple to charge into Leyte Gulf. But

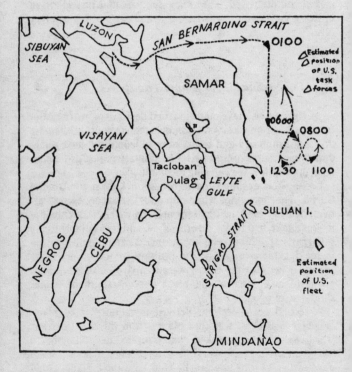

Track Chart of Kurita Fleet, 25 October 1944

was there any chance of success in making the penetration? Could he expect favorable battle results? Would it not end in futile death and perpetual disgrace for the Japanese Navy? The question was not one of losses, but could a responsible fleet commander justify the loss of ten of his own ships while sinking only one of the enemy's?

Kurita first judged that during the two or three hours of his further approach to the mouth of Leyte Gulf his ships would be subjected to even more attacks from land- and carrier-based planes than they had suffered in the Sibuyan Sea. Also, since the initial enemy landings had occurred seven days earlier and since Kurita was familiar with the enemy's great ability in carrying out landing operations, he judged that the transports, which were his principal target, would already have been unloaded and withdrawn.

If Kurita searched out these empty ships and sank them, it would have little effect on the general war situation. Furthermore, when high-powered shells hit an empty ship they penetrate and pass through without exploding, causing a minimum of damage and few sinkings. This was a standing joke among men who had had just such experiences in the Indian Ocean in 1942. I do not know if this thought occurred to Kurita at the time, but it was well-known that empty transports are most unprofitable targets.

Empty ships are certainly a part of the enemy's strength, but Kurita's judgment was that his fleet would be annihilated in attacking such targets. It would be like sacrificing battleship *Yamato* for a third-rate merchant ship. Ever since the training at Lingga Anchorage it had been the fleet consensus that there would be no suicide pact with empty transports, and this sentiment had a powerful influence on Kurita's decision not to lead his ships in a penetration of Leyte Gulf.

16. *Final Glory of the Japanese Navy*

Kurita's orders from Imperial Headquarters were to charge into the Gulf, but he questioned the intent behind these orders. Imperial Headquarters certainly expected that the fleet would go forward to certain death if battle goals were within reach. However, if favorable battle results seemed unobtainable, and if annihilation of the fleet was almost inevitable, Kurita felt it would not be a violation of orders for him to shift his target of attack. On the contrary, that is what a responsible commanding officer should do.

If there was any hesitation on Admiral Kurita's part about not obeying his basic order, it quickly disappeared when he realized that his fleet might be annihilated. One fact and one hypothesis weighed heavily in his decision: he was totally without help from any friendly forces. The land-based air forces, whose help had been promised by Combined Fleet, provided no assistance whatsoever. With the arrival of Fukudome and Ohnishi (both the great hope of the Navy) Kurita had expected to receive some aid. But up to this point they had not flown a single plane. Nor had they provided one bit of information. Understandably, the men of the fleet were angered.[8]

Kurita also wondered what had happened to the Ozawa Force, which was supposed to have lured the enemy task force northward. Having received no word from General Headquarters, or from Ozawa, Kurita concluded that his weak hodgepodge fleet had been sunk along the way.

Kurita assumed that he was fighting alone, and that the other two parts of the Leyte battle trinity had made no move at all. Furthermore, he had fought against submarines on 23 October, had suffered aerial attack all day on the 24th, and engaged a carrier fleet in the morning of the 25th, and was

---

[8] Bad weather, insufficient training and other such considerations had caused a delay in aerial support for the battle. It was about 1630 on 25 October that Japanese planes first appeared in the sky over Kurita's ships. But by that time the fleet was withdrawing from the battlefield. Of the planes which did arrive at this time, two mistook battleship *Yamato* for an enemy and dropped bombs. In addition to underlining the anger of the fleet, this incident is evidence of how poorly the pilots were trained.

about to enter the decisive battleground with less than half his original strength. He was literally alone and helpless.

Kurita knew of no support from any of his intended supporting forces. It was probable that his fleet was already surrounded by enemy task forces. Possibly the two carrier groups which he had chased southward that morning would pursue him at a safe distance of about 100 miles. And the force which had said it could provide help "within two hours" would certainly have arrived by this time. Moreover, it was already five and a half hours since the whereabouts of Kurita's ships had become known to the enemy. It did not take a naval strategist to realize that all enemy task forces, including the one whose plane had hit Kurita hard the day before in the Sibuyan Sea, would now be concentrating toward Leyte Gulf.

Such being the case, Kurita's force, by stubbornly pursuing the scheduled westward course, would have found itself completely enveloped by the time it reached the mouth of Leyte Gulf. There would then be no escape except to the bottom of the sea.

This was the conclusion that Admirals Kurita, Koyonagi, and Morishita each arrived at independently. Based on the above hypothesis, this was clearly a correct judgment. Kurita suddenly decided to crash against the nearest task force of the enemy. If annihilation was to be his fate, he preferred to fight against carriers on the high seas rather than against empty transports in Leyte Gulf.

If he could avenge the debacle of Midway by sinking carriers *Enterprise* and the new *Hornet*, the late Admiral Yamamoto would smile from his grave. Far wiser than shooting holes in empty transports. From the standpoint of giving meaning to battle, there was no comparison. Thus it was that Admiral Kurita issued the order to turn northward from the eastern coast of Samar Island on a course of 0 degrees to "engage in decisive battle with the enemy task force which is in position bearing 5 degrees, distant 113 miles from Suluan lighthouse."

17. Search for the Enemy

Earlier, on the way from Brunei to Leyte, there had been discussions about what the fleet should do if it encountered a powerful enemy task force. Should the penetration of Leyte Gulf be abandoned to engage the enemy? Kurita's chief of staff, Rear Admiral Koyanagi, had raised this question at the end of August when Captain Shigenori Kami, a Combined Fleet staff officer, had brought the *Sho* 1 operation plans to a battle conference in Manila. Captain Kami answered affirmatively. The ranking officers of the Southwest Area Fleet agreed, saying that this was not only a matter of course, but also that the engagement of an enemy task force took precedence over all other considerations.

Of battleship *Yamato*'s supply of 1,080 main battery (18.1-inch) shells, only 81 had been expended. She had enough left to display her mighty fire power in four or five additional sea battles. One of these shells was enough to sink a carrier, and several such shells could easily disperse any escort force. The Kurita Force was vibrant with fighting spirit as it headed north northeast.

At 1315 a great formation of about 70 planes appeared overhead. Their attack was briefer than the first and the skill of the pilots was inferior. The third and fourth waves came at 1400 and 1500. Fortunately, there were no casualties, but, judging by the frequency and direction of these carrier plane strikes, the enemy was obviously nearby, to the east northeast of the Kurita Force. A lack of scouting planes prevented Kurita from pinpointing the exact location of the enemy ships. Kurita was anxious to engage, but the enemy launched planes from a safe distance, and stayed beyond range of his big guns.

Three hours more and it would be sundown. Night engagements were the specialty of the Japanese Navy, but a night action is possible only when the location and movement of the opponent can be determined with some certainty. At 1615, for the first time, a formation of about 60 Japanese planes appeared over Kurita's ships and requested the location of the enemy. They flew away in the direction indicated by the fleet according to its best estimate. When they reappeared it was to report that they had been unable to make contact.

Admiral Kurita realized that his search for the enemy task force had failed because of a lack of aerial reconnaissance. Should he return to base by again traversing San Bernardino Strait? Or should he charge into Leyte Gulf and then return to base by way of the Mindanao Sea? Kurita had already abandoned the latter choice as foolhardy.

There were two prevailing attitudes in the Japanese Navy concerning life and death in battle. The first maintained that when one does not know whether to go to the right or the left, he should head in the direction of death. According to the other view, one should be cautious in order to make death as meaningful as possible. Vice Admiral Tamon Yamaguchi, in his decision for death at Midway, represented the former school; Vice Admiral Takeo Kurita the latter. At a moment of crisis the actual difference in viewpoint may be very slight. The choice of one school over the other is, however, extremely delicate since the consequences may make a tremendous difference.

When Kurita started in search of the enemy task force, he did not expect to survive the engagement. But once he missed the chance of engaging in surface battle, he must have believed it useless to turn again to penetrate Leyte Gulf and venture his ships in such a futile operation. Kurita did not mind long odds but he was opposed to any operation which offered no chance. He knew how long it takes to train a fighting man, that battle losses can never really be replaced, and therefore each man's life must be protected as much as possible. Death in war is inevitable, but it should not be pointlessly courted. It was a basic tenet of the Japanese Navy to avoid any operation which offered no chance of survival. The volunteers who went to blockade the mouth of Port Arthur in the Russo-Japanese War knew that a boat was ready to receive them after they had scuttled merchant ships to block the passage, and a warship was standing by to rescue them. Even in the case of the midget submarines which became famous for their attempted attack on Pearl Harbor, plans were made for their return to mother ships. The probable outcome of these and other similar operations was death, but in each case there was a possibility of survival. This tradition was not violated until the adoption of the tactics which called for the Kamikaze Special Attack Force (suicide pilots) and the *kaiten* (human torpedoes), at a time when Japan realized that the war was lost.

18. *Kurita Upholds Tradition*

It was in keeping with Japanese Naval tradition that Kurita did not penetrate Leyte Gulf. Kurita's decision was also consistent with his previous actions in this war.

The situation against Japanese forces had become critical in Guadalcanal in October, 1942, when the Army and Navy were cooperating in trying to maintain this strategic island. Admiral Yamamoto, Commander in Chief Combined Fleet, proposed that a powerful battle squadron should penetrate Lingga Anchorage at night and bombard the enemy air base with Type-3 incendiary shells. Each of these 14-inch shells exploded in the air would scatter some 600 incendiary balls and burn everything on the ground. Combined Fleet was then anchored at Truk, where tests were made with the Type-3 incendiaries. When the shells proved to be satisfactory, Yamamoto approved their use for Guadalcanal. In order to fire these shells accurately a straight-line approach of at least 10 miles was required. The gunnery ship could not turn from this course, no matter how much enemy interference there might be, or the shells would miss the target. Our supply of 1,000 Type-3 bombs, that is to say 600,000 incendiaries, were to be used at Guadalcanal.

It was something more than risky, however, to enter enemy territory at night with the purpose of going back and forth along a straight line for an hour and a half to fire at land targets. The mission was certain to be strongly opposed, and, indeed, the possibility of annihilation could not be ignored. The assignment was given to the commander of Battle Division (Batdiv) 3, Vice Admiral Takeo Kurita. Batdiv 3 consisted of *Kongo* and *Haruna*. The commanding officer of battleship *Kongo* was Captain Tomiji Koyanagi. (By coincidence Koyanagi was Kurita's chief of staff in the Leyte operation.)

In accepting this mission, Kurita raised one condition for Admiral Yamamoto's consideration. He asked that his crews be equipped with land-warfare weapons such as helmets, rifles, machine guns, and hand grenades. If his ships were fatally damaged by enemy bombs and torpedoes he would want to ground them and put all hands ashore to fight as land forces. If they were fortunate they might have a chance of joining the regular ground forces. Only with such a provision for survival could Kurita willingly accept a mission to a death-filled battlefield. Admiral Yamamoto approved Kurita's proposal, and made arrangements for Kurita's crews to be provided with the requested equipment.

This is an eloquent example of Kurita's chance-for-survival philosophy, which was also demonstrated early in 1943. At Truk Admiral Yamamoto ordered Kurita to use his squadron of heavy cruisers in support of Army operations at Bougainville. Kurita suggested that there should be air cover and that it would be costly to risk cruisers in this job which could be done perfectly well by destroyers, but Yamamoto wanted cruisers too. On the way to Bougainville, the ships stopped at Rabaul for fuel and were there subjected to a severe enemy air attack, in which the cruisers were badly damaged, but managed to escape. There had been no fighter support as promised. Kurita thought it foolish to expose heavy cruisers to such dangers on worthless missions, and sent a message to headquarters saying that he was returning to base. On his arrival at Truk, he was greeted by Admiral Yamamoto with a knowing smile. Admiral Kurita's straightforward action and expression of resistance in this instance tallied with his later action at Leyte Gulf.

One other episode which reflected Kurita's philosophy and personality occurred on the occasion of the death of Captain Nobuyoshi Nakaoka, the skipper of heavy cruiser *Atago*.

Flagship *Atago* was the principal target of the enemy bombing in the Rabaul action referred to above. While Captain Nakaoka was standing on the bridge a large bomb fragment tore away half of his abdomen. As he was being carried away on a stretcher, he passed Admiral Kurita and said farewell. He died a few minutes later with a smile on his face, for he had said his last banzai. This man's unnecessary death left a lasting impression on Kurita, and it must have strengthened his feeling of resistance toward any useless sortie.

This same regard for the value of life was shown the night of 24 October when Kurita sent a message to Admiral Nishimura telling him to rendezvous with Kurita's own ships ten miles north of Samar at 1000 the next day. As a reply to Nishimura's message reporting the time when he would penetrate Leyte Gulf from the south, this message seemed odd. Did Kurita mention this rendezvous—to take place six hours after Nishimura's hazardous run-in—merely by way of encouragement? It seems to me that the message was sent as a word of caution to Nishimura that he should do his best to come through the action alive.

Kurita wanted to convey the idea that, although both admirals had their orders from General Headquarters, death should not be invited unnecessarily. From Nishimura's use of the words "charge in," Kurita knew that he intended to penetrate deep into the Gulf. Kurita meant to tell Nishimura that he should enter the Gulf but approach the enemy only near enough to fire his big guns, and that he should then withdraw for the indicated rendezvous. At the time he sent that message, Kurita was transiting San Bernardino Strait, with the clear intention of charging directly into Leyte Gulf. Thus after their intended rendezvous, both Kurita and Nishimura would dash into Leyte Gulf, fire their guns, and escape through the Mindanao Sea to return to Brunei Bay. In summary, Kurita read in Nishimura's message the latter's determination for death, and thus sent the message advising against it.

Kurita adhered rigidly to orders, but he also placed great value on and had great respect for human life. Surrounded by the enemy and without any support, he opened up a route which led to survival.

Psychologists explain that a fighting man engaged in a life-and-death struggle does not fear death. The tension and excitement of battle create an abnormal condition which subdues thoughts and fears of dying. But, once free of the struggle, he cherishes life and, consequently, fears death.

In considering Kurita's decision, this explanation does not apply. He was well known in the Navy for his cool-headedness. Is it not likely that the notorious turn-away from Leyte Gulf was the product of a combination of Kurita's judgment of the battle situation, his principle of avoiding certain death, consideration for his subordinates, and resistance to useless sacrifice?

19. Interview with Admiral Kurita

Admiral Kurita has always been known as a taciturn man. This is particularly true regarding his statements about the battle at Leyte Gulf. For many years after his fateful decision of 25 October 1944, he refrained from comment. It would appear that he has been trying to forget a bad dream. His attitude seems to have been that "A defeated general should not talk about his battles." Because of my long acquaintance with him, however, it was easy for me to question him about the essential points of his decision, and I took the occasion of one of our friendly meetings to do so.

"Why, after getting so close, did you turn away?"

"At the time I believed it was the best thing to do. In thinking about it since that time, I have concluded that my decision may have been wrong. I had been given orders and, as a military man, I should have carried them out."

I was reluctant to drop the issue at this point. "Looking back on your decision, do you still feel today that it was the right one?"

"As I consider it now, my judgment does not seem to have been sound. Then the decision seemed right, but my mind was extremely fatigued. It should probably be called 'a judgment of exhaustion.' I did not feel tired at the time but, under great strain and without sleep for three days and nights, I was exhausted both physically and mentally."

The reader will recall that Kurita's force had endured torpedo attacks on the first day of its sortie, devastating aerial attacks the next day, and a surprise encounter with carriers in the morning of 25 October. By noon of the 25th he must have been living on nerve alone.

"Is it true that you held a staff meeting to consider the various reports you had received and that the decision to reverse course and retire was the result of this meeting?"

"After the last meeting with my staff I had no thought of retiring. I did not discuss the decision with any member of my staff. The decision was entirely my own. The incoming reports were unconfirmed, and I had no time to confirm them. My belief at the time that enemy task forces were in the immediate vicinity was mistaken."

"But the enemy did have a task force nearby. You had been subjected to steady attacks by carrier-based planes."

"True, my misjudgment, however, lay in the belief that we would be able to get within range of this enemy. But his carriers were 100 miles away. No matter how much we pursued we could not engage this force. It was a mistake on my part to think that we could. The destruction of enemy aircraft carriers was a kind of obsession with me, and I fell victim to it."

At this point your writer ventured the statement that thousands of lives had been spared because Kurita had not penetrated Leyte Gulf, and that, from this point of view, the decision was fortunate. To this the Admiral replied simply, "Yes, I suppose that could be a point." And indeed it was a very big point.

I then asked if he had considered going back to Leyte Gulf upon realizing at 1630 (25 October) that it was impossible to overtake the enemy task force. Kurita's straightforward answer to this was, "By that time I believe that Leyte was no longer in my thoughts. As I recall, my mind was filled with such problems as enemy air attacks in the Sibuyan Sea next day, and the state of our fuel supply."

"They say that a man who escapes the jaws of death would not again court the same danger. Did you, Admiral Kurita, have any such thought at Leyte?"

"I don't know because the thought of turning back never occurred to me."

I had expected that my prepared questions would have provided a full day of conversation and writing, but such was plainly not the case. Admiral Kurita sat silent and thoughtful after his brief answer to my last question, before he volunteered, "Leyte Gulf was stationary, the enemy task force was not and so the chances of finding it were an unknown quantity. If one says it was an error in judgment for me to have reversed course for an unknown quantity, then I have no excuse."

I then asked his opinion on such subjects as the basic operation orders and the fact that Commander in Chief Combined Fleet had directed the operation from Hiyoshidai in the homeland instead of being in the front lines. To these questions Admiral Kurita remained silent and merely smiled a wry smile.

He did volunteer one other remark. He said, "I was, so to speak, the pitcher of the losing team." And finally, "You appear to be fond of statistics. Well, my fleet holds the world record for the number of air attacks sustained. *Yamato* alone was the target of 19 such attacks during the Leyte operation."

9

THE BATTLES FOR LEYTE: PHASE THREE

1. Cripples Return to Base

BEGINNING AT 1600 ON 25 OCTOBER, Admiral Kurita, having abandoned the engagement, spent the next two hours wondering how to transit San Bernardino Strait and avoid deadly air attack. Up to this point he had been pursuing the enemy, but the situation was suddenly reversed and from now on he would be pursued. Kurita directed a course slightly to the east, as though he were still seeking an enemy, until sundown at 1830, when he turned sharply westward and headed for San Bernardino. By 2130 the fleet had traversed the strait. Kurita's message that he was abandoning the Leyte penetration was received at Hiyoshidai by Combined Fleet at 1600. The staff officers were flabbergasted and barren of ideas, but finally issued an order at 1647: "Engage in night battle tonight if there is a chance. If not, proceed to base at your discretion." Kurita received this message at 1925 but, not having lo-

180

cated the enemy by daylight, it was impossible to engage him that night. The issuance of the order thus appears to have been purely perfunctory.

That night Admiral Kurita sent a message of request and recommendation to Admirals Fukudome and Ohnishi, commanding the land-based air forces. "I believe that the enemy, suppose to be to the east or north of Legaspi Peninsula, will air attack this fleet on 26 October. This is an excellent chance for you to strike and thus regain control of the air."

Thereupon Kurita proceeded westward through the Sibuyan Sea.

As expected, at 0834 on 26 October, 30 enemy carrier planes came to attack the fleet. Cruiser *Noshiro* was disabled by a torpedo, and battleship *Yamato* took two bomb hits. At 1040 a second attack wave arrived. This time 30 B-24s, the enemy's largest bombers, concentrated on *Yamato*, as if determined to finish her off. *Yamato*'s anchor room was flooded and a big hole was opened in her port side at the waterline abreast her forward main turret.

A third wave, made up of 60 planes, came presently. *Noshiro* was sunk. *Yamato* was hit with three bombs forward, letting in 3,000 tons of water. As a counterflooding measure, an additional 2,000 tons of water was taken into her stern sections. In other words, *Yamato* took in a total of sea water equal to almost the tonnage of a cruiser.

Several near misses caused *Yamato* to tremble like a fragile building in an earthquake, and water spouts rose to a height twice that of the Marunouchi Building (which is about 10 stories), drenching everyone on the bridge. The smell of gunpowder lingered in the ship for days. *Nagato* had a similar experience, suffering four direct hits and nine near misses.

Kurita's ships left a telltale trail as they departed the Sibuyan Sea. Three days of heavy fighting had loosened rivets and seams to the point where every ship leaked oil. They had to pass through the same waters where enemy submarines had knocked out three of Kurita's heavy cruisers on the sortie. And now the exhausted fleet was completely vulnerable, like

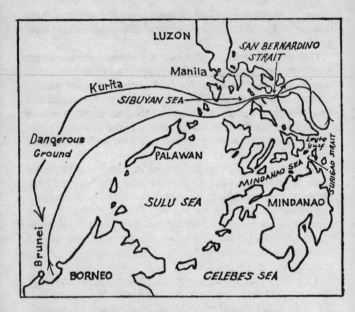

Track Chart of Kurita Fleet, Battles for Leyte Gulf

wounded soldiers straggling back to camp. Accordingly, after passing Palawan Strait at 1800, Kurita deliberately led his ships north of Shinnan Island and then south through the "dangerous ground," where, because of rocks and shoals, even enemy submarines did not go. He finally returned to Brunei Bay at 2130 on 28 October. Despite the amount of water taken on, *Yamato* had returned 1,000 miles to base under her own power. *Yamato* was, after all, the unsinkable battleship.

When the fleet had sortied from Brunei six days earlier, with flags fluttering in the morning breeze and hopes high for victory in decisive battle, it was an imposing force of 7 battleships, 11 heavy cruisers, 2 light cruisers, and 15 destroyers.

There now remained 4 battleships, 2 heavy cruisers, 1 light cruiser, and 8 destroyers. Destroyer *Yukikaze* was the only ship to come through the battles unscathed.

One might expect that a fleet suffering such terrible losses would be too demoralized for thoughts of future battle. The eager young officers and men, however, were still full of fighting spirit. They spoke animatedly of new ships and future battles. *Katsuragi* was nearing completion, and *Unryu* and *Amagi* would soon be commissioned. With these three new aircraft carriers, the talk went, we will not so easily be defeated again. Staff officers, who better knew the war situation, said nothing. They realized that the end of the Imperial Japanese Navy was at hand.

2. Criticism of Battle Off Samar

The battle off Samar was one of the several naval actions fought between the two forces engaged in the "Battles for Leyte." This engagement itself was not on a large scale, but is of interest for the following reasons:

1. The encounter was a surprise to both sides. Withdrawal and pursuit took place immediately, and ended indecisively.
2. Both sides lost the opportunity for a decisive victory.
3. For the first and only time 18.1-inch shells were fired in action from a ship's guns.

All Japanese misfortunes in this battle sprang from lack of reconnaissance, resulting in a paucity of information about the enemy. Off Samar occurred Japan's only opportunity of the Leyte battles to inflict great damage on the enemy. The opportunity was missed because of three tactical errors:

1. Pursuit broken off too soon.
2. Destroyers not used aggressively.
3. Disunity of command.

1. *Lack of pursuit*

The enemy fled on the arc of an inner circle, at a speed of only 18 knots. By 0925 on the 25th he was being hard pressed by our cruisers and, had the pursuit continued for another half hour, more of his tiny escort carriers would have been sunk. Cruiser *Haguro* was low on ammunition by the time of her nearest approach to the fleeing enemy force of five small carriers. The Japanese destroyers had barely come within torpedo-firing range of the carriers when the cease-fire order was issued.

This opportunity was missed because of the Japanese failure to know the strength of the enemy. As described earlier, Admiral Kurita judged his targets to be regular carriers, capable of more than 30 knots. He abandoned pursuit because he thought it would be impossible to overtake them. If the truth had been known and the pursuit continued, this entire enemy force could have been annihilated. Thus the American force, fleeing in confusion at its unexpected encounter with the Japanese, was saved. It should be noted that the planes which flew from the defenseless escort carriers packed a wallop out of all proportion to the weakness of their mother ships. These planes sank four Japanese heavy cruisers.

2. *Destroyers not used aggressively*

This was the result of an order from Admiral Kurita as soon as the enemy carriers were sighted. He thought that the enemy could be crushed by gunfire alone, and wanted to conserve his destroyers for use in mopping-up operations. If the destroyers had steamed full speed to the attack, there was danger that their supply of precious fuel would be exhausted. Accordingly Kurita ordered the destroyer units to follow after the battleships and heavy cruisers. They reduced speed from 35 to 22 knots, but were still able to overtake the enemy, whose speed was limited to 18 knots. At 0905 they fired torpedoes, but the first firing at a great range could not be expected to hit.

3. *Disunity of command*

This occurred because the Kurita Force sighted the enemy at 0640 while shifting from night cruising formation to day anti-aircraft formation. Most American historians are critical of Kurita for not having put the fleet formation in order before starting the pursuit. Actually there was no time to do so. Kurita was doing his utmost not to miss this heaven-sent opportunity. His best chance to get within gunfire range of the enemy was by having each ship move independently, but this meant their gunfire was unconcentrated and ineffective.

Limited visibility was further reduced by rain squalls and smokescreens, and Japanese ships were forced to fire their guns by radar control at ranges generally under 3,000 meters. This was the first time that the Japanese Navy had used fire-control radar in combat, and many misses must have been caused by lack of familiarity with the new technique. Moreover, fire-control radar had been developed for only six months in Japan, and was not nearly as reliable and effective as American radar which had been in combat use for two years.

Americans cite the abandonment of the breakthrough into Leyte Gulf as another failure on Kurita's part. They say that if Kurita had pushed through against the United States Seventh Fleet at the head of the gulf, he might have annihilated it since most of its ammunition had been exhausted against the Nishimura Force. Moreover, there were many transports within the gulf which had not yet unloaded their cargoes, and General Douglas MacArthur himself was on the beach. The Americans were thus exposed to far more danger than Admiral Kurita realized.

There is room for doubt concerning the validity of these speculations. It is inconceivable that the Seventh Fleet had actually exhausted its ammunition, for its engagement with *Fuso* and *Mogami* that morning had been a very brief one. Battleships *West Virginia* and *Maryland*, with their 16-inch guns, and the four others with their 14-inch guns must have had enough ammunition for more than one brief engagement.

American logistics planners would not have permitted such an error. In short, this whole claim sounds like a speculative afterthought effort to exaggerate Kurita's error.

3. Halsey Taken in by Decoys

Admiral Kurita believed that every movement of his fleet was known to the enemy. On the contrary, the Americans were caught completely off guard by the emergence of the Kurita Force off Samar. This manifestation of U.S. negligence continues to be a matter of great discussion as a tactical failure.

Rear Admiral Thomas L. Sprague's escort carrier force, which encountered the Kurita Force, was approaching Samar Island in a leisurely fashion, secure in the idea that the approaching ships were friendly. Even if Sprague did not know that the Japanese force had been repulsed in the Sibuyan Sea, he had been assured by Admiral Halsey that no Japanese fleet would emerge from San Bernardino Strait. It was his understanding that any Japanese ships attempting to come through the strait would be subject to an attack by torpedoes, bombers, and surface gunfire that none could survive.

Admiral Kinkaid, under whose command Sprague's carrier groups were operating, insists that it had been agreed that he was to protect the transports and supply lines to Leyte, while Halsey's fleet was to defend the mouth of San Bernardino Strait. When Sprague arrived off Samar he saw not Halsey's fleet, as anticipated, but the Kurita Force. It is not unreasonable, therefore, that Admiral Kinkaid became enraged at this turn of events.

It was a mistake on the American side to have allowed Kurita to have exited from San Bernardino Strait. Certainly it seemed improbable to them that the retreating Kurita would turn again and resume his original course for Leyte. However, as long as such a possibility existed, the wise opponent should have taken it into consideration. Japanese military forces have been known to take extreme measures from time to time. Had aerial contact been maintained over Kurita's fleet for another two hours, that is, until sundown, either the turnaround would have been detected, or Kurita might have delayed the turnaround for another day until he could be sure of the cooperation of land-based air forces.

Furthermore, submarine contact should have been maintained with the Kurita Force during the night. Since the end of 1943 the Americans had become more and more skilled in submarine warfare, and beginning in 1944 Japanese destroyers were being sunk in greatly increasing numbers. Japanese naval officers, chagrined at these submarine actions, lamented that the mice were catching the cats. At the time of the Marianas battles of June 1944, American submarines were employed with deadly effectiveness. Had they also been employed in the Leyte battles, they alone could have blocked any sortie from San Bernardino Strait.

Another American failure must be considered. To point out this failure is to praise Admiral Ozawa for his successful decoy operation. The American commander fell victim to it because of the following misjudgments:

1. He far overestimated the strength of the Japanese Mobile Force.
2. He allowed the Kurita Force freedom of movement for twelve daylight hours while he pursued the Ozawa Fleet with his entire force.

Around 1500 on 24 October American scout planes had reported the presence of a powerful Japanese task force proceeding southward. Admiral Halsey should have entertained some doubt as to the actual existence of a powerful Japanese task force at that time. In the Marianas battles four months earlier, Halsey himself had sunk the leading Japanese carrier *Taiho*, as well as *Shokaku* and *Hiyo*. He must have known that only *Zuikaku* remained to Japan as a regular fleet carrier. Japan's other few carriers were second-rate ones with speeds of less than 25 knots. Halsey should have realized that these remaining Japanese carriers were not worthy of the attention of even half of the carrier forces under his command. Under the circumstances Admiral Halsey should properly have kept at least half of his carrier forces to guard San Bernardino Strait.

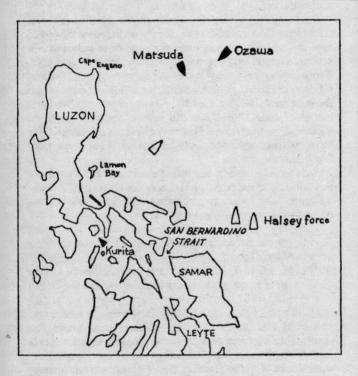

The Battle for Leyte: 1600/24 October 1944

Here we are reminded of the American criticism mentioned before, that "Kurita missed a golden opportunity." In other words, it was said that because Kurita did not carry out his original plan of dashing into Leyte Gulf, American forces

The Battle for Leyte: 0400/25 October 1944

were saved from a great loss. The American landing operations might even have been thwarted. Thus grave were the possible consequences of Admiral Halsey's chase to the north.

On the other hand, Admiral Halsey would mention that the Kurita Fleet did not have carriers. A fleet without carriers is not the main force. The main force is the mobile fleet, and it is common sense that it should be the target of an all-out attack. With hindsight one may argue that the actual fighting strength of the Ozawa Force made it an unworthy target, but Halsey would maintain that there was no way of his knowing what its actual strength was at the time. Japanese carriers which had been under construction for the past two or three years, might well have been added to the fleet. Furthermore, once the Japanese mobile fleet was destroyed, the United States would have complete control of the air and sea in the Pacific Ocean.

The Battle for Leyte: 1300–1700/25 October 1944

Halsey regarded the battle off Cape Engaño as the golden opportunity to achieve this. Halsey would state that it is a tradition of American strategy to proceed to the main target and not be diverted by minor distractions. Kurita did not go into Leyte Gulf because U.S. carrier groups were in the neighborhood. Had he gone into the Gulf, he would surely have been destroyed.

Arguments on both sides will never be exhausted. The American forces, with their great concentration of strength, overwhelmed the Japanese, it is true, but the fact remains that Halsey's great force was lured to the north by Ozawa's decoy fleet and thus absented itself for one day from the assigned battlefield off San Bernardino Strait and Leyte Gulf.

4. Ruinous Defeat

The Japanese defeat at the battle of Leyte Gulf was indeed miserable. Losses came to 3 battleships, 4 aircraft carriers, 9 cruisers, 13 destroyers, and 5 submarines, for a total of 34 ships; while the enemy lost only four. The score was one-sided to an extent rarely seen in warfare. It was a complete revenge for Pearl Harbor.

A fundamental cause of this debacle must be attributed to the operation objective, which was really an invitation to disaster. The *Sho* 1 Operation orders were the death warrant of the Combined Fleet. It was beyond common sense to think that a surface force could sortie for enemy territory 1,000 miles distant, without air cover, and hope to have a chance of attacking transports which were protected by vastly superior enemy forces. If the Japanese commander had been an inflexible person, his force would have been destroyed to the last ship and man.

In April 1945, the Emperor asked his Naval Chief of Staff, "Was not the use of our warships inappropriate at Leyte Gulf?" Ordinarily the question would have been asked by using the word "appropriate" and in a positive way. The Emperor's phrasing of this question, which I learned of from a close friend in the Emperor's naval entourage, indicates that he was deeply concerned about the reasons for the tremendous losses inflicted on the Japanese Navy at Leyte.

The answer given to the Emperor's question is not known, but I am sure that it was rendered with profound embarrassment and guilt. There is no excuse for committing warships and people to suicide. When a battleship sinks, 2,000 men die. To order a fleet into an operation where there is sure death with no expectation of worthy results is an act of desperation.

In Army Colonel Sako Tanemura's *A Secret Diary of Imperial General Headquarters*, mention is made of the decision for the Leyte operation. Every member of the Army General Staff opposed it, but the Navy was insistent. Since it was a Navy matter, the Army withdrew its opposition and left the decision to its proper jurisdiction. The recklessness of the Leyte operation is obvious from the fact that even the Army, often criticized for its own recklessness, called it reckless.

Admiral Soemu Toyoda, who issued the operation order, explained his position to a member of the United States Strategic Bombing Survey. He said that with Japan's supply of oil from the south cut off, the fleet, in home waters, would have been immobilized by lack of fuel; in the south the ships could not have been supplied with ammunition. It was a dilemma and the Japanese Navy decided to risk this one last engagement.

That is one way to look at it. The Navy may have wanted to respond to the unspoken question of the people: "What is the Fleet doing?" Since Japan's defeat was inevitable, the Naval High Command might have seized on this opportunity for a final all-out effort. The problem was that, in this battle area so far distance from any port of safety or supply, there was no place for the fleet to retire to lick its wounds. All the sky was under enemy domination.

It is astonishing that Admiral Kurita was able to accept his orders for this battle calmly. He later remarked, "The plans of staff officers ashore sometimes seem reckless to those who are experienced in combat at sea. In the case of Leyte, I knew it would be difficult, but decided to try."

This was a noble gesture on the part of Admiral Kurita. He set out with great determination but, when he had had enough, he was able to acknowledge defeat and withdraw. That, too, was noble.

5. *Special Attacks Come Too Late*

Admiral Kurita would have had a better chance if air support had been available to him in the four days of the Leyte battle. With land-based air cooperation for his fleet, the enemy air attacks would not have been so successful. He also regretted his fleet's lack of fighter and scout planes. The commander of Japanese air forces in the Philippines, Vice Admiral Takijiro Ohnishi, was deeply concerned about the recklessness of sending the fleet into enemy territory without air protection, as evidenced by his 23 October message to Combined Fleet Headquarters:

> Air protection must be given to the Kurita Fleet, but we cannot have fighters ready by the target date. Please postpone the operation for two or three days.

But Kurita had already sortied, and there was so little fuel that the fleet simply could not mark time for two or three days. Moreover, Ozawa and Nishimura had also departed for the battle area. Thus Kurita entered the Sibuyan Sea unprotected.

What is more important, Kurita's operational area would have been an ideal location for effective action by the land-based air forces. Their role was a major consideration in the Leyte operation planning. But Ohnishi had only 100 planes of all types, and his flight crews were inexperienced. The land-based Fifth Air Force of Vice Admiral Shigeru Fukudome was transferred from Formosa to the Philippines. When it became clear that even this did not improve the situation substantially with regard to air capability against targets far at sea, Ohnishi decided to adopt Special Attack tactics.

Because Special Attacks meant certain death for the pilots, the missions were purely voluntary. In the Imperial Navy a man could be ordered into action only where there was a chance for survival. After the Battle of the Marianas the war situation was so grave that the possibility of crash-diving tactics began to be discussed among Navy men.

At about the same time, training accidents increased markedly. Almost daily men were killed in practice landings and takeoffs from carrier decks. Observing these accidents, the pilots themselves began to feel that if they were going to die on carrier decks, it would be much better to die crashing the decks of enemy carriers. And if the planes contained bombs, the enemy ships could be sunk as well. This idea fired the enthusiasm of many men, until finally, Rear Admiral Sueo Obayashi, ComCarDiv 3, and Captain Eiichiro Jyo, skipper of carrier *Chiyoda*, proposed to Admiral Ozawa the formation of Special Attack forces.

Admiral Toyoda vigorously opposed this idea, saying the situation was not that desperate. But one man could not wait —Rear Admiral Masafumi Arima, commanding officer of the 26th Flotilla based at Nichols Field in the Philippines. On 14 October, during the air battle off Formosa, he dove his plane toward an enemy warship. The crash damaged the ship (probably light cruiser *Reno*), and Arima was killed. This act gave strong impetus to the Special Attack spirit of Arima's subordinates. Vice Admiral Ohnishi finally gave in to the apparent demands of the moment and called for the organization of a Special Attack Force. On 21 October two planes of the Yamato Special Attack Unit departed from the airfield at Cebu, on the island of the same name. On 23 October two other volunteers for death also took off on a suicide mission. The fate of these four planes is unknown. On 24 and 25 October, five planes from the Shikishima Unit, two from Yamazakura, seven from Yamato, four from Wakazakura, two from Kikusui, two from Asahi (for a total of 22 planes), sortied in search of enemy carriers in the Leyte and Tacloban areas. Except for one plane of the Wakazakura Unit, whose pilot radioed that he was crash-diving on an enemy ship in Leyte Gulf, nothing was heard from these planes.

No report of Special Attack results was obtained unless a cover plane was assigned to observe the action. But fighter planes were so scarce that even a carrier fleet did not have them. As a matter of fact, the few fighter planes available were being converted into Special Attack planes. Thus nothing is known of the early Special Attack efforts, except from American reports. These reports show that on 24 October, ocean tug *Sonoma* was sunk by a suicide plane. And on 25 October suicide planes accounted for the sinking of escort carrier *St. Lo* and the damaging of escort carriers *Sangamon, Suwannee, Santee, White Plains, Kalinin Bay,* and *Kitkun Bay*.

Admiral Ohnishi had no word of these results, but he launched another 19 suicide planes on 26–27 October. Again he learned nothing of their accomplishments. American records show that they succeeded only in damaging light carrier *Suwannee* once again.

Even in Special Attacks, pilot skill is required. It is no easy task to detect an enemy surface force, get past his protective air and antiaircraft screens, and come in on the target for a direct hit. Special Attacks did not become an integral part of Japanese Naval strategy until after the Leyte Operation.

Japan had 64 submarines in December 1941. In the course of the war she built an additional 126. What did she accomplish with these 190 submarines? What were they doing at the time of the Leyte Gulf battle? During three years of war, the Press Section of Imperial General Headquarters rarely had any announcement about the achievements of Japan's submarines. Actually a submarine fleet did exist, commanded by Vice Admiral Yoshishige Miwa. The numerical strength of this Sixth Fleet dwindled so alarmingly throughout the war that its squadron commanders such as Rear Admirals Owada, Ishizaki, Uozumi, and Kudo could only huddle over the conference table and sigh at the ever-shrinking numbers of their charges. At the time of Leyte Gulf Japan had only 32 operational submarines, plus 20 antiquated ones which were good only for training purposes. Of the 32, 2 were being used as transports, 4 were in the Indian Ocean, and 13 newly constructed ones were on shakedown maneuvers, leaving only 13 available for the Leyte Operation.

Since Operation *Sho* 1 was an all-out battle, and since it was especially suitable for submarine action, these thirteen submarines should have put to sea ahead of the main force to precede the surface ships into the battle area. The fact that they were ordered to depart after the Ozawa Fleet was an indication that Combined Fleet Headquarters was not relying on submarines in this battle. There were actually eleven that sortied under a plan which placed three of them on station off Lamon Bay, four off Samar Island, and four off Surigao Strait. However, it took longer than expected for them to reach their assigned locations, and they did not arrive on station until 25–26 October. Among them they reported sighting many ships during the battle, but the only submarine to make any offensive move was *I-56*, which fired torpedoes at one transport and one aircraft carrier. The enemy reported only one escort carrier slightly damaged by submarine action, while three Japanese submarines were lost in this operation.[1]

A preview of this miserable showing may be seen in the part that submarines played in the attack on Pearl Harbor. There were 27 crack submarines stationed in Hawaiian waters to torpedo any ships which might come out from the harbor. Great things were expected of these submarines in the Hawaiian operations, but their participation ended in failure. The submarine fleet reported, "We have discovered that it is extremely difficult for submarines to attack warships and blockade a well-guarded harbor. We are of the opinion that the main operational targets of submarines are merchant ships, and not warships." The Navy High Command was flabbergasted at this report, but was forced to admit that the traditional use of submarines in the Japanese Navy had been merely to effect attrition on the enemy fleet as surface forces

[1] *I-46* sunk 28 Nov. by DDs *Saufley, Waller, Pringle, Renshaw* at 10°48′ N, 124°35′ E; sunk 28 Oct. were *I-45* by DE *Whitehurst* at 10°10′ N, 127°28′ E, and *I-54* by DDs *Gridley* and *Helm* at 10°56′ N, 127°13′ E.

closed for decisive battle. Even recognizing this, the Imperial Navy went on throughout the war forcing submarines into unreasonable missions and operations for which they were never intended, resulting in unnecessary losses. Another striking cause for Japanese submarine failures was the great progress made by the enemy in antisubmarine measures, plus Japan's outdated and antiquated weapons. A contest between a submarine equipped with modern underwater detection gear and one without was like a contest between a rifle and a spear. The Leyte battle was a golden opportunity for Japanese submarines to regain their lost prestige, but, instead, it added to their record of ignominy. The blame lay not with the men but with the machine.

It is reported that German experts, after making a study of Japanese submarines, reported to Hitler on several of their major shortcomings. Thereupon, Hitler sent two German submarines as gifts to the Imperial Navy. One managed to reach Kure but was never put into operation since the war was already drawing to a close. Time was running out for Japan in all things, and the chance of revising the design and concept of submarines was no exception.

10

"SPECIAL ATTACK" OPERATIONS

聯合艦隊

1. Kikusui[1]

THE FALLING CHERRY BLOSSOMS seemed to be mourning the fate of the Imperial Navy. On 5 April 1945 Vice Admiral Ryunosuke Kusaka, Chief of Staff of the Combined Fleet, came to Vice Admiral Seiichi Ito on board Second Fleet flagship *Yamato* and personally delivered the *Kikusui* Operation order from Commander in Chief Toyoda. He explained the necessity for this extreme tactic and urged Admiral Ito to act promptly. The order read:

Second Fleet is to charge into the enemy anchorage of Kadeno, off Okinawa Island, at daybreak of 8 April. Fuel for only a one-way passage will be supplied. This is a Special Attack operation.

[1] Literally "floating chrysanthemum," *Kikusui* was the banner of the 14th century patriot Masashige Kusunoki. Under this banner he led his men to certain death in the battle of Minatogawa.

The name was applied to a series of ten aerial suicide operations carried out between 6 April and 22 June 1945. The first of these mass attacks (6–7 April) was to be coordinated with the sortie of *Yamato* and her cohorts, and thus the name came to be applied also to the surface ship effort.

If, by chance, the crews of the participating ships were able to make their way to shore on Okinawa, they could join in the land fighting and there find glory. But it was clear that such a hope was impossible, and that *Kikusui* was a suicide operation.

Vice Admiral Ito, an outstanding officer, had been Vice Chief of Naval Operations at the start of the war. He understood the dire position of the Navy in 1945 and accepted this reckless venture with no sign of disturbance. The Naval General Staff had opposed this operation, maintaining that even though Japan was on the verge of total defeat, it was inhuman to order men into such a suicidal activity. Since it was inconceivable that the fleet could even reach Okinawa, the loss of these men and ships was a wasteful sacrifice.

Combined Fleet Headquarters, which had originated the operation, refuted these arguments by stating that the loss of Okinawa would be disastrous for Japan. In so desperate a situation the Navy could best cooperate with the Army by carrying out this operation. The fleet might not reach Okinawa but it would attract many enemy planes. With fewer enemy planes on the island, a counterattack by the land forces on Okinawa might have a good chance of success. Battleship *Yamato* was to serve as a lure for the enemy's planes. I have read the story of a devoted son who, to save his parents from suffering mosquito bites during their sleep, covered his body with rice wine to attract the bothersome insects to himself. Heaven, observing this act of filial piety, was moved to banish all mosquitoes from the neighborhood. Would a merciful Heaven be similarly impressed by the *Kikusui* Operation, which forced men to pointless suicide?

All commanding officers in Second Fleet were summoned to *Yamato* immediately. When the operation order had been read the meeting was opened to discussion. There was vehement objection by everyone except *Yamato*'s skipper, Captain Kosaku Aruga, who remained silent throughout the conference. Commander Yoshiro Sugihara, of destroyer *Asashimo*, was particularly vocal in his opposition. He said, "I object to an operation which demands the destruction of its participants before they have even a chance of reaching their assigned des-

tination. I am opposed to squandering the last of our Navy."
Even the taciturn Captain Kiichi Shintani voiced objection,
"This operation does not offer us a proper place to die. A
more fitting place will present itself when we can engage the
enemy in hand-to-hand combat as we oppose his invasion of
the homeland. The proposed plan is idiocy!" Captain Hisao
Kotaki, Commander Destroyer Division 21, who was known
for his hot temper and sarcasm, said, "Combined Fleet Headquarters stays in its air-raid shelter at Hiyoshidai. What can
they be thinking of at this critical time? Why don't they come
out and take personal command of the fleet?"

Utterance of such heated remarks by Navy officials was
most unusual. Traditionally, though such differences of opinion often existed about tactics and strategy, they had never
been disputed in this manner. Six months earlier, in the Leyte
Operation, there had been expressions of dissatisfaction
among the commanders, but they had never reached a point of
explosion. The fact that such strong opposition was raised at
that 5 April *Kikusui* conference was indicative of the senseless-
ness of the whole operation. A surface fleet without fighter
protection, in an area completely under enemy domination,
was certain to be destroyed. Perhaps it could cruise for a few
hours under the temporary protection of darkness, but by day
the enemy's air forces could not possibly miss it. Already
B-29s appeared daily to observe the fleet anchorage, and
enemy submarines were known to be patrolling in the Bungo
Straits. Furthermore, the allotted fuel, sufficient for only a
one-way passage, showed that the fleet was not expected to
return.

This Second Fleet had been dominated by the philosophy of
"fight bravely, but die not in vain." It had long been commanded by Vice Admiral Takeo Kurita, and his respect for
human life permeated the organization. The fleet lost ships
but it was proud of its survivor record. The sentiment behind
this pride was also responsible for the strong objections to the
proposed operation plan.

The conference on board *Yamato* was closed by Chief of
Staff Kusaka and Commander in Chief Ito who explained in

detail the reasons for this sortie. The attitude of the conferees suddenly changed completely. They then acquiesced to a man, saying, "Very well, let us do what we can."

2. Eve of Fatal Sortie

The skippers returned to their ships. Preparations to sortie were begun immediately. Many crewmen sharpened bayonets in the belief that they would see hand-to-hand combat ashore at Okinawa. The men were full of fighting spirit. Pitifully uninformed, it did not occur to them that their ships were apt to be sunk on the way by enemy planes.

Orders were issued to disembark midshipmen who had come on board a few days earlier, fresh from the Naval Academy. These young men objected vigorously, and one of their spokesmen said, "We are proud of this chance to shed our blood for the homeland. We are mortified at the thought of being left out of this operation. How can we face our families if you do not take us along?"

Deeply moved, the commanding officers said to the youngsters, "Only veterans are permitted in this operation. Inexperienced hands might handicap our effort."

The young men went forlornly into waiting boats and ashore. There they lined up to look longingly at the fleet until darkness closed the ships from sight.

That night there were farewell parties. In cruiser *Yahagi* the host was Rear Admiral Keizo Komura, Commander Destroyer Squadron 2, who entertained his division commanders and skippers. They consumed many bottles of *saké*, but thoughts of the morrow kept the alcohol from having its customary effect. The skippers returned to their own ships where there were smaller parties in the officers' quarters. These broke up with the singing of *"Doki no Sakura"*[2] whose familiar strains spread out on the quiet waters of the Inland Sea, with the

---

[2] Literally, "Cherry Blossoms of the Same Rank." An Academy song which alludes to the officers as cherry blossoms, the emblem of the Japanese Navy.

voices from each ship blending into a chorus of goodnights and farewells. The commanding officers bowed their heads and forced back tears as they thought of the young "cherry blossoms" that were about to fall.

When *Yahagi*'s skipper, Captain Tameichi Hara, was going to his quarters that night, he came across Machinist Mate 1st Class Yamamoto, who was laboring on a generator in his oil-soaked work clothes. Captain Hara asked Yamamoto what he was doing and the young man replied, "I do not want a power failure on so significant an occasion, and so I have traded this watch with my buddy who likes to drink." There were many men like Yamamoto in *Yahagi*, and in the other ships as well. Battles will be fought and ships destroyed but man's spirit survives.

3. The Ten-Ship Second Fleet

Just as Masatsura Kusunoki had inscribed on the walls of the Nyoirindo Temple the names of the men who were about to follow him into fatal battle, so the names of these ships that were approaching fatal battle must be inscribed. They were battleship *Yamato*, light cruiser *Yahagi*, destroyers *Fuyutsuki, Suzutsuki, Yukikaze, Isokaze, Hamakaze, Kasumi, Hatsushimo,* and *Asashimo*. These ten were all that could be mustered for this fateful operation. Battleship *Kongo* had been torpedoed and sunk by an enemy submarine in the early morning of 21 November 1944 in the Formosa Strait.[3] Battleship *Haruna* was under repair, *Nagato* was tied up in Yokosuka, and two heavy cruisers remained in the South Seas.

This, then, was the Second Fleet. There had been no First Fleet since May 1944 when Admiral Soemu Toyoda, as the new Commander in Chief, had moved his headquarters to a shore base.

This total remaining strength of the Japanese Navy sailed

[3] By submarine *Sealion II* (Commander Eli T. Reich), which also sank *Kongo*'s escorting destroyer *Urakaze* at the same time.

from Mitajiri in the Inland Sea at 1500 on 6 April 1945. A feeble sun shone through the spring mist. It was a perfect day for cherry blossoms to fall.

No sooner had the fleet assembled into cruising formation than two enemy B-29s appeared and dropped bombs from a high altitude as if in prelude to battle. The ships passed through Bungo Strait at 2200, and four hours later, as they negotiated Osumi Channel, the presence of two enemy submarines was detected. The B-29s, watching from above by day, and submarines on hand to follow close behind at night, made it a virtual certainty that these ships would never reach Okinawa. But they had no alternative to proceeding at full speed.

4. Yamato *Sinks*

The fleet passed Tanegashima and Yakushima that night, and, at 0600 entered the open sea southwest of Kyushu. The ships shifted to a ring formation, with *Yamato* at the center, and headed due south for Okinawa on a zigzag course. The ring formation, devised by the United States Navy in 1929 as a proper defensive disposition for high-seas cruising, was intended for multi-ship fleets. It was grotesque for these few paltry ships to resort to this grouping.

For a brief time there were ten friendly planes in the sky over the ships. They soon departed for land bases, as did scout seaplanes from *Yamato* and *Yahagi* which were flown off to prevent their destruction in battle. There was no need for reconnaissance; the location of the enemy was well known. At a distance of 10,000 meters a surfaced enemy submarine followed the formation. Overhead, reconnaissance planes kept a watchful eye. Ahead lay enemy carriers with hundreds of planes waiting to attack. The enemy was everywhere.

There was no thought of altering course. The men of the fleet prayed only that they might charge into Okinawa the next morning, and there pump shells into the enemy positions.

Yamato's huge guns were capable of throwing projectiles a distance of 35 miles and piercing 16 inches of steel plate. One such shell could knock out a battalion of troops, and *Yamato* carried more than 1,000 of them.

At 1230 the ubiquitous enemy planes appeared from clouds some 20 kilometers on the port hand. At first there were two, then five, ten, then by the dozens. Suddenly there were hundreds of planes filling the sky. The fleet shifted into antiaircraft formation with 5,000-meter intervals. Speeding at 27 knots, the ships opened fire against their aerial foes.

The bombing and torpedo attacks against *Yamato* were daring. This was the fourth time that United States naval air forces had attacked this giant battleship. In the earlier actions at least ten direct hits and numerous near missess had failed to ruffle her. This time the enemy was determined to do a thorough job. *Yamato*'s 150 antiaircraft and machine guns raised a curtain of shellfire into the sky. Planes were shot down, but new attack waves came on incessantly. It was simply a question of how long *Yamato* could endure their onslaught.

The first bomb struck *Yamato* at 1240, and ten minutes later the first torpedo found its mark. Thereafter, countless bombs and at least fifteen torpedoes struck home. Three hours of steady attack by bombs and torpedoes finally doomed the great battleship.

Staff officers gathered on the bridge to die with their ship, but Admiral Ito directed that they save themselves to continue serving the nation. His stern tone, which they were hearing for the first time, influenced the officers to turn obediently and leave the bridge. A great explosion rent the ship, putting the main decks awash and trapping hundreds of men below. Captain Aruga spoke to his Executive Officer, Captain Jiro Nomura, "I am one with *Yamato*, but, once in the water, I might swim and survive. Take this rope and tie me to the binnacle. This is my last request, and it is an order!"

Nomura, who knew his skipper well, obeyed. While Captain Aruga was being tied, he turned toward Admiral Ito and said, "You are indispensable. Please leave the ship."

Admiral Ito nodded, with his usual gentle smile, but he did

as the British Admiral Tom Phillips had done on board his flagship *Prince of Wales* in the battle off Malaya. Nomura was still tying his skipper to the compass stand when he was washed from the sinking ship.

Ito and Phillips were both highly regarded for their ability. Both had become fleet commanders after serving as Vice Chief of Naval Staff. Both died as the result of aerial attacks upon "unsinkable" battleships.

Thus Captain Aruga went down with his *Yamato*. In the same way, Captain Toshihira Inoguchi had gone down with *Musashi*, and Captain Toshio Abe with carrier *Shinano*. It is curious that these three—the greatest warships in the world—should all have suffered the same fate. At 1500 hours on 7 April 1945 the giant *Yamato* disappeared beneath the waves, 90 miles south of Bo no Misaki.

After the battle a message came from Combined Fleet Headquarters: "Owing to the brave and sacrificial fighting of the Second Fleet, our Special Attack planes achieved great result." This message was delivered to the skippers of the five destroyers—all that remained of the Second Fleet—when they returned to port. These words of commendation were received with bitter smiles.

I wish that *Yamato* might have survived and been placed under United Nations custody as a memorial to man's naval ingenuity. It is regrettable that she was sacrificed in a futile *Kikusui* operation which achieved nothing.

5. Special Attack Sacrifice

On 21 October 1944 two planes flew from Cebu airfield in the southern Philippines. Their pilots, Lieutenant (jg) Yoshiyasu Kuno and Ensign Chisato Kunihara, had volunteered to crash their planes into enemy aircraft carriers. It was the beginning of *Kamikaze* (Divine Wind) Special Attacks.

From 23 to 26 October an additional 55 planes, loaded with bombs, flew out to attack enemy carriers in crash-dive attacks.

Unfortunately, they could find no targets, and most of these planes ran out of fuel and were lost at sea. But later, especially during the naval actions around Okinawa, these strange suicide tactics sank or damaged many ships. Another very important effect of these attacks lay in the fear that they created in the enemy.

These desperate efforts could not possibly have changed the tide of war. But they did inspire greater patriotism in the people of Japan, and that must serve as consolation for the noble youths who thus died for their country.

Ensign Masahisa Uemura, who had been captain of the football team at St. Paul's University in Tokyo, died in kamikaze plane Number 3. There were dozens of young men like him who, drafted from school into the Army, volunteered for Special Attacks. We should mourn their precious sacrifice with the same spirit that we mourn the loss of great ships. More than two thousand Navy men died in kamikaze attacks.

The Japanese believed that in the battles off the Philippines and Formosa they sank four and damaged fourteen carriers, and that nine other ships were sunk and twelve damaged. The Americans announced their casualties with more accuracy. Fleet carriers *Intrepid, Franklin, Essex, Lexington* and escort carriers *Independence, Belleau Wood, St. Lô* received direct hits. At least forty other ships were damaged. The over-all results were five ships sunk, 23 heavily damaged, and 12 with moderate damage. Of the later battles off Okinawa, Admiral Ernest J. King reported as follows: "From 25 March to 21 June, 250 ships including carriers, battleships, cruisers, destroyers, and landing craft were damaged by Japanese aerial attack. Most of these were Kamikaze Special Attack planes, and they sank a total of 34 destroyers and smaller ships."

These were the rather considerable results. Unfortunately, this extraordinary attack method came to be accepted by the Japanese. While conventional air attacks envisaged the return of men and planes after they had launched their bombs and torpedoes, this frightful tactic called for the expenditure of men and planes as well as bombs and torpedoes. Such tactics were bound to be criticized from the standpoint of both economy and humanity.

At the time there was no leisure for such consideration. Imperial General Headquarters, which had planned for "The Decisive Battle of the Homeland"—the very idea of which today appears so repugnant—had taken the further step of hiding 3,500 naval planes throughout Kyushu to be used in Special Attacks against enemy landings in the main islands. Additionally, 1,300 Army planes were to be placed under command of the Navy. If one out of five of these planes could have hit a target, they would have damaged 1,000 enemy ships. This ratio was established on the basis of the 902 planes which sortied at Okinawa and damaged 200 enemy ships.

Considering that the enemy's antiaircraft effectiveness was increasing day by day, it was more likely that one out of each ten planes might succeed in hitting a ship. Of more import than the ratio, however, was the fact that the Headquarters plan called for throwing the *entire* force against the enemy's *initial* landing effort. Nothing would then be left to counter subsequent enemy attack waves. This seems to have been given no consideration in the plan.

6. Special Attack Year. 1945

One retired admiral observed this new development and was gravely concerned. He was Prime Minister Kantaro Suzuki. He invited the Naval General Staff to his official residence for a discussion in which he stressed one point:

"Using men in a situation where there is no chance of survival is not a proper military operation. The Japanese Navy has always opposed such undertakings."

There is no way of knowing if he foresaw that the end of the war was at hand, but he was plainly disturbed at the sacrifice of Japan's promising young men in suicide attacks.

Admiral Suzuki had commanded a torpedo boat at Wei-hai-wei in the Sino-Japanese War of 1894–95. Ten years later he was in command of a destroyer squadron in the Russo-Japanese War. His guests therefore listened carefully to his words.

As the war situation became more desperate, so did the strategy and tactics of the Japanese High Command, until finally they accepted Special Attacks. Japan's resources and productive ability were rapidly becoming exhausted, as was the supply of skilled pilots. The High Command realized that Special Attacks were inhuman, but there was no apparent alternative.

Thus 1945 was the year of the Special Attacks. Designs were drawn for special fighter planes, the *Shusui* and *Reppu*, for attacking B-29s. But the war ended before they ever went into production. *Ohka* and *Shinyo*, however, joined with kamikaze planes in the battle of Okinawa, and these two weapons remained in production until the end of the war.

Ohka was a rocket-assisted glider weapon carried to the target vicinity by a twin-engined bomber and then released to smash against an enemy ship. These deadly missiles were easily mass produced, but utterly useless without mother-ships to bring them within striking range of targets.

Shinyo was an ordinary motorboat with explosives in the bow. The idea behind this simple craft was that so many could be used against each enemy warship that one or two would surely get in for a kill. Great numbers of them were built and stored away in seaside caves, against the day of a homeland invasion.

Another extreme plan hatched in the closing part of the war was to have skilled swimmers carry an explosive charge beneath enemy ships, where the divers would detonate their burden in hope of doing some damage to the enemy vessel. The war ended while the first of these *Fukuryu* (hidden dragon) units were still being trained.

The idea of using human divers with explosive charges did not originate in Japan. The British had devised a two-man midget submersible vehicle to blow up a German pocket battleship in the fiords of Norway. Italy also used human torpedoes in 1941 to slip into the harbor at Gibraltar, where they blew up British tanker *Denbydale*. On 19 December 1941, British battleships *Valiant* and *Queen Elizabeth* were damaged by human torpedoes in Alexandria Harbor and incapacitated for many months. These torpedoes were carried to the harbor mouth by submarines. Two men mounted on a torpedo guided it to the hull of a target ship and there fastened the warhead. A delayed-action fuse was set to allow the men time to slip safely out of the harbor, or ashore to be taken prisoner. In the attack on Alexandria two officers were captured while they were swimming among the other British ships. They refused to disclose their mission, but their objective was achieved.

In 1943 Italian divers entered Gibraltar harbor and attached delayed-action charges to Allied ships. These men swam safely out of the harbor and as a result of their handiwork one Allied ship was sunk and two damaged. There were a total of seven such Italian forays, which sank or damaged fourteen Allied ships, at a cost of three divers killed and three captured.

The Italian human torpedoes could range sixteen kilometers at a speed of three knots. The crew strode their vehicle in equestrian fashion. It was a deadly game, but allowance was made for the survival of the valiant crews. In contrast the Japanese *kaiten* used at the end of the war allowed no consideration for the survival of crews.

7. *Japan's Unique Torpedoes*

Immediately after the war, representatives of the Japanese Foreign Ministry, Army and Navy were called to Manila to arrange for American occupation of the homeland. One of General Richard K. Sutherland's first questions to them was, "Are *kaiten* still at sea?" When he learned that seven *kaiten*-laden submarines were at that moment on patrol, he ordered their immediate surrender.

Japan's Naval representative knew that *kaiten* had been achieving effective results from June 1945 until war's end, but he was surprised to learn that they were such a great threat to the enemy. People in Japan, hard-pressed by the bombing of homeland cities, knew little about the successes of the *kaiten*.

A news broadcast at 2000 hours on 6 May 1945 reported

that within one month two Japanese submarines commanded by Lieutenant Commanders Orita and Sugamasa had managed to sink one enemy light cruiser, two destroyers, five large transports, and damage three other ships. It is interesting to note that this announcement was one of only three news releases by Imperial General Headquarters which were not falsehoods. The other two accurate ones had been the announcements of the attack on Pearl Harbor and the battle off Malaya. Aside from these, the Press Section of Imperial General Headquarters released nothing but lies and exaggerations. Accurate Japanese reports of World War II were limited to the beginning and the end.

The Type-93 torpedo, basis of the *kaiten*, remained unexcelled to the end of the war, and this Japanese achievement was never matched by the enemy. This special torpedo used oxygen under high pressure as its fuel. It had a range of 22,000 meters at 50 knots, and 40,000 meters at 36 knots.

For comparison and reference, the following table gives the characteristics of this Japanese torpedo along with the best American and British torpedoes:

NATION	DIAMETER (cm.)	SPEED (knots)	RANGE (meters)	EXPLOSIVE CHARGE (kilograms)
Japan	61	36	40,000	500
United States	53	32	8,000	300
Great Britain	53	30	10,000	320

It was the use of oxygen as a propellant which made Japanese torpedoes superior to any others. Where conventional torpedoes leave a tell-tale bubbly wake, an oxygen-fueled one has the great advantage of leaving no track whatsoever.

The French Navy first conceived of oxygen as a propellant, but abandoned the idea because of the hazard of accidental explosion. The British tried oxygen as a torpedo fuel, but they also gave it up as dangerous. Japan engaged in research with these torpedoes, with such men as Vice Admiral Toshihide

Asaguma, Rear Admiral Kaneji Kishimoto working on its development. They experienced a few accidents but finally perfected this weapon, named Type-93 because it was successfully produced and approved 2,593 years after the founding of the Japanese Empire, which was 1933 A.D. Admirals Asaguma and Kishimoto received special awards for their achievement.

A torpedo which had greater range than the biggest guns of a battleship provided the opportunity for a revolution in surface actions. In some Japanese cruisers, guns were replaced by extra mounts for the Type-93 torpedoes, and bulky oxygen-producing equipment was installed in both cruisers and destroyers. The Type-93 torpedo was so potent a weapon that it alone could have made up for the enemy's advantage of the 5-to-3 ratio in warship strength in conventional surface actions. However, the advent of aerial tactics as the primary striking power in naval actions changed the picture entirely. The expected maximum distance between opposing forces had been about 20 miles, but combat airplanes placed the opposing forces at distances which averaged something like 200 miles. Under these circumstances the advantage of even a vastly superior torpedo was lost.

8. Kaiten *Sortie*

The Type-93 torpedoes, at first the great hope of the Japanese Navy, lay in warehouses like corpses. After the surface actions in the Solomons, two young officers, Lieutenant (jg) Kuroki and Ensign Nishina, conceived the idea of converting them into human torpedoes. They figured that human torpedoes would be far more accurate, and thus more effective, than midget submarines.

An experimental model completed in early 1944 was not then acceptable for operational purposes. Toward the end of October 1944, however, when volunteers were being taken for the Kamikaze Special Attack Corps, human torpedo volunteers were also accepted. Aerial suicide was far more dramatic than unseen death beneath the waves, but there were plenty of volunteers for each. In the beginning, when volunteers were grateful at being accepted, this weapon was called *kyukoku heiki* (national salvation weapon), next it was called Zero-6, and finally *kaiten* (heaven-shaker).

The placid Inland Sea waters off Otsushima were broken daily by wakes from high-speed motor boats, operating in and out of Tokuyama Bay. These busy craft followed *kaiten* as they went through submerged practice drills. From the time of the first *kaiten* sortie on 20 November 1944 until the end of the Okinawa campaign the *kaiten* took 7 lives in training and 48 in action, without achieving any significant confirmed results.

These pitiful sacrifices were a bitter disappointment. The cause for the failure was not the weapon, but rather the manner in which it was employed. Combined Fleet Headquarters had been using submarines in static patrols around enemy bases rather than, as they were intended, on roving patrols to disrupt enemy lines of communication and shipping. Sun-tze said that there are four areas in which an enemy can be defeated. In order of importance they are: his strategy, his alliances, his troops, and his fortresses.[4] Attacks on fortresses or bases were assigned the lowest priority, as being the least effective method of defeating the enemy. Thus, the most inferior of tactics was assigned to submarines. Japanese submarines made their attacks on enemy ships only within or immediately outside of well-defended harbors. All too often they proved to be steel coffins as a result of the enemy's alert antisubmarine defenses.

Properly used, the *kaiten* was an excellent weapon. Basically it was the superb Type-93 torpedo, and its characteristics were:

---

[4] Sun-tze, *On the Art of War*, Chapter 3, paragraph 3. "Thus the highest form of generalship is to balk the enemy's plans; the next best is to prevent the junction of the enemy's forces; the next in order is to attack the enemy's army in the field; and the worst policy of all is to besiege walled cities." Translation by Lionel Giles, London: Luzac & Co., 1910, pp. 17–18.

Length: 14.7 meters
Diameter: 1 meter
Weight: 8 tons
Crew: 1 man
Warhead: 1.25 tons of TNT
Range: 23 kilometers at 30 knots, 78 kilometers at 12
        knots

It was a remarkable weapon! General Sutherland's special concern about this weapon was understandable and justified.

A fleet submarine carried six *kaiten*. During the approach to a target the weapon was made ready and the pilot entered it through a special hatch which was then sealed off. The submarine skipper continued to close, informing the pilot by telephone regarding the relative position of the target ship. At the optimum moment the *kaiten*'s engine was started, and it was released from the mother ship. The pilot observed the target during his approach by means of a short periscope which could be raised for periodic spot checks. At about 500 meters from the target the pilot put his vehicle on automatic control for the final dash at full speed, submerged at a depth of about four meters.

Had Japanese submarines and *kaiten* been properly employed, they would have presented a terrible threat to the enemy. The approach of the *kaiten* could not be detected, its explosive charge was enough to sink a big ship, and its control to the target was almost infallible.

9. *Final Submarine Activities*

By April 1945 some corrections were finally made in the employment of Japanese submarines. Instead of attacking enemy fleets and bases, the submarine was beginning to be used to stalk enemy shipping and disrupt lines of communication. After neglecting their proper use throughout the war until this time, Combined Fleet Headquarters still continued this misapplication with *kaiten* in early 1945, tending to use them also in conjunction with kamikaze attacks against enemy fleets and fleet bases. But Commander Takenosuke Torisu, the torpedo expert on the staff of Sixth Fleet, at the risk of his position, argued for the proper use of submarines and finally received permission to employ two craft experimentally to attack enemy lines of supply. As a result, submarines *I-47* and *I-36* sortied on 20 and 23 April from the *kaiten* base, which had then been moved from Otsushima to Hirao, in Yamaguchi prefecture.

I-47 assumed its patrol station between Okinawa and Ulithi, and *I-36* on a line between Okinawa and Saipan. At dawn of 26 April, *I-36* discovered a great convoy of 30 ships bound for Okinawa. As it approached the convoy to within 7,000 meters it released four *kaiten* manned by Lieutenant (jg) Yagi, Petty Officers Abe, Matsuda, and Ebihara. Twelve minutes later skipper Sugamasa of *I-36* raised his periscope and observed tremendous explosions and heard four detonations in rapid succession, which violently shook the submarine.

On May 1 *I-47*'s skipper, Lieutenant Commander Zenji Orita, released four *kaiten* at a convoy sinking three Liberty-ship transports. The following day his two remaining *kaiten* were released, and they sank one enemy destroyer and damaged another. The pilots of these *kaiten* were Lieutenants (jg) Kakizaki and Maeda, Petty Officers Yamaguchi, Furukawa, Yokota, and Shinkai.

Both Combined Fleet and Imperial General Headquarters had to acknowledge that submarine employment should be left to the control of Sixth Fleet. Sixth Fleet immediately launched *kaiten* operations in the Western Pacific with all available submarines, a total of nine. These operations achieved the following results in the last three months of the war: 15 tankers and transports, 2 cruisers, 5 destroyers, 1 seaplane tender, and 6 unidentified ships sunk; and 2 ships damaged. Thus the deadly effectiveness of the *kaiten* posed a great threat to the United States Navy, even at this late stage of the war and with Japan's greatly reduced facilities.

Submarine *I-58* (Commander Mochitsura Hashimoto)

achieved a notable success, on 29 July 1945. At 2327 hours surfaced *I-58*'s lookout spotted the black outline of a warship on the horizon and called attention to it. The submarine submerged and made an approach to within 1,500 meters of this target. There six torpedoes were fired at two-second intervals, sinking cruiser *Indianapolis* with three direct hits. It was learned after the war that this ship had transported to the Marianas some parts of the atomic bombs dropped on Hiroshima and Nagasaki.

There is a question as to whether a third atomic bomb was on board the ship at the time of her sinking. After the war, Secretary of War Stimson announced that the two bombs used on Hiroshima and Nagasaki were the only ones the United States had. President Truman, however, says in his *Memoirs* that there was a plan to drop a third bomb on Niigata, but it was cancelled because that city was so far from Tinian. According to information put out by the United States Navy, there was a plan to drop the third bomb on either Sapporo or Niigata, but it was called off because the cruiser which carried the third bomb had been sunk.

We cannot know which of these reports was right, but it is certain that the sinking of *Indianapolis* was regarded as a grave incident. Commander Hashimoto was eventually summoned to a military trial of *Indianapolis'* commanding officer held in Annapolis, Maryland, to testify concerning the circumstances of his attack. It is unusual for a skipper to be tried in court martial for the sinking of his ship in time of war.

At any rate, it is a fact that these *kaiten* achieved a brilliant record. That must stand as consolation to the 98 men who gave their lives in these operations. Ten enemy ships were sunk as late as 10 August, 1945, by *kaiten* torpedoes. But when Japan was left with only seven submarines, even the "heaven-shakers" could not change the tide of the war.

11

CONCLUSION

聯合艦隊

JAPAN'S DESTINY IN MODERN TIMES had been closely aligned with the United States and Great Britain. The Imperial Japanese Navy had been modeled after the Royal British Navy. Both countries had assisted Japan in her wars against China and Russia, and she had been allied with them in World War I. They had contributed greatly to her modernization. In declaring war against them Japan broke close ties of many years, violated her destiny, and brought on her own defeat.

The Japanese Navy had good ships and good men; it was loved in the homeland and respected throughout the world for its competence and integrity. Unfortunately, the Japanese Navy lacked sufficient courage to repudiate the Army's reckless plan for war. Having no allies in the Far East and limited resources, Japan's defeat was inevitable. Her highly trained forces fought hard for three and a half years, only to go down in defeat. It was a shock to learn suddenly that even her great Navy, which had been building steadily for seventy years, was obliterated.

The 5-5-3 naval ratio allowed Japan only 60 per cent of the strength of either of her potential opponents. For a brief time before the war Japan's naval strength rose above that percentage of U.S. strength, but it did not reach the 70 per cent which Japan felt was barely adequate for a strategy of defense. As against the combined British-U.S. strength, Japan never reached more than 40 per cent. Britain, to be sure was greatly involved in Europe, but her Navy would be free for action in the Pacific as soon as Germany and Italy were defeated.

Japan had no chance of winning a war against the combined strength of the United States and Great Britain. Her leading Naval officers knew this, as witness their prewar remarks about how long Japan could last against those opponents. Had the same men been asked if Japan should enter such a war, there is not a doubt in the world that their answer would have been negative.

The men who strove to avoid war as a line of national policy were Admiral Mitsumasa Yonai, Navy Minister; his Vice Minister, Admiral Isoroku Yamamoto; and Vice Admiral Shigeyoshi Inoue, Chief of the Naval Affairs Bureau. In January 1939, soon after Kiichiro Hiranuma became Prime Minister, the Army Minister, Lieutenant General Seishiro Itagaki, insisted on the need for a tripartite pact with Germany and Italy as a bulwark against Communism. Admirals Yonai, Yamamoto, and Inoue knew that any pact of alliance with Germany would lead to a risk of war between Japan and the United States. Regarding such a risk as unbearable, they endangered their lives by opposing the Army. Their clear and insistent opposition, which lasted for eight months, saved Japan temporarily from the trap of a pact with Germany and Italy. Admiral Yonai fought so vigorously that seventy ensuing Cabinet meetings produced no resolution. In August, when Germany concluded a non-aggression pact with the Soviet Union, the Hiranuma Cabinet fell. Thus the anti-Comintern pact was tabled and one dark cloud was cleared from the horizon.

The second Konoye Cabinet, formed in July 1940, made another ominous bid for the tripartite pact. Since this was primarily a military alliance and it was relatively certain that the United States would join with Great Britain in opposing it, Japan's chances of being involved in war against the United

States were increasingly great. Prime Minister Prince Konoye was optimistic, however, because he expected the Navy to reject such a proposal. But where the Navy had at first loudly opposed joining the pact, it had now become silent and was moving toward acquiescence.

The Navy Ministry under Koshiro Oikawa, Vice Minister Teijiro Toyoda, and Chief of Naval Affairs Bureau Takazumi Oka was entirely different from what it had been the year before under Yonai, Yamamoto, and Inoue. Prince Konoye in his *Memoirs* reveals that Toyoda told him, "The Navy is actually opposed to the Tripartite Pact; but national politics is applying heavy pressure. The Navy, however, is still reluctant about going to war against the United States."

Navy leaders lacked the courage to resist political pressure, and they lacked the force to check young but vocal naval officers who went along with the Army's struggle for power in the cabinet. In September 1940, when the time came for a decision, Yonai was retired and Yamamoto was at Kure as Commander in Chief Combined Fleet. Admiral Yamamoto attended one of the last Naval conferences on the Tripartite Pact, but walked out when he was not invited to speak. Thus the Navy faction, lacking positive leaders, retrogressed and compromised.

With the signature of the Tripartite Pact the crisis deepened. Unaware of the real facts, the masses were agitated and aroused to the possibility of war. As the new year arrived, no efforts were made to check this inclination, and the only hope of resolving the crisis between Japan and the United States was the slender thread of direct negotiations. The Foreign Minister was indifferent to these efforts, initiated while he was visiting in Europe; but the Nomura-Hull conversations in Washington were undertaken with the support of General Hideki Tojo, the Minister of War. He feared that war with the United States at this time would be a great danger to Japan, engaged as she was in conflict on the mainland of China. But suddenly in August 1941, Tojo raised vigorous objections to the negotiations in Washington. This change in attitude was the result of his inability to check the younger military officers.

It became apparent that war or peace was in the balance. Naval leadership at this critical juncture was, unfortunately, in the hands of the same three men who, a year earlier, had favored the military alliance with Germany and Italy. Navy Minister Oikawa and his colleagues showed the same stripe in this crisis as they had when the Tripartite Pact was concluded. Prime Minister Prince Konoye called for a ministerial conference to be held at his Tokyo residence on 12 October 1941. Early that morning Oikawa sent a note to Konoye: "The Navy does not wish to break off negotiations, because war with the United States must be avoided if at all possible. But I cannot say so at the conference table. Please understand this today when I propose that the decision for peace or war be left to you."

At the conference that afternoon Oikawa said, in substance, "The Navy will leave the decision for peace or war to the discretion of the Prime Minister. If he decides for peace, the Navy will go along with him to the end, and compromise if necessary. If we are not going to war we must insure that present negotiations are successful. If we are going to war, the decision must be made now." Thus the Navy Minister hoped that the Japan-United States negotiations would be successful, but he did not have courage enough to say unequivocally that they must be continued and war avoided at any cost.

Prince Konoye shared Oikawa's hope, but he too lacked the courage for action. He had to make the decision, and accept responsibility for Japan's going to war. Perhaps it was unreasonable to expect such great courage from this nobleman. He wanted the Navy to say that negotiations with the United States must be continued, with compromises if necessary, but the Navy failed to do so.

One condition upon which the United States insisted in the negotiations was withdrawal of all Japanese forces from the mainland of China. Even the military felt that this idea provided a good opportunity for preserving the Japanese Army from the bottomless quicksands of China, and hoped that negotiations with the United States might be concluded favorably. So Prime Minister Konoye was not alone in looking to the Navy for opposition to war against the United States. The

Army also secretly hoped that the Navy might make such a declaration. Tojo was reported to have asked Konoye, "Why doesn't the Navy Minister clearly declare against war with the United States?" He even sent Major General Akira Muto to the Navy Minister to learn the real intention of the Navy. Tojo was also groping for a way out of the crisis.

War against the Soviet Union would have been an Army responsibility, just as the decision for war against the United States and Great Britain rested with the Navy. Army men were either ignorant of or indifferent to the Navy's strategic province, but there was a small group of Army officers, including Premier Tojo, who were genuinely disturbed about the prospect of war against the United States.

At the same time the Army was fanning a fire whose sparks fell everywhere. The leadership of the Army was dominated by young trigger-happy officers. If the road to Chungking was too long, they were willing to turn northward. If Soviet Russia was too strong, they would encamp in the fields of French Indochina. They were content only if they had targets in their gunsights. In such a bellicose atmosphere peaceful initiative was impossible.

Maintaining that naval warfare was beyond the scope of Army judgment, the Army left it to the Navy to interdict war with the United States. The Navy, however, held that it was in no position to make such a declaration, and asked: "Who started the Manchurian Incident? Who enlarged the Sino-Japanese Incident? Who pressed for the Tripartite Pact? Who invaded French Indochina? Who dubbed the Japan-United States negotiations 'coquette diplomacy'? Who spread war fever among the people by mobilizing sycophant scholars, commentators, and writers to publicize the Greater East Asia Co-Prosperity Sphere, to agitate against Great Britain and the United States as Japan's irreconcilable enemies? Who denounced peace efforts through negotiation as 'humiliation diplomacy'?" In each case the Army had been responsible, and was now anxious for the Navy to assume the consequences. The Navy saw through the Army's efforts to escape responsibility, and did not want to fall victim to this Machiavellian scheming.

At the same time, the Navy was not without blame. The Navy first meddled in the civil government as early as the London Disarmament Conference of 1930 when Admiral Hiroharu Kato, Chief of the Naval General Staff, exercised his prerogative of by-passing the cabinet and appealing directly to the Emperor. On 15 May 1932, Naval officers were responsible for the assassination of Prime Minister Inukai and other high government officials. In 1940, by failing to take a firm stand against the Tripartite Pact, the Navy aided in its creation. And in 1941 some Naval officers were included in the group of hot-blooded military men who urged for war against the United States and Great Britain.

In the autumn of 1941, when the Naval General Staff advised the Navy Minister to state frankly that there was no chance of winning a war against the United States, Oikawa replied, "Having boasted of our invincible fleet, we cannot now insist on compromise and say that we are unable to fight. We would lose face everywhere."

Oikawa and other Navy leaders were unaware of their impaired judgment. They could not see that the nation was more important than the Navy. Perhaps this opinion is too harsh; we must also understand how unbearable the stigma would have been if Japan was forced to yield because the Imperial Navy lacked strength. History might have placed things in proper perspective, but the Army in 1941 would have concentrated the entire blame on the Navy.

Nevertheless, the Navy, knowing that Japan would lose any war with the United States, should have shown the courage expected of leaders, and accepted humiliation in order to preserve the nation from defeat. Such a sacrifice would have proven that the Navy was worthy of the people's high regard and confidence.

The juggernaut of national destruction was rolling down Miyakezaka Hill in front of the War Ministry, and it seemed that nothing could alter its course. Even the Emperor, with his earnest prayers for peace, had no effect on the move toward war.

The question of peace or war was squarely posed for the first time in an Imperial Conference on 6 September 1941.

When the military representatives failed to clarify their stand as to whether diplomacy or war preparation was their dominant consideration, the Emperor, in a rare departure from precedent, expressed his regret at the situation and read aloud a verse composed by his grandfather, the Emperor Meiji:

> Since all the waters of the world
> are one,
> Why seethe the waves and rage
> the winds?

The assemblage was startled by this dramatic utterance, which was followed by the Emperor's remark that he had always tried to spread the peace-loving spirit of the late Emperor by reciting this poem. But the Army, having decided to gamble on war, was deaf to his plea.

Admiral Osami Nagano, with his thorough knowledge of American character and productive capacity, was overly optimistic in his estimate that Japan could wage aggressive war against the United States for two years. Consider how much more erroneous was the estimate of Army leaders, who knew far less about the intended enemy. Nothing but a resolute stand by the Navy could stop the explosive-laden juggernaut on Miyakezaka Hill. The Emperor and the civilian government prayed to hear the voice of salvation from the Navy's red brick headquarters at Kasumigaseki, but they prayed in vain.

At this point let us recall Admiral Gonnohyoe Yamamoto, the builder of the Combined Fleet, who served four terms as Navy Minister and two as Prime Minister, and twice saved Japan from a major crisis. In 1900, when General Aritomo Yamagata headed the Cabinet, the Emperor's permission was obtained to send troops to Amoy. Prime Minister Yamagata then convened a conference to get the Navy Minister's approval for this move. When General Taro Katsura, the War Minister, explained the reasons for sending the troops, Navy Minister Yamamoto not only expressed his vigorous opposition but, after several hours of heated argument, dropped a bombshell by saying, "Any troop-laden ship on the high seas without cause will be sunk as a pirate by the Japanese Navy. Please understand that this is perfectly in accord with the rules of international law." This ended the conference, whereupon the Army Chief of Staff, General Oyama, had to go back to the Emperor and request that his approval of the Army's proposal be withdrawn. The problem was thus solved in one day. In 1903 Admiral Yamamoto again resolved a national crisis by preventing the sending of troops to Korea. Naval textbooks still cite him for his considered opinions and firmness.

Had Admiral Oikawa possessed half the courage of Admiral Gonnohyoe Yamamoto, Japan's war with the United States would never have taken place. There might have been uprisings by hot-headed young militarists, but the horror of the Pacific War would have been avoided.

Yamamoto was resourceful as well as courageous. He took a broad view of problems and solved them realistically. He cautioned against placing undue reliance on divine assistance in war, saying that battles are based on logistics, and strategy must be determined only after a careful analysis of comparative strengths.

The United States, recognizing the power of the Japanese Navy, did its utmost to avert war. Admiral Stark, the United States Chief of Naval Operations, had since February 1941 twice refused to send a fleet of one aircraft carrier, four cruisers, and several destroyers to Manila or Singapore, on the ground that this would provoke the Japanese Navy. Later, when British Foreign Minister Anthony Eden suggested that there was nothing provocative about the presence of the United States fleet in waters of Hawaii, its own territory, Admiral Stark used the same argument to oppose this idea.

As late as 20 November 1941, eighteen days before the attack on Pearl Harbor, President Roosevelt drafted the following compromise plan, which Secretary of State Cordell Hull showed to Great Britain, the Netherlands, and China:

1. The United States will resume the export of petroleum to Japan.
2. The United States will assist in direct negotiations between Japan and China.

3. Japan will send no more troops overseas, and will not carry out the Tripartite Pact, even if the United States enters the European conflict.

This proposal was opposed by China. When Churchill, who at first favored the plan, shifted to the support of China, Roosevelt was forced to withdraw this compromise effort. In its place the Hull memorandum, containing much stiffer clauses to satisfy China, was sent to Japan as a trial balloon. Japan considered it an ultimatum.

The Combined Fleet, under discerning and courageous leaders, had developed a glorious tradition. Its popularity at home increased with Japan's early successes in the Pacific War. Under Admiral Isoroku Yamamoto the glory of the Combined Fleet continued in World War II even through setbacks and defeats. His untimely death in April 1943 shocked Japan and was a loss to the Imperial Navy, but Admiral Mineichi Koga carried on in the great tradition until his own unfortunate death in March 1944. The loss of two commanders in chief within eleven months was a staggering blow to Naval Headquarters and caused grave concern for the welfare of their successor, Admiral Soemu Toyoda.

Koga, like Yamamoto, established his headquarters in flagship *Yamato*. Early in 1944, however, he decided to move to a shore base in order to best control his forces in the threatened areas of the Marianas, Palaus, and Philippines. This gave rise to consideration of where the supreme naval command should be based.

Dispute on the subject of command location first arose in 1937 during the autumn war games. There were heated arguments on each side of the question. The admirals, entertaining no thought of imminent war with the United States, left the controversy unresolved. In April 1944 the subject again came up for serious consideration, and this time it was a vital and pressing matter.

There were strong opinions that the commander in chief should be located centrally at a fixed place, to be in touch with all areas and maintain a consistent picture of the situation. Times had changed, and so had the character of naval actions. No longer were battles determined in a single engagement or area; instead they were often fought simultaneously on several fronts over distances of thousands of miles—on the land, at sea, and in the air. With these changes had come increased responsibilities for the Commander in Chief Combined Fleet. Until 1944 his command had consisted only of naval forces outside home waters, but that year his jurisdiction was expanded to include the homeland naval districts as well as part of the Army Air Force. This added breadth and multiplicity of responsibilities demanded that his headquarters be on shore.

While the arguments for a stationary Combined Fleet Headquarters were logical, there were strong counter-arguments. Some maintained that as long as Combined Fleet existed, the flagship should be at its center. The morale of a fleet was better, the argument continued, when the leader was embarked with his men, and it suffered when he was ashore. His place was with the fleet, and there he should be to command and assume responsibility in decisive battles. A commander in chief had to know minute-by-minute changes in the battle area so that he could give orders for the proper movement of his forces. He could not direct an action by radio from thousands of miles away. If responsibility was transferred to a subordinate commander on the scene, the Combined Fleet would no longer be necessary, and the Naval General Staff would suffice. Tactical orders issued without knowledge of the changing battle situation were bound to lead to difficulties, confusion, and needless losses.

On 30 April 1944 Combined Fleet Headquarters was established in cruiser *Oyodo*, anchored off Kisarazu in Tokyo Bay. Such a compromise of the two opposing views soon proved to be unsatisfactory, and was to be another major factor in Japan's defeat. *Oyodo*'s radio facilities were inadequate and her operations room was not as complete as that of former flagship *Yamato*. These disadvantages became evident during the Marianas battles and *Oyodo* moved to Hiroshima Bay.

Combined Fleet Headquarters remained in *Oyodo* for only five months. In mid-September 1944, against much opposition, the move was made to Keio University in Hiyoshidai, a Tokyo suburb. Underground headquarters accommodations there were so strong that not even an atom bomb could have disturbed them.

Admiral Soemu Toyoda had flown to Formosa to take personal command of the 12–15 October air battles off Formosa. Regarding this as a golden opportunity, Toyoda threw in most of his air strength, and much of it was lost in these actions. He returned promptly to Hiyoshidai.

Thereafter real problems arose. Could naval actions at Leyte Gulf be directed properly from an air-raid shelter in Tokyo? The Leyte Gulf area was included in one part of the Combined Fleet's *Sho* Operation plan, whose main objective was to thwart the enemy's next offensive, wherever it came. It was to be Japan's largest single naval effort of the war. When the enemy struck at Leyte it was clear that the diverse areas of battle would require close cooperation and coordination of all naval forces involved. It was hoped that the surface effort could be supported by land-based air forces and the submarine fleet.

There were great difficulties involved in providing a unified command. Ideally the orders to each unit should have been based directly on observations of local commanders. The widespread battle areas defied direct observation by an overall commander, so orders and commands had to depend on the observations of individual local commanders as relayed by radio. It was impossible to fight a skillful and coordinated battle without knowing in detail the movements of all friendly units.

Had Kurita known of Ozawa's success in luring the enemy task force to the north, he would have acted differently. Kurita received no help, nor even any word, from land-based air forces in the Philippines. He had to operate independently and unassisted. No wonder the battle went amiss.

In the Leyte naval actions there were four Japanese vice admirals at sea and two ashore, all sharing independent command responsibility. On 25 October, the decisive day, these six officers were all located within a radius of 100 miles and yet each fought his own battle, uncoordinated with any of the others. The commanders in chief, who should have been at Davao or Manila, acting as a focal point for these scattered commands, were at Hiyoshidai, 2,000 miles away. Admiral Toyoda himself considered flying to the Philippines to take direct local command of the situation, but his staff dissuaded him by pointing out that communications facilities there could not compare with those at Hiyoshidai. A unified command and timely orders were thus impossible.

There were harsh comments in the fleet that the Leyte operation leaders were reckless in throwing the still-great surface force of the Japanese Navy into an enemy-controlled gulf. For the 9 battleships, 4 aircraft carriers, 11 heavy and 6 light cruisers, and 35 destroyers involved it meant almost certain destruction. Some said that if the intent and purpose of the operation had been sacrificial, then the commander in chief should have led these contingents in person, determined to perish with his fleet. The argument had merit but, no matter where his flag flew, Admiral Toyoda could not possibly have been a winner in the Leyte battles.

The fleet situation was again completely changed in the *Kikusui* surface operation of April 1945. Japan's entire naval strength was then the Second Fleet which comprised one battleship, one light cruiser, and eight destroyers. With fuel enough for only the outward passage, this was so obviously a death march for the Japanese Navy that here too it was said that the commander in chief should have died gloriously with the last of his warships. This opinion, voiced at the time, still finds expression today.

While most of the ships of Combined Fleet rested at the bottom of the sea, its headquarters survived impotently ashore at Hiyoshidai. Admiral Toyoda became Chief of the Naval General Staff on 29 May 1945, and Admiral Jisaburo Ozawa was then made Commander in Chief Combined Fleet. With no ships to command, he could do little more than stand and look at the waning moon.

. Did he recall colleagues who had been sunk with their ships? Or comrades in arms who had gone down in stricken planes? Many of his flag-rank colleagues and many more of his subordinates had died in this war.

Fleet Admirals Yamamoto and Koga; Admirals Ito, Nagumo, Takagi, Nishimura, Yamaguchi, Goto, Inoguchi, Ban, Shinoda, Nakaoka, and Aruga, who have appeared in these pages, were dead. In World War II Japan lost a total of 315 flag-rank Naval officers.

A *kaiten* pilot from submarine *I-36* wrote a letter to his mother before his midget craft went on its fatal sortie:

> My heart breaks when I think of how you will be provided for. Your words that one should die nobly for our country are strong in my mind as I leave on a mission from which there is no return. Please take good care of yourself.

In reading the letter his commanding officer wished he could provide some words of solace for the petty officer, but the *kaiten* was already gone. Within minutes of its departure the *kaiten* exploded on target and the shock waves reached submarine *I-36*.

More than 400,000 men of the Imperial Japanese Navy, each in his own way, shared the fate of this petty officer.[1] The war in which they died was not of their choosing. Japan will never forget their noble patriotism.

The Japanese Navy should have stood firmly opposed to war with the United States. For lack of courage to do so, it was dragged into a reckless war which led to the total defeat of the Imperial Navy. The Combined Fleet will never return. Its existence and achievements are now but a page in history which will show that blame for the loss of Combined Fleet must rest, not on the enemy who destroyed it, but on Japan itself.

---

[1] The Economic Stabilization Board *Taiheiyo Senso ni yoru waga kuni no higai sogo hokokusho* [*Over-all Report of Japan's Losses in the Pacific War*] (Tokyo, 1949) pp. 52–54, gives Imperial Navy's losses in action as 300,386 officers and men, 114,493 civilians attached to the Navy, for a total of 414,879.

See Appendix for principal Japanese warship losses in World War II.

APPENDIX I

Major Japanese Warships in World War II

BATTLESHIPS

SUNK

Date	Name	Tonnage*	Location	Agent
13 Nov 42	*Hiei*	32,250	9°00'S, 159°00'E	air & surface
15 Nov 42	*Kirishima*	32,250	9°10'S, 159°55'E	surface
8 Jun 43	*Mutsu*	38,900	34°05'N, 132°20'E	magazine explosion
24 Oct 44	*Musashi***	64,000	12°50'N, 122°35'E	air
25 Oct 44	*Fuso*	34,000	10°25'N, 125°20'E	surface

* Standard or Washington Treaty tonnage.
** Commissioned during the war.
*** U.S. statisticians regard these ships as sunk in the air attacks of July 1945 on Kure.

BATTLESHIPS (continued)

SUNK (continued)

Date	Name	Tonnage*	Location	Agent
25 Oct 44	*Yamashiro*	34,000	"	"
21 Nov 44	*Kongo*	32,250	26°09′N, 121°23′E	*Sealion* (SS-315)
7 Apr 45	*Yamato***	64,000	30°54′N, 128°10′E	air

NOT SUNK

Date	Name	Tonnage	Location	Agent
18 Jul 45	*Nagato*	38,900	Yokosuka	medium damage
28 Jul 45	*Haruna*	32,250	Kure	foundered***
24 Jul 45	*Hyuga*	35,400	"	"
28 Jul 45	*Ise*	35,400	"	"

AIRCRAFT CARRIERS

SUNK

Date	Name	Tonnage	Location	Agent
7 May 42	CV *Shoho* (ex *Tsurugizaki*)	11,200	10°29′S, 152°55′E	*Lexington* air attack
4 Jun 42	CV *Soryu*	17,500	30°38′N, 179°13′E	carrier-based air attack
4 Jun 42	CV *Kaga*	36,800	30°20′N, 179°17′E	"
5 Jun 42	CV *Akagi*	36,000	30°30′N, 179°08′E	"
5 Jun 42	CV *Hiryu*	17,500	31°38′N, 178°51′E	"
24 Aug 42	CV *Ryujo*	10,500	6°10′S, 160°50′E	*Saratoga* air attack

Date	Name	Tonnage*	Location	Agent
4 Dec 43	CVE *Chuyo*** (ex *Nitta Maru*)	16,700	32°37′N, 143°39′E	*Sailfish* (SS-192)
19 Jun 44	CV *Shokaku***	27,000	11°50′N, 137°57′E	*Cavalla* (SS-244)
19 Jun 44	CV *Taiho***	29,300	12°22′N, 137°04′E	*Albacore* (SS-218)
20 Jun 44	CV *Hiyo* (ex *Izumo Maru*)	24,100	15°30′N, 133°30′E	carrier-based air attack
18 Aug 44	CVE *Taiyo* (ex *Kasuga Maru*)	16,700	18°16′N, 120°20′E	*Rasher* (SS-269)
16 Sep 44	CVE *Unyo* (ex *Yawata Maru*)	16,700	19°18′N, 116°26′E	*Barb* (SS-220)
25 Oct 44	CV *Zuikaku*	27,000	19°20′N, 125°51′E	carrier-based air attack
25 Oct 44	CV *Chiyoda***	11,200	18°37′N, 126°45′E	"
25 Oct 44	CV *Zuiho* (ex *Takasaki*)	11,200	19°20′N, 125°51′E	"
25 Oct 44	CV *Chitose***	11,200	19°20′N, 126°20′E	carrier-based air and surface attack
17 Nov 44	CVE *Shinyo*** (ex *Scharnhorst*)	17,500	33°02′N, 123°33′E	*Spadefish* (SS-411)
29 Nov 44	CV *Shinano***	62,000	32°00′N, 137°00′E	*Archerfish* (SS-311)
19 Dec 44	CV *Unryu***	17,300	28°59′N, 124°03′E	*Redfish* (SS-395)

NOT SUNK

Date	Name	Tonnage	Location	Agent
9 Dec 44	CVE *Junyo* (ex *Kashiwara Maru*)	24,100	Torpedoed by *Seadevil* (SS-400) & *Redfish* (SS-395) off Nagasaki	medium damage
19 Mar 45	CV *Ryuho*** (ex *Taigei*)	13,400	Kure	air attack; slight damage
19 Mar, 24, 28 Jul 45	CV *Amagi***	17,100	Kure	carrier-based air attack; foundered
"	CVE *Kaiyo*** (ex *Argentina Maru*)	15,400	Beppu	carrier-based mine and air attack; foundered

AIRCRAFT CARRIERS (continued)

NOT SUNK (continued)

Date	Name	Tonnage	Location	Agent
19 Mar, 24, 28 Jul 45	CV *Katsuragi***	17,100	Kure	air attacks; medium damage
24 Jul 45	CVL *Hosho*	7,500	Kure	air attack; slight damage

HEAVY CRUISERS

SUNK

Date	Name	Tonnage	Location	Agent
6 Jun 42	*Mikuma*	12,500	30°00′N, 173°00′E	carrier-based air attack
10 Aug 42	*Kako*	8,800	2°15′S, 152°15′E	*S-44*
11 Oct 42	*Furutaka*	8,800	9°00′S, 159°50′E	surface
14 Nov 42	*Kinugasa*	9,000	8°45′S, 157°10′E	carrier-based air attack
23 Oct 44	*Atago*	13,400	9°28′N, 117°17′E	*Darter* (SS-227)
23 Oct 44	*Maya*	13,400	9°22′N, 117°07′E	*Dace* (SS-247)
25 Oct 44	*Chokai*	13,400	11°30′N, 126°30′E	carrier-based air attack
25 Oct 44	*Suzuya*	8,500	"	"
25 Oct 44	*Chikuma*	12,500	"	"
25 Oct 44	*Mogami*	12,500	9°40′N, 124°50′E	carrier-based air & surface
5 Nov 44	*Nachi*	13,000	14°23′N, 120°25′E	carrier-based air attack
25 Nov 44	*Kumano*	12,500	15°45′N, 119°48′E	"

Date	Name	Tonnage	Location	Agent
16 May 45	*Haguro*	10,000	5°00'N, 99°30'E	British surf. attack
8 Jun 45	*Ashigara*	10,000	1°59'S, 104°57'E	British sub *HMS Trenchant*

NOT SUNK

Date	Name	Tonnage	Location	Agent
13 Nov 44	*Myoko*	13,000	damaged off Cape St. Jacques, Indochina by submarine torpedo; limped to Singapore and was still there at war's end.	
23 Oct 44	*Takao*	13,400	heavily damaged at Leyte by submarine torpedo, but reached Singapore and was there at war's end.	
27 Jul 45	*Tone*	11,200	heavily damaged near Kure by carrier-based air attack.	
28 Jul 45	*Aoba*	9,000	heavily damaged at Kure by air attacks.	
24 Jul 45	*Iwate*[1]	9,200	slightly damaged by air attack near Kure.	
24 Jul 45	*Izumo*[1]	9,200	capsized as result of air attack at Kure.	
	Yakumo[1]	9,100	undamaged.	

LIGHT CRUISERS

SUNK

Date	Name	Tonnage	Location	Agent
25 Oct 42	*Yura*	5,760	8°40'S, 160°00'E	U.S. Marine & Army air attack
18 Dec 42	*Tenryu*	3,300	5°11'S, 145°57'E	*Albacore* (SS-218)
13 Jul 43	*Jintsu*	5,850	7°36'S, 157°06'E	surface
2 Nov 43	*Sendai*	5,850	6°20'S, 154°20'E	surface

[1] *Izumo* (built in 1900) and *Iwate* and *Yakumo* (1901) were classified as "1st class cruisers" in July 1942, but were not used in combat.

LIGHT CRUISERS (continued)

SUNK (continued)

Date	Name	Tonnage	Location	Agent
11 Jan 44	*Kuma*	5,700	6°00′N, 99°00′E	Brit. sub *Tallyho*
16 Feb 44	*Agano*	6,651	10°11′N, 151°42′E	*Skate* (SS-305)
17 Feb 44	*Naka*	5,850	7°15′N, 151°15′E	carrier-based air attack
17 Feb 44	*Katori*	6,000	7°45′N, 151°20′E	air & surface
13 Mar 44	*Tatsuta*	3,300	32°58′N, 138°63′E	*Sandlance* (SS-381)
27 Apr 44	*Yubari*	3,500	5°20′N, 132°16′E	*Bluegill* (SS-242)
19 Jul 44	*Oi*	5,700	12°45′N, 114°20′E	*Flasher* (SS-249)
7 Aug 44	*Nagara*	5,760	32°09′N, 129°53′E	*Croaker* (SS-246)
18 Aug 44	*Natori*	5,760	12°29′N, 128°49′E	*Hardhead* (SS-365)
19 Sep 44	*Ioshima* (ex *Ning-hai*)	2,500	33°40′N, 138°18′E	*Shad* (SS-235)
25 Oct 44	*Tama*	5,700	21°23′N, 127°19′E	*Jallao* (SS-368)
26 Oct 44	*Kinu*	5,760	11°46′N, 123°11′E	carrier-based & Army air attack
26 Oct 44	*Noshiro*	6,651	11°35′N, 121°45′E	carrier-based air attack
26 Oct 44	*Abukuma*	5,760	9°20′N, 122°32′E	Army air & surface
13 Nov 44	*Kiso*	5,700	14°35′N, 120°50′E	carrier-based air attack
25 Nov 44	*Yasojima* (ex *Ping-hai*)	2,500	15°40′N, 119°45′E	"
12 Jan 45	*Kashii*	6,000	13°50′N, 109°20′E	"
7 Apr 45	*Yahagi*	6,651	30°40′N, 128°03′E	"
7 Apr 45	*Isuzu*	5,760	7°38′S, 118°09′E	*Gabilan* (SS-252) *Charr* (SS-328)

NOT SUNK

Date	Name	Tonnage	Location	Agent
24 Jul 45	*Kitakami*	5,760	damaged at Kure by air attack.	
24 Jul 45	*Oyodo*	8,200	capsized at Kure from damage inflicted by air attack.	
	Kashima	6,000	undamaged.	
	Sakawa	6,651	at Maizuru, undamaged.	

SUBMARINES

SUNK

Date	Name	Location	Agent
1941			
10 Dec	*I-70*	23°45′N,155°35′W	*Enterprise* (CV-6) aircraft
17 Dec	*RO-66*	approx. 19°N, 166°E	*RO-62* collision
29 Dec	*RO-60*	Kwajalein	stranded
1942			
17 Jan	*I-60*	Sunda Strait	HM DD *Jupiter*
20 Jan	*I-124*	off Pt. Darwin, Australia	*Edsall* (DD-219) & HMA minesweepers *Deloraine, Lithgow, Katoomba*
27 Jan	*I-73*	28°24′N, 178°35′E	*Gudgeon* (SS-211)
Feb	*I-23*	south of Oahu—unheard after 14 Feb 42	
26 Apr	*RO-30*	18°11′N, 166°54′E	*Tautog* (SS-199)
17 May	*I-28*	6°30′N, 152°00′E	*Tautog* (SS-199)
17 May	*I-164*	29°25′N, 134°09′E	*Triton* (SS-201)
28 Aug	*I-123*	9°21′S, 160°43′E	*Gamble* (DM-15)
29 Aug	*RO-33*	9°36′S, 147°06′E	HMA DD *Arunta*
late Aug	*RO-35*	Espiritu Santo area	(Dep. Truk 16 Aug. for Espiritu Santo. Last heard from by radio on 25 Aug.)

SUBMARINES (continued)

SUNK (continued)

Date	Name	Location	Agent
1942			
31 Aug	RO-61	52°36′N, 173°57′W	Reid (DD-369) & air
28 Sep	RO-65	Kiska, Aleutians	U.S. Army air
13 Oct	I-30	1°00′N, 105°00′E	British mine
10 Nov	I-172	10°13′S, 161°09′E	Southard (DMS-10)
12 Nov	I-22	8°32′S, 148°17′E	PT-122
9 Dec	I-3	off Guadalcanal	PT-59
16 Dec	I-15	9°10′S, 159°30′E	air (VS-55)
20 Dec	I-4	5°02′S, 152°33′E	Seadragon (SS-194)
1943			
2 Jan	I-18	8°49′S, 157°09′E	Grayback (SS-208)
29 Jan	I-1	off Guadalcanal	HMNZ trawlers Kiwi & Moa
4 Apr	RO-34	8°15′S, 158°58′E	O'Bannon (DD-450)
mid May	RO-102	(Milne Bay area)	(Dep. Rabaul 29 Apr. for Rabi to strike enemy. Radio failure 9 May after reporting absence of enemy in area. Unheard from thereafter)
29 May	RO-107	15°35′S, 167°17′E	SC-669
May–June	I-178	(E. of Australia)	(Dep. Truk in early May for patrol E. of Australia. Unheard from.)
10 Jun	I-9	53°16′N, 174°24′E	PC-487
13 Jun	I-31	52°08′N, 177°38′E	Frazier (DD-607)
22 Jun	I-7	51°49′N, 177°20′E	Monaghan (DD-354)
12 Jul	I-25	8°00′S, 157°19′E	Taylor (DD-468)
14 Jul	I-179	Inland Sea, Japan	training accident
27 Jul	I-24	2°50′S, 149°01′E	Scamp (SS-277)
19 Aug	I-17	23°26′S, 166°50′E	US air & HMNZ Tui
25 Aug	RO-35	(Espiritu Santo)	(last heard this date)
3 Sep	I-168	13°10′S, 165°28′E	Ellet (DD-398)
9 Sep	I-182	10°33′N, 125°31′E	Trout (SS-202)

Date	Name	Location	Agent
10 Sep	RO-101	(S. of San Cristobal)	(Dep. Rabaul 10 Sep. to disrupt enemy SE of San Cristobal. Attacked enemy but was sunk by counterattack)
15 Sep	RO-103	10°57′S, 163°56′E	Saufley (DD-465) & air
1 Oct	I-20	7°40′S, 157°10′E	Eaton (DD-510)
12 Nov	I-34	5°17′N, 100°05′E	HMSS Taurus
19 Nov	RO-38	(Gilberts area)	(Dep. Truk 19 Nov)
22 Nov	I-35	1°22′N, 172°47′E	DD Frazier & Meade
25 Nov	I-19	3°10′N, 171°55′E	Radford (DD-446)
25 Nov	RO-100	(Buin N. Channel)	Air
27 Nov	I-21	(vic. Tarawa)	(last heard this date)
late Nov	I-40	(vic. Makin Is.)	(Dep Truk 22 Nov)
23 Dec	I-39	9°23′S, 160°09′E	Griswold (DE-7)
1944			
16 Jan	I-181	vic. Vitiaz Str., New Guinea—missing after this date	
22 Jan	RO-37	11°47′S, 164°17′E	Buchanan (DD-484)
30 Jan	I-175	en route Wotje from Truk	unheard from
1944			
31 Jan	I-171	5°37′S, 154°14′E	Guest (DD-472) & Hudson (DD-475)
1 Feb	RO-39	9°24′N, 170°32′E	Walker (DD-517)
11 Feb	RO-110	Bengal Bay	Indian sloop & RAN minesweeper
12 Feb	I-27	1°25′N, 72°22′E	HM DDs Paladin & Petard
15 Feb	I-43	12°42′N, 149°17′E	Aspro (SS-309)
15 Feb	RO-40	9°50′N, 166°35′E	Phelps (DD-360) & Sage (AM-111)
17 Feb	I-11	10°34′N, 173°31′E	Nicholas (DD-449)
23 Mar	I-42	6°40′N, 134°03′E	Tunny (SS-282)
24 Mar	I-32	8°30′N, 170°10′E	Manlove (DE-36) & PC-1135
4 Apr	I-169	7°25′N, 151°50′E	accident
7 Apr	I-2	2°17′N, 149°14′E	Saufley (DD-465)
20 Apr	RO-45	15°19′N, 145°31′E	Seahorse (SS-304)
26 Apr	I-180	55°10′N, 155°40′W	Gilmore (DE-18)
28 Apr	I-183	32°07′N, 133°03′E	Pogy (SS-266)
29 Apr	I-174	6°13′N, 151°19′E	Monterery (CVL-26) aircraft, MacDonough (DD-351) Stephen Potter (DD-538)

SUBMARINES (continued)

SUNK (continued)

Date	Name	Location	Agent
1944			
13 May	*RO-501* (ex U 1224)	18°08′N, 33°13′W	Francis M. Robinson (DE-220)
16 May	*I-176*	4°01′S, 156°29′E	Franks (DD-554), Haggard (DD-555)
19 May	*I-16*	5°10′S, 158°10′E	England (DE-635)
22 May	*RO-106*	1°40′N, 150°31′E	England (DE-635)
23 May	*RO-104*	1°26′N, 149°20′E	England (DE-635)
24 May	*RO-116*	0°53′N, 149°14′E	England (DE-635)
26 May	*RO-108*	0°32′S, 149°56′E	England (DE-635
31 May	*RO-105*	0°47′N, 149°56′E	Hazelwood (DD-531), McCord (DD-534), England (DD-635), George (DE-697), Raby (DE-698)
10 Jun	*RO-42*	10°05′N, 168°22′E	Bangust (DE-739)
11 Jun	*RO-111*	0°26′N, 149°16′E	Taylor (DD-468)
13 Jun	*I-33*	Iyo Nada, Inland Sea	training accident
13 Jun	*RO-36*	15°21′N, 147°00′E	Melvin (DD-680)
16 Jun	*RO-44*	11°13′N, 164°15′E	Burden R. Hastings (DE-19)
16 Jun	*RO-114*	15°02′N, 144°10′E	Melvin (DD-680), Wadleigh (DD-689)
17 Jun	*RO-117*	11°05′N, 150°31′E	VB-109 aircraft from Eniwetok
20 Jun	*I-184*	13°01′N, 149°53′E	Suwannee (CVE-27) aircraft
22 Jun	*I-185*	15°50′N, 145°08′E	Newcomb (DD-586), Chandler (DMS-9)
24 Jun	*I-52*	15°16′N, 39°55′W	Bogue (CVE-9) aircraft
4 Jul	*I-10*	15°26′N, 147°48′E	David W. Taylor (DD-551), Riddle (DE-185)
14 Jul	*I-6*	15°18′N, 144°26′E	Wm. C. Miller (DE-259)
17 Jul	*I-166*	5°10′N, 100°00′E	HM SS Telemachus
19 Jul	*I-5*	off Saipan	by U.S. counterattack
19 Jul	*RO-48*	13°01′N, 151°58′E	Wyman (DE-38)
26 Jul	*I-29*	20°10′N, 121°50′E	Sawfish (SS-276)
28 Jul	*I-55*	14°26′N, 152°16′E	Wyman (DE-38), Reynolds (DE-42)
3 Oct	*I-364*	7°48′N, 133°28′E	Samuel S. Miles (DE-183)

Date	Name	Location	Agent
1944			
28 Oct	I-45	10°10′N, 127°28′E	*Whitehurst* (DE-364)
28 Oct	I-54	10°56′N, 127°13′E	*Gridley* (DD-380), *Helm* (DD-388)
12 Nov	I-37	8°04′N, 138°03′E	*Nicholas* (DD-499)
13 Nov	I-38	31°55′N, 139°45′W	USCGC *Rockford* (PF-48), *Ardent* (AM-340)
17 Nov	I-26	12°44′N, 130°42′E	*Anzio* (CVE-57) aircraft, *Lawrence C. Taylor* (DE-415)
19 Nov	I-177	8°07′N, 134°16′E	*Conklin* (DE-439), *McCoy Reynolds* (DE-440)
28 Nov	I-46	10°48′N, 124°35′E	*Saufley* (DD-465), *Waller* (DD-466), *Pringle* (DD-477), *Renshaw* (DD-499)
28 Nov	I-365	34°44′N, 141°01′E	*Scabbardfish* (SS-397)
1945			
18 Jan	RO-47	12°08′N, 154°27′E	*Fleming* (DE-32)
23 Jan	I-48	9°45′N, 138°20′E	*Corbesier* (DE-438), *Conklin* (DE-439), *Raby* (DE-698)
Jan	I-362	(Caroline Is. area)	(Dep. Yokosuka 1 Jan., to reach Mereyon I. 21 Jan., but never made it.)
1 Feb	RO-115	13°20′N, 119°20′E	*Jenkins* (DD-447), *O'Bannon* (DD-450), *Bell* (DD-587), *Ulvert, M. Moore* (DE-442)
7 Feb	RO-55	15°27′N, 119°25′E	*Thomason* (DE-203)
9 Feb	I-41	18°50′N, 121°40′E	*Batfish* (SS-310)
11 Feb	RO-112	18°53′N, 121°50′E	"
12 Feb	RO-113	19°10′N, 121°23′E	"
mid-Feb	I-371	(unknown)	(Dep. Truk 31 Jan. for Yokosuka but failed to arr. 22 Feb. as scheduled)
26 Feb	I-368	24°43′N, 140°37′E	*Anzio* (CVE-57) aircraft
26 Feb	I-370	22°45′N, 141°27′E	*Finnegan* (DE-307)
26 Feb	RO-43	24°07′N, 140°19′E	*Anzio* (CVE-57) aircraft
late Mar	RO-49	SE of Kyushu	(Dep. Japan for Okinawa, last reported 25 Mar.)

SUBMARINES (continued)

SUNK (continued)

Date	Name	Location	Agent
1945			
31 Mar	*I-8*	25°29′N, 128°35′E	*Morrison* (DD-560), *Stockton* (DD-646)
5 Apr	*RO-41*	26°22′N, 126°30′E	*Hudson* (DD-475)
9 Apr	*RO-46*	26°09′N, 130°21′E	*Mertz* (DD-691), *Monssen* (DD-798)
12 Apr	*RO-64*	34°14′N, 132°16′E	mine
17 Apr	*RO-56*	19°17′N, 166°35′E	*Sea Owl* (SS-405)
18 Apr	*I-56*	26°42′N, 130°38′E	*Bataan* (CVL-29) aircraft, *Heerman* (DD-532), *McCord* (DD-534), *Uhlmann* (DD-687), *Mertz* (DD-691), *Collett* (DD-730)
25 Apr	*RO-109*	21°58′N, 129°35′E	*Horace A. Bass* (APD-124)
29 Apr	*I-44*	24°15′N, 131°16′E	*Tulagi* (CVE-72) aircraft
30 May	*I-12*	22°22′N, 134°09′E	*Anzio* (CVE-57) aircraft
May–Jun	*I-361*	SE of Okinawa	no contact after 24/5/45 dep.
10 Jun	*I-122*	37°29′N, 137°25′E	*Skate* (SS-305)
27 Jun	*I-165*	15°28′N, 153°39′E	land-based air (VPB-142)
14 Jul	*I-351*	4°30′N, 110°00′E	*Bluefish* (SS-222)
16 Jul	*I-13*	34°28′N, 150°55′E	*Anzio* (CVE-57) aircraft, *Lawrence C. Taylor* (DE-415)
28 Jul	*I-372*	33°00′N, 133°00′E	carrier-based aircraft
13 Aug	*I-373*	29°02′N, 123°53′E	*Spikefish* (SS-404)

APPENDIX II

Japanese Combatant Ships
Numbers Added and Sunk during the Pacific War * (tentative)

Type	On Hand 7 Dec. 1941	1941 8 Dec. and After			1942			1943			1944			1945		On Hand 15 Aug. 1945
		Added	Sunk	Total	Added	Sunk	Total	Added	Sunk	Total	Added	Sunk	Total	Added	Sunk	
Battleships	10	1	0	11	1	2	10	0	1	9	0	4	5	0	1	4
Cruisers	38	0	0	38	4	6	36	3	2	37	2	23	16	0	5	11
Aircraft Carriers	9	1	0	10	6	6	10	3	1	13	5	12	6	0	0	6
Destroyers	112	0	4	108	10	19	99	12	34	77	24	61	40	17	15	42
Submarines	64	0	3	61	20	18	63	37	23	77	39	59	57	30	29	58
Total	233	2	7	228	41	51	218	56	61	213	70	159	124	47	50	121

* Data furnished Mr. Susuma Nishiura, Chief, War History Office, Defense Agency, Tokyo, 22 February 1962.

INDEX